34.95

SAVING FORESTS,
PROTECTING PEOPLE?

D0797131

Colo. Christian University Library
8787 W. Alameda Ave.
Lakewood, CO 80226

GLOBALIZATION AND THE ENVIRONMENT SERIES

SERIES EDITORS

Richard Wilk, Department of Anthropology, 130 Student Building, Indiana University, Bloomington, IN 47405, USA, or wilkr@indiana.edu

Josiah Heyman, Department of Sociology & Anthropology, Old Main Building #109, University of Texas, 500 West University Avenue, El Paso, TX 79968, USA, or jmheyman@utep.edu

This AltaMira series publishes new books about the global spread of environmental problems. Key themes addressed are the effects of cultural and economic globalization on the environment; the global institutions that regulate and change human relations with the environment; and the global nature of environmental governance, movements, and activism. The series will include detailed case studies, innovative multi-sited research, and theoretical questioning of the concepts of globalization and the environment. At the center of the series is an exploration of the multiple linkages that connect people, problems, and solutions at scales beyond the local and regional. The editors welcome works that cross boundaries of disciplines, methods, and locales and span scholarly and practical approaches.

BOOKS IN THE SERIES

Power of the Machine: Global Inequalities of Economy, Technology, and Environment, by Alf Hornborg (2001)

Confronting Environments: Local Environmental Understanding in a Globalizing World, edited by James Carrier (2004)

Communities and Conservation: Histories and Politics of Community-Based Natural Resource Management, edited by J. Peter Brosius, Anna Lowenhaupt Tsing, and Charles Zerner (2005)

Globalization, Health, and the Environment: An Integrated Perspective, edited by Greg Guest (2005)

Cows, Kin, and Globalization: An Ethnography of Sustainability, by Susan A. Crate (2006)

Global Visions, Local Landscapes: A Political Ecology of Conservation, Conflict, and Control in Northern Madagascar, by Lisa L. Gezon (2006)

Globalization and the World Ocean, by Peter Jacques (2006)

Rethinking Environmental History: World-System History and Global Environmental Change, edited by Alf Hornborg, John McNeill, and Joan Martínez-Alier (2007)

The World's Scavengers: Salvaging for Sustainable Consumption and Production, by Martin Medina (2007)

Saving Forests, Protecting People? by John W. Schelhas and Max J. Pfeffer (2008)

Capitalizing on Catastrophe: Neoliberal Strategies in Disaster Reconstruction, edited by Nandini Gunewardena and Mark Schuller (2008)

World in Motion: The Globalization and the Environment Reader, edited by Gary M. Kroll and Richard H. Robbins (2009)

SD
414
.C8
S34
2009

SAVING FORESTS, PROTECTING PEOPLE?

Environmental Conservation in
Central America

JOHN SCHELHAS AND MAX J. PFEFFER

ALTAMIRA PRESS
A Division of Rowman & Littlefield Publishers, Inc.
Lanham • New York • Toronto • Plymouth, UK

AltaMira Press
A division of Rowman & Littlefield Publishers, Inc.
A wholly owned subsidary of The Rowman & Littlefield Publishing Group, Inc.
4501 Forbes Boulevard, Suite 200, Lanham, MD 20706
www.altamirapress.com

Estover Road, Plymouth PL6 7PY, United Kingdom

Copyright © 2008 by AltaMira Press
First paperback edition 2009

All rights reserved. No part of this publication may be reproduced, stored in a retrieval system, or transmitted in any form or by any means, electronic, mechanical, photocopying, recording, or otherwise, without the prior permission of the publisher.

British Library Cataloguing in Publication Information Available

Library of Congress Cataloging-in-Publication Data

Schelhas, John.
  Saving forests, protecting people? : environmental conservation in Central America / John Schelhas and Max J. Pfeffer.
    p. cm.—(Globalization and the environment series)
  Includes bibliographical references and index.
  1. Forest conservation—Economic aspects—Costa Rica. 2. Forest conservation—Economic aspects—Honduras. 3. Land use, Rural—Costa Rica. 4. Land use, Rural—Honduras. I. Pfeffer, Max John. II. Title.

  SD414.C8S34 2008
  333.75'16098—dc22
                    2007026006

  ISBN-13: 978-0-7591-0946-9 (cloth : alk. paper)
  ISBN-10: 0-7591-0946-X (cloth : alk. paper)
  ISBN-13: 978-0-7591-0947-6 (pbk : alk. paper)
  ISBN-10: 0-7591-0947-8 (pbk : alk. paper)
  ISBN-13: 978-0-7591-1357-2 (electronic)
  ISBN-10: 0-7591-1357-2 (electronic)

Printed in the United States of America

♾™ The paper used in this publication meets the minimum requirements of American National Standard for Information Sciences—Permanence of Paper for Printed Library Materials, ANSI/NISO Z39.48-1992.

To Susie and Robinson, for all the time spent in the field and writing.

—JS

To Pilar and Danny, who supported and encouraged me despite many long stays far from home.

—MP

CONTENTS

ILLUSTRATIONS

Figures

Tables

Preface

TWO STORIES CAN PERHAPS BEST introduce the early roots of this book: First, in early 1989, one of us (John Schelhas) was beginning field research on the material basis of land use choice in a frontier community adjacent to a national park in Costa Rica. In the process of picking my research site, I had visited a number of national parks and communities adjacent to them and had discussions with many development and conservation practitioners. It was clear that local people often resented national parks and forest conservation and that it would be important to make initial contacts with rural people in a way that focused on their needs and interests and not those of conservationists. I had decided to focus my research on the material logic of local people's land use choices, which meant that I was most interested in a careful empirical evaluation of what people did on their land, given their resources and opportunities. I hoped to later use my understanding of the logics of land use choices to suggest ways that forest conservation could be more successfully integrated into local land use practices.

I had spent several hours over several days with a local landholder, and he had shown me his land, talked about his crops and cattle, and told me about his future goals. I felt that we had developed a good relationship. I had been careful not to initiate discussion about, or show enthusiasm for, forests or the national park, even when the farmer brought them up several times in our conversation. Thus, when near the end of our visit, he asked if I thought it could be a good idea to leave forests on one's land, I let my guard down slightly and carefully replied that it was obvious to me that landowners needed to meet their family's economic needs from their lands, but if one had enough land, it could be good to leave some forest standing. For the next half hour, I stood in stunned silence through the landowner's diatribe on how the problem with North Americans was that they loved trees too much, that people could not eat trees, and that he was tired of North Americans coming around telling him that he should not fell trees.

Clearly my earlier impression that the topic of forest conservation was best researched obliquely by first focusing on agricultural land use was accurate. It would only be at the end of my field research, after nearly a year of living in the community, that I would again talk with people about trees and reforestation. As it turned out, there was interest in reforestation for timber and in conservation of forest patches for environmental services. People remained very sensitive to any hints that forest conservation should take precedence over their livelihood needs, but by this time they knew that I was as interested in their land use systems and household economies as I was in forest conservation.

For the second story, we need to fast-forward less than ten years. I had continued to focus my research on the material basis for land use choice in Costa Rica, although reports from several graduate students working in Costa Rica suggested that land-owners were increasingly interested in forest conservation. Around this time, I was with several other researchers taking some global positioning system (GPS) readings for a study of forest cover in southern Costa Rica. As we were taking one reading, we could hear someone chopping brush with a machete in the interior of the adjacent coffee plantation. After a while, the chopping stopped, and a little later a grizzled, short, stocky man dressed in the worn clothing and the traditional white hat of an almost prototypical Costa Rican *campesino* emerged from the dense coffee where he had been pruning back some of the branches on the shade trees. We had talked only a few minutes about his coffee when he informed us that he had a patch of native forest nearby that he had conserved on his land and that it was a beautiful piece of forest that had never been cut. I was quite surprised to hear this older and most traditional of Costa Rican *campesinos* boasting about his forest when we were trying to talk to him about his coffee. I knew that North Americans had increasingly been purchasing forested land in Costa Rica, and it occurred to me that perhaps he was hoping to sell it to us for a handsome price (like people used to offer their pasture land to me). But this experience, and its contrast with my earlier experience, nevertheless made clear that a significant change had taken place in rural people's attitudes toward forests in Costa Rica over a very short time period. Later visits to my 1989 research site confirmed this, when people I knew from my earlier research quickly brought up the topic of trees and forests in our conversation, eager to tell me about their reforestation plots and the forest patches they had conserved on their land.

When I mentioned that I had been noticing this change to a Costa Rican friend from San José, he found it interesting because he had recently noticed that in the evening, after the late news, when a television station was signing off in the traditional way by playing the national anthem and showing pictures of the country, the pictures had changed. Before the pictures had been of *campesinos*—with their oxcarts, picking coffee, cultivating crops. Now they were pictures of national parks, beaches, and tropical forests. It was clear something had changed dramatically in Costa Rica in terms of the way people looked at forests and perhaps in the national identity. Because it had changed so rapidly, it was accompanied by very little change in the material basis of rural life in Costa Rica. This raised of the question of how attitudes toward forests could change so quickly and what this change meant.

At about this time, the two of us began to discuss this change. One of us (Schelhas) was working in Costa Rica, and the other (Max Pfeffer) was working in Honduras, on issues related to national parks and adjacent communities. Costa Rica was generally regarded at the time as an environmental success story, a stark exception to the rest of Central America, while Honduras had less tourism and environmentalism and got serious about national park management much later. We began to think that we could learn more about how this change had come about in Costa Rica by doing a comparative study of the forest values of rural people in Honduras and Costa Rica. The two countries presented contrasts in general level of attention to, and action on, environmental issues, as well as in overall level of development. There were several important touchstones for our thinking. We were intrigued by Steven R. Brechin and Willett Kempton's 1994 paper that argued that environmentalism was no longer limited to the wealthy people and countries and proposed several possible explanations for this ranging from cultural transformation of environmental values to a new conception of environmentalism—sustainable development—that saw environmentalism as linked to livelihood concerns. We were influenced by Kempton et al.'s book *Environmental Values in American Culture*, both in the general approach of cultural models and in the methodology of mixing qualitative and quantitative research. We later turned to the theoretical and empirical work on cultural models of Dorothy Holland, Naomi Quinn, and Claudia Strauss to more fully develop our approach.

Our research took place in communities in or near national parks in these two different countries with and near two national parks that had different management histories. The park in Costa Rica was what we will call a conventional park, along the lines of the stereotypical U.S. national park model of strictly protected boundaries with communities lying outside the park on private lands with no legal relationship to the park. The park in Honduras reflected recent parks-and-people thinking and was a zoned park, similar to the biosphere reserve model,[1] with a core "untouchable" zone surrounded by human-occupied buffer zones. The contrast between these two management styles was built into our research project from the beginning, although we did not anticipate the degree of polarization that would soon emerge between international "neoprotectionists" and "parks-and-people" advocates.[2]

On the one hand, efforts begun in the late 1980s to develop integrated conservation and development projects and community-based conservation programs had come under harsh criticism from some conservationists for being ineffective and irrelevant wastes of conservation resources, with seemingly little recognition that parks-and-people approaches came about because protectionist approaches were losing traction in lesser developed countries. On the other hand, many social scientists seemed to increasingly see conservation programs as only harming people or as little more than extensions of state power into remote areas, with little recognition that international conservation goals were legitimate or that conservation might have some benefits for local people in either the short or long term.

While there is no doubt that this debate produced some new insights and clearer thinking, the degree of polarization that became common in many discussions seemed counterproductive and to hinder both conservation and development practice. We see a much more complex picture not easily divided into clear conservation versus people terms. Most people we have met in the field seem to be seeking a more pragmatic balance between the environment and development, and the global survey data on environmentalism summarized in Brechin and Kempton (1994) also seemed to support this. Since we find our perspective spanning this polarized debate, we should make explicit some of our views.

First, we see the national park concept and related perspectives of nature conservation as generally originating in the developed countries and being transferred to (and, in some cases, imposed on) people in lesser developed countries. At the same time, we believe that much of this has been done in an effort to conserve species and ecosystems for human well-being and appreciation or, in rarer cases, because people believe nonhuman species have rights to exist. We consider these to be worthwhile goals, although we feel they should be carried out fairly and justly. We recognize that this has not always been the case, either in the developed or lesser developed countries, and that local people worldwide have often objected to national park formation. Early work related to parks and people was notable for listing the many benefits to people from conservation (see, for example, Ledec and Goodland 1988, Oldfield 1984, Raven and McNeely 1998) but paying little attention to the distribution of costs and benefits or the ability of local people to bear short-term, tangible losses in exchange for long-term, diffuse benefits. But the fact that conservation can involve lost opportunities for some in the short run does not make it a bad idea altogether. In the pursuit of their short-term goals, people have in some places destroyed elements of the natural environment essential to their very existence. The human situation fundamentally requires meeting short-term needs for products and services while at the same time maintaining the ability of our environment to produce these indefinitely into the future. Conservation by its very nature requires forgoing some short-term uses of natural resources, although fairness suggests that these costs should be shared across social groups in ways consistent with the benefits of conservation.

Second, globalization seems to be a widespread, all-encompassing process. While we see the worldwide rise of parks as a phenomenon of globalization, we note that it is also accompanied by increasing globalization in natural resource extraction, forestry, agriculture, and consumption. It seems that it should be viewed within this larger context, rather than focusing on simply environmentalism. Costa Rica and Honduras have both been subject to rapid deforestation and forest degradation as a result of the globalization of agriculture and forestry, and the people we interviewed were not indigenous people or long-term residents but, rather, relatively recent colonists who had been forced into forest landscapes as large-scale agricultural operations took over more fertile agricultural lands. At the same time, there has been a complex set of reactions of local people to conservation. Rural people's engagement with conservation ranges from cases of violent opposition to alliances with conservation programs to resist against outside resource extraction. Clearly, understanding why and how conservation programs play out so differently and provoke such different responses in different places at different times is an important job for social scientists.

With all this in mind, we have endeavored to conduct a careful and systematic analysis of what happens when globally driven conservation programs encounter local communities using local resources to earn their livelihoods. We have focused on questions related to environmental values because we believe that they are contested by competing interests and, because of this, it is important to understand how they are formed and operate. We have sought to address the question of environmental values in a way that involves careful and sympathetic listening and, through excerpts from our transcribed interviews, gives voice to local people. We believe that understanding these processes in our study sites, combined with similar work carried out by other researchers in other places, is critical work in the global and local efforts to promote biodiversity conservation in ways that are fair and effective today and long into the future.

Organization of the Book

The book begins with an introduction that provides an overview, based on social science and conservation literature, of the issues related to globalization, national parks, and forest conservation, as well as a brief discussion of schema theory and cultural models, which provide the conceptual framework for our research. Chapter 2 describes the two research sites, discusses their conservation history, and provides some basic sociodemographic analysis of our respondents. Chapter 3, for Costa Rica, and chapter 4, for Honduras, lead the reader through our analysis of environmental values using excerpts from our transcribed qualitative interviews supplemented by data from our questionnaires. In each of these chapters, we proceed through a discussion of forest values, value change, and sources of values, followed by briefer discussions of the national parks and their benefits and then hunting. After this, we consider the different ways that people dealt with conflicts between forest conservation and their livelihood interests. Finally, we discuss the preferred land use patterns of our respondents and their forest-related behaviors. In the final chapter, we draw on the analyses from the two countries to discuss the nature, formation, and force of environmental values in a globalizing world and end with some brief comments about the insights from our work for studying environmental values and for practical forest conservation efforts. The appendixes contain our open-ended interviewing guide, as well as our questionnaires with summaries of responses.

Acknowledgments

This book is the culmination of a project instigated long ago with a grant from the National Science Foundation (NSF). We are extremely grateful for the generous support offered by the NSF in funding our project, "Policy, Norms and Values in Forest Conservation: Protected Area Buffer Zone Management in Central America" (Grant #SBR-9613493). This project was seeded with generous support for travel and exploratory research from the Central America Committee of the Cornell International Institute for Food, Agriculture, and Development (CIIFAD). Committee members Robert Blake, Margaret Smith, Phil Arneson, and David Lee were our kind and enthusiastic supporters, and we are most grateful for their support. Additional preliminary work was done under Cornell's NSF-funded Research Training Group, "Ecological and Social Science Challenges of Conservation" (Grants BIR-9113293 and DBI-9602244). Other faculty members at Cornell University were supportive of our efforts in numerous ways that we cannot begin to recount here. But one person stands out as being especially generous and helpful. Stephan DeGloria played a very important role in guiding our work with satellite images and their analysis. Not only is Steve a knowledgeable and careful researcher, but he is a supportive and kind colleague without parallel. Our collaboration with Steve led to the publication of an article in *Agriculture, Ecosystems and the Environment* (vol. 110, 2005), "Population, Conservation and Land Use Change in Honduras."

CIIFAD also provided support to a number of Cornell University graduate students who worked in Central America. One of those students stands out as especially significant for our project. Alan Barton conducted his own dissertation research in Honduras and teamed up with us on occasion. Alan had extensive experience in Latin America and, with his experience, provided invaluable assistance on our project. We spent a great deal of time conducting interviews with Alan in the Cerro Azul Meambar National Park (CAMNP). These were always very productive and enjoyable times. In addition to lending a hand on our project, he independently completed his dissertation, "Regulatory Authority and Participatory Protected Areas Management at Cerro Azul Meambar National Park, Honduras."

We benefited from the assistance of a number of students who completed their own thesis and dissertation research using data from our project. Two students had a special hand in our project. Leyla Day and Caroline Stem spent extended periods in the field in both Honduras and Costa Rica conducting in-depth interviews and, in this way, made a major contribution to our project. We are most grateful for their help. Perhaps most memorable was their interview with José Punta Pistola, a pseudonym for one of the most humorous interviewees in our project. Leyla Day completed her M.S. thesis, "Conflicting Values in Forest Conservation: The Cerro Azul Meambar Park in Honduras," with data from the in-depth interviews. Leyla also coauthored an article with us that appeared in *Rural Sociology* (vol. 66, 2001), "Forest Conservation, Value Conflict and Interest Formation in a Honduran National Park." Caroline Stem went on to do further research in Costa Rica and completed a Ph.D. dissertation entitled "The Role of Local Development in Protected Area Management: A Comparative Case Study of Eco-Tourism in Costa Rica." Catherine (Kayte) Meola provided us with assistance in data management and analysis and used our project data to complete her own M.S. thesis, "Parks and Patriarchy: The Effects of Educational Practice on Gendered Environmental Attitude Formation in a Honduran Biosphere Reserve," and coauthored with us an article in *Rural Sociology* (vol. 71, 2006), "Environmental Globalization, Organizational Form and Expected Benefits from Protected Areas in Central America." Carylanna Bahamondes also played a helpful part in our project by completing her M.S. thesis, "Closing or Opening Space? Global and Local Water Conservation Discourse in Cerro Azul Meambar National Park, Honduras."

Our work could not have been completed without the cooperation of numerous collaborators in Honduras and Costa Rica. In Honduras, Chet Thomas, executive director of *Proyecto Aldea Global*, provided advice and encouragement, as well as access to the CAMNP and the buffer zone communities. At the time of our field work, Alexis Oliva was director of the CAMNP. Alexis was always gracious and helpful despite the demands we put on his already demanding workload. Teodoro Calles introduced us to the park guards and provided introductions in communities throughout the park that paved the way for us meet and interact with the people living in the CAMNP buffer zone. Teodoro was an asset to us just as he was to the park administration because of his extensive knowledge of the local communities and the park's natural resources. Park guards in all the communities we worked in were helpful, kind, and generous hosts, but we are especially grateful for the assistance provided us by Filadelfo Calix and Hector Flores.

We were able to draw on the resources of two important institutions in Honduras because of the assistance provided by two individuals. Jorge Gomez of the *Corporación Hondureño de Desarollo Forestal* (COHDEFOR, the national forest development corporation) completed analysis of satellite imagery and spent considerable time ground-truthing our findings from that analysis. Jorge also produced the maps of CAMNP for us. His knowledge of geographic information systems, forests, and the geography, history, and communities of CAMNP was of immense importance to our project, and it is hard to think of how we would have completed the work without his assistance. In addition to numerous hours in front of computer monitors and out in the field, Jorge worked with us to coauthor the article mentioned above that appeared in *Agriculture, Ecosystems and the Environment.* Ivan Guillén played a leading role in helping one of the most daunting tasks in our project, completing interviews with more than six hundred randomly selected householders in eight communities within the CAMNP buffer zone. Ivan, a professor of extension education, mobilized a large group of students at the *Escuela Nacional de Ciencias Forestales* (*ESNACIFOR*, the national forestry school) to conduct the interviews. Ivan supervised this large effort above and beyond his regular duties at *ESNACIFOR*, and he did this with great success. The data were carefully and completely collected thanks to Ivan's efforts.

In Costa Rica, we were assisted by three institutions, the Organization for Tropical Studies (OTS), the National System of Protected Areas (a branch of the Environment and Energy Ministry, *MINAE*), and by the National Autonomous University (*Universidad Nacional*). OTS helped with many of our logistics in Costa Rica as we began our work out of the Las Cruces Biological Station (LCBS). Discussions with several Costa Ricans working for OTS provided us with important insights on environmentalism in Costa Rica, particularly Luis Diego Gómez, at the time the director of LCBS, and José María Rodríguez, at the time the environmental policy coordinator. Later, Guillermo Durán Sanabria provided us with the land cover maps used in the book. Arturo Sanchez of the University of Alberta also did some land cover analysis for us. From *MINAE*, park rangers Eddie Aguilar, José Manuel Fernández, and Ronald Chan Fonseca provided us with information and community contacts that were crucial in getting our work started. From the *Universidad Nacional*, we owe a great debt of thanks to professors Claudia Charpentier and Dora Rivera for getting together a group of fourteen students to administer the survey in Costa Rica. We also want to thank all the students for their diligent work during the month we were in the field. We also thank Jimmy Ureña, Adolfo and Yali Solano and family, and José Manuel Fernández and family for logistical help, friendship, and valuable discussions when we were in the field.

Notes

1. Confusingly, the Costa Rican park was a biosphere reserve, while the Honduran park was not.

2. For a brief review, see Schelhas, Buck, and Geisler 2001.

Parks and Protected Areas in the Process of Environmental Globalization

1

MOST NATIONAL PARKS in the tropics are surrounded by human populations that interact with the forests that the parks protect. These interactions include human use of resources within the protected area and conversion of forests to agriculture on private lands adjacent to parks. The ability of parks to protect biodiversity often depends on the amount and pattern of forest cover surrounding core protected areas, as well as on the use and management of these forests (Brandon et al. 1998, Ceballos et al. 2005, Freese 1997, Kramer et al. 1997, Laurance and Bierregaard 1997, Redford 1992, Robinson 1996, Schelhas and Greenberg 1996, Schroth et al. 2004). Therefore, biodiversity conservation must focus on several things, including protecting tropical forests from clearing, limiting or managing extractive forest uses, and promotion of forest cover on private lands adjacent to core protected areas.

From a social point of view, protection of old growth forests and wildlife and the promotion of forest cover in human-occupied landscapes often brings about conflict between conservation and other interests of local people (Pfeffer et al. 2001, 2005). More general goals of biodiversity conservation are often promoted by those living far from tropical forests, those in urban areas, and those able to meet their economic needs without forest use and destruction. Local people may find that biodiversity conservation hinders their ability to meet their livelihood needs and ambitions. Park managers have addressed this issue in a number of ways, including (1) programs for local awareness and environmental education, (2) cross-boundary natural resource management programs, (3) promotion of compatible economic development in neighboring communities, (4) programs to promote conservation on farms near national parks, and (5) involvement of local people in protected area management (Brandon et al. 1998, Brosius et al. 2005, Buck et al. 2001, Dugelby and Libby 1998, Kramer et al. 1997, Western and Wright 1994). In spite of these efforts, tensions between parks and local people are common. The ways that forest conservation impacts rural people's livelihoods, rights to resources, and related political and power relationships have been extensively explored in the social science literature on conservation (e.g., Brechin et al. 2003, Peluso 1992). It is now generally recognized that there are complex links between local and global material, power, and ideological interests (Hannerz 1992, Ortner 1997), and analyses of conservation discourse have been addressing convergence and conflict between these different interests (Carrier 2004, Dove et al. 2003, Gezon 2005). But there remains a need for fine-scale studies of the global-local cultural interactions that take place around environmentalism and conservation ideology near protected areas.

The Global Rise of Environmentalism

Conventional wisdom long held that environmental concern was limited primarily to residents of wealthy industrialized nations, who had what have been called "postmaterialist values" (Dunlap and Mertig 1997). However, this notion has been directly challenged by recent research and events. Global environmental concern and action have increased markedly over the past four decades, as indicated by a number of measures (Brechin and Kempton 1994, Brosius 1999). First, international public opinion surveys, including a Gallup survey using representative samples of whole country populations in twenty-two countries, have found high levels of environmental concern in both developed and less developed countries (Brechin and Kempton 1994, Dunlap et al. 1993, Dunlap and Mertig 1997). Second, there have been rapid increases in grassroots environmental movements; in local, national, and international environmental nongovernmental organizations (NGOs); in government agencies dealing with environmental issues; and in international organizations concerned with global environmental governance (Brechin and Kempton 1994, Brosius 1999, Buttel and Taylor 1992, Dunlap and Mertig 1997, Frank et al. 2000, Terborgh et al. 2002). Governments, NGOs, and international agencies have also implemented a wide variety of policies and programs in support of environmental conservation (Brechin et al. 2003, Frank et al. 2000). Third, there has been a continual increase in the establishment of national parks and protected areas around the world and participation in international environmental agreements, organizations, and meetings (Brandon et al. 1998, Buttel and Taylor 1992, Frank et al. 2000, United National Development Programme et al. 2003). Fourth, environmental messages have become ubiquitous, not only those specifically promoting environmentalism but also product advertisements and other aspects of popular culture (Cronon 1996, Smith 1996, Yearley 1996).

Steven R. Brechin and Willett Kempton (1994), in seeking a new explanation of environmentalism to replace the postmaterialist hypothesis, offered five possible explanations for the global rise in environmentalism: (1) environmental concern and action in poorer nations as part of larger patterns of conflict over macrolevel domination and local resistance; (2) diffusion of environmental values, often in conceptually consistent packages, through mass media and personal communication; (3) direct observation of environmental problems, which are widespread and experienced by people everywhere; (4) communication of environmental values and policies through formal organizations such as states, NGOs, and multi- and bilateral aid agencies; (5) a change in the way environmental quality is viewed—now as integral to the economic development process rather than as a luxury. Evidence indicates that the global trends in environmental concern are emerging from all of these sources, and Brechin (1999) suggests that environmentalism is a complex phenomenon that is a mix of social preferences, local histories and environmental realities, international relationships and influences, and unique cultural and structural features. Under this interpretation, environmentalism is not an undifferentiated universal phenomenon. Rather, environmental concern is expressed in a variety of social constructs that emerge from complex interactions of locally unique historical, political, and environmental factors confronting global environmental values and action. Local factors encourage differences in environmentalism, while exposure to common phenomena, such as the global spread of environmental values, induces greater similarity. Thus, it is particularly important that we understand different environmentalisms and their construction through relationships between the global and local.

Globalization and Environmentalism

The recent literature often closely links the spread of environmentalism to globalization. Globalization can be defined as the intensification of worldwide social relationships, characterized by the global spread of ideas, practices, and technologies (Milton 1996). Drawing on world systems theory, some scholars have seen globalization as a spread of ideas, practice, and technologies from the more developed core regions (both globally and within countries) to the periphery, following patterns of economic, political, and ideological power (Hannerz 1992, Milton 1996). Core-periphery relations are structured by terms of trade, foreign aid, international agreements, and cultural dominance (Milton 1996). World systems theory views the peripheral regions as being shaped by these relationships in ways that make them different from core areas, rather than simply being at different points on a universal path to development (Milton 1996). For example, data suggest that forest cover is increasing in the developed world and decreasing in much of the developing world, and pollution is decreasing in the developed world and increasing in the developing world.[1] World systems theory, rather than seeing the developing countries as lagging behind developed countries, sees these phenomena as intimately linked—developed countries are transferring their environmental ills, or the responsibility for forest conservation, to developing countries (Robbins and Fraser 2003, Yearley 1996).[2] Similarly, regarding environmental values, rather than a transfer of environmental values from developed to developing countries, some environmental anthropologists suggest that unique environmental values emerge in the core and periphery as a result of the different positions they occupy in material and power relationships (Milton 1996, Pulido 1996). As an example, Michael Redclift (1984) suggests that environmentalism in the developed industrialized countries focuses on a pleasant countryside and outdoor recreation, whereas that of rural Latin America is about people's ability to survive in a degraded environment.

A second focus of scholarship on globalization and the environment has been the construction of environmental problems as global problems universally affecting all people (Brosius 1999, Carrier 2004, Frank et al. 2000, Little 1999, Taylor and Buttel 1992, Yearley 1996). Frederick H. Buttel and Peter J. Taylor (1992) suggest that understandings of global environmental problems are shaped as much by science and the media as they are by biophysical reality. While some environmental problems are inherently global, such as global warming, other environmental problems, such as habitat degradation and pollution, may have global implications, but their causes and consequences are locally concentrated (Yearley 1996). Kay Milton (1996) suggests that the depiction of the earth as a single ecosystem with global environmental problems, combined with an emerging view of humanity as a single moral community, is used to justify a wide range of environmental conservation actions and policies that give precedence to broad public interests (i.e., environmental conservation) over narrower interests of individuals and groups. The key point is that "global" environmental issues may be construed in ways that benefit the interests of certain groups of people and that developed country constructions of environmentalism may be skewed to benefit developed country interests (Buttel 1992, Carrier 2004). Thus, environmentalism cannot be understood apart from its social context, and environmentalism is often intimately tied in with other social issues, dramas, and contests (Agrawal 2005, Gezon 2005, Haenn 2005).

With more frequent global-local encounters, global constructions of both environmental and nonenvironmental issues are more prominent in struggles for resources and power in a globalizing world. While there are a number of instances where defining environmental issues as global issues has facilitated the imposition of core region values and practices on local people in peripheral regions (Carrier 2004), there are also cases where local communities on the periphery have appealed to global environmental values to counter the imposition of outside resource extraction regimes (Heyman 2004). In other cases, appeal to global values such as human rights is used to counter globally inspired initiatives like expansion of national parks and protected areas (e.g., Geisler 2002). Appeal to the global, then, is not limited to environmentalism. Rather, it is a more general tool that may be used both by globalizers to achieve their agendas and by communities in defense of their interests in the face of globalization (Heyman 2004). It is important to note, though, that appealing to the global is not always the best way to seek advantage in disputes and in pursuit of agendas. In some cases, reference to the local, rather than the global, can more effectively confer legitimacy; for example, indigenousness and long-term occupancy can be judged to give people a special voice or power in environmental disputes (Milton 2002). But Melissa Leach and James Fairhead (2002) suggest that because they develop in response to globalist discourses, many localized discourses are themselves defined by the dominant global discourse. In summary, ideas of global and local are useful as tools in advancing all sorts of agendas, and it is important to pay attention to the way that they are used in environmental discourse.

A third focus of scholarship considers the ideological content of global environmentalism. Redclift (1984) suggests that environmentalism emerged in industrialized countries, and one important strand of it often has a utopian element that contrasts a pure nature or wilderness against the ravages of civilization. This form of environmentalism, often represented by the romantic protectionism of John Muir and his intellectual descendants, coexists with a more pragmatic strand that emphasizes conservation, often characterized by the utilitarianism of Gifford Pinchot (Milton 1996, Nash 2001, Redclift 1984). Milton (1996) suggests that this difference is more evident in theoretical discussions and in the philosophical statements of environmentalists than in the environmentalism of the general public, which studies show is often based on diverse justifications. Milton (1996) also suggests that global environmentalism is more likely to be seen as a separate domain of life, whereas in premodern cultures, environmental knowledge was often embedded in the context of its use.

While some of the literature sees environmentalism as originating in the core, industrialized countries (Redclift 1984), another strand of research has seen resource conservation as fundamental to any society's long-term sustainability, and thus something that all societies have grappled with (Allen et al. 2003, Diamond 2005, Redman 1999). There is a body of research, based in anthropology and ethnoscience, that examines indigenous and traditional conservation practices. This research has stimulated an intense and far-reaching debate over whether indigenous, traditional, and other local people are conservationists (Alcorn 1998, Krech 1999). One question is whether indigenous people who have lived in some form of balance or harmony with their environment over long periods of time have done so because they have taken good care of the environment purposefully or simply have not had the capacity (tools and technologies, population density) to degrade the environment (Krech 2005). Thus, for some authors, including Milton (1996) and Shepard Krech (2005), one of the key questions is whether or not local people have had specific ideologies that favor environmental conservation.

Others (e.g., Alcorn 1989, Atran et al. 2002, and Gerritsen and Wiersum 2005) have argued that traditional conservation is often encoded in scripts like agricultural procedures or deeply embedded in culture. This perspective suggests that traditional environmentalism is not always a separate, conscious domain, but rather has over time become deeply entwined with other aspects of culture, such as religion, social organization, and subsistence practices. Sacred groves, agricultural rituals, and complex agroforestry systems often have clear conservation benefits, but it is often not clear that they are explicitly environmental conservation practices because they may be undertaken as much for other social and cultural reasons (Barucha 1999, Laird 1999, Milton 1996). It is also important to note that conservation intent, whether explicit or deeply embedded, and conservation outcomes do not always go together. There are several types of actions: (1) actions not related to conservation that have positive conservation outcomes, (2) actions not explicitly taken for conservation but which may have an adaptive history that in effect results in conservation, (3) actions taken explicitly for conservation that have conservation benefits, and (4) actions explicitly stated as related to conservation that have little or no conservation benefit.

While this issue of lack of explicit conservation intent has been raised mostly with reference to traditional and indigenous conservation practices (e.g., Krech 2005, Laird 1999), it has less often been recognized that it applies nearly as well to "modern" conservation. There are many examples of intended and unintended conservation practices and outcomes: (1) National parks—one of the prime modern vehicles for biodiversity conservation—have their origins more in cultural preservation (scenery, grandeur, tourism, romanticism) than in biodiversity conservation (Runte 1997, Schelhas 2001a, Sellars 1999). (2) Professionally trained foresters have socially derived myths and practices of their own (Burch 1999). (3) The conservation ideology and practice of scientists and agencies may have social and cultural biases built in (Leach and Fairhead 2002). (4) Religion and environmentalism can become intertwined in the modern world (Giner and Tábara 1999, Hessel and Ruether 2000). Scott Atran et al. (2002) believe that sociocultural features that have become intertwined with conservation ideologies or behaviors in indigenous and traditional people have important lessons for developing successful conservation in the modern world and can function to maintain common pool resources even under conditions of open access.

Thus, in all places, people's environmental beliefs, values, and practices are likely to be intimately tied to other social, economic, and political spheres. Local people generally have their own environmental and conservation beliefs and values. These beliefs and values may have complex relationships to practical issues of sustainable agricultural practices, social and power relations, and symbolic and ideological systems of religion and culture. Local people's ideologies may also have varying degrees of relationship to the actual conservation value of land use practices (Campbell 2005, Laird 1999, Lebbie and Freudenberger 1996, Parajuli 1999). At the same time, local people confront an expanding global environmental force that originates in the institutions of core regions and has its own complex relationships to conservation.

In summary, there are at least three important dimensions of globalization and environmentalism. One refers to a certain global environmentalism that may be imposed by more powerful social groups (core) upon local people living in remote areas. The nature of this environmentalism may be more to the benefit of people from core areas than those from the periphery. Second, global and universal constructions may be used to impose core environmentalism on people of the periphery, and resistance to this imposition may be couched either in appeals to other global values (e.g., human rights) or in the value of the local (although perhaps a globalized valuing of the local). Third, global and local environmentalism may have differing content, rooted in various social, cultural, political, and economic interests.

Global-Local Interaction in Environmentalism

The processes of globalization—both the view of the earth and its people as one world and the compression of relationships among people across the globe—are seen by some to be a homogenizing process that will transform diverse cultures to be more like the West (e.g., Igoe 2004). Milton (1996, 155) notes, however, that while some see globalization as eroding cultural differences due to the flow of cultural values outward from core areas, others have suggested that it can also generate cultural diversity as new forms are generated in the interactions between core and periphery. Compression of economic and political spaces and the rise of a global media certainly mean that many objects and ideas are simultaneously experienced worldwide, where before products and information spread more gradually and were subject to more adaptation (Luke 1996, Watson 1997, Wilk 1994). However, Milton (1996) and Marshall Sahlins (1994) have both argued that we should take care in assuming that because the same products and ideas are available, they are also always perceived and used the same ways worldwide. Imported cultural forms—both material and ideological—are often adapted to local purposes as they cross cultural boundaries (Milton 1996). Thus, expanding global trends do not necessarily represent a hegemonic force for cultural homogenization. A number of social scientists have explored ways in which globalizing practices, ideas, and values interact with the local to produce unique, socially constructed cultural forms at specific places that have elements of both global and local culture (Calhoun 2004, Hannerz 1992, Milton 1996, Pfeffer et al. 2001, Sahlins 1994, Watson 1997, Wilk 2006).

While the global spread of fast food may seem an unlikely place to look for parallels to the global spread of environmentalism, James L. Watson's (1997) edited volume on the spread of McDonald's restaurants in East Asia provides a thorough discussion of global-local interactions and generates some important insights for our study of environmentalism. Like national parks and environmentalism, McDonald's is often seen as a homogenizing, imperialistic global force running roughshod over the local (Dove 2003, Milton 1996, Ritzer 1996, Watson 1997). Yet Watson's (1997) book shows that while McDonald's restaurants in different countries have indeed changed local food ways, they also have been changed by local people into local—or localized—institutions in important ways. The authors in Watson's volume describe complex interactions of the global and local that result in unique menus, changes in operating procedures, unique patterns of use, and unique meanings in different places—sometimes to such an extent that younger consumers may be unaware of the restaurant's foreign origins (Watson 1997). The changes brought about by fast food restaurants occur not in static and unchanging local cultures, but rather in cultures that are already very dynamic and in which people are carrying out their own social and cultural projects (Carrier 2004, Milton 1996, Watson 1997).

Differences and similarities in the cultural processes at play when the global meets the local have important lessons for our general understanding of global-local interactions, environmentalism, and practical conservation efforts. Conservation as implemented in many lesser developed countries under the influence of biological scientists and professionals from core countries was often exclusionary (West 1991). However, facing limits to adoption in lesser developed contexts, adjustments were made in developed country conservation models intended to better integrate conservation into the new local contexts (Lucas 1984). At the international level, these changes have been controversial and criticized for losing a conservation focus while addressing human needs (e.g., Oates 1999, Terborgh et al. 2002). But in conservation practice, many hybrid forms have emerged (see, for example, Buck et al. 2001, Western and Wright 1994).

As an example, in Costa Rica, Lisa M. Campbell (2002) found that a traditional, exclusionary parks and protected area conservation agenda had been promoted by international scientists and allied locals, often with international funding. Exclusionary approaches ignored the social-economic constraints of many families living in or near protected areas, and the failure to acknowledge these limitations created conflict. To avoid or reduce tensions, the government did not enforce rules and regulations. Eventually, an ecodevelopment approach emerged. This approach, supported by major economic interests, promoted ecotoursim and bioprospecting. In the end, parallel, local-level, populist, sustainable development and conservation perspectives arose and supported the ecodevelopment approach (Campbell 2002, Nygren 1998).

In conservation, many hybrid approaches were formally categorized under new globalized counter-discourses and policies of sustainable development, ecodevelopment, and integrated conservation and development projects. But, similar to the fast food example, there are also many examples of parks and conservation programs that have made their own idiosyncratic local adaptations, such as allowing access to certain resources, to make conservation success possible (see McNeely 1995, Sharma and Shaw 1993, Zube and Busch 1990). This may be necessary, since, as Steven Yearley (1996) discusses, universalized approaches, especially in an unequal and divided world, may not be successful unless they are adapted to address specific local needs.

Park Management and Forest Conservation as a Globalizing Phenomenon

The creation of parks and other protected areas is a global phenomenon that has gained momentum over the past few decades. Throughout the world, 104,792 total protected area sites cover 12.2 percent of the earth's land surface (Chape et al. 2005). National parks make up 3,881 of these sites; nature reserves, wilderness areas, national monuments, wildlife refuges, protected landscapes, and protected managed ecosystems account for the rest (Chape et al. 2003). This phenomenon is relatively recent: more parks have been created since 1970 than ever before (Brandon et al. 1998). The parks protect a wide range of environments, but their inspiration and the strategies used in their management are part of a global process (Brandon et al. 1998, Western and Wright 1994). Parks in many cases are interpreted by local people as impositions from an alien force over which they have no control (Igoe 2004).

The proliferation of protected area management is global in two important ways. First, park management strategies, although typically deployed under the authority of national governments, are internationally inspired. They emerge from an international environmental discourse that emphasizes the universal quality of certain environmental problems and a purportedly common interest in resolving them (Hannigan 1995, Rocheleau and Ross 1995, Yearley 1996). Second, although nation-states are involved in this discourse, it transcends their boundaries, and they do not dominate it. Environmental NGOs are an active and increasingly important force in discussions of global environmental problems. Their importance was quite evident at the United Nations Conference on Environment and Development, more commonly known as the Earth Summit, held in Rio de Janeiro in 1992 (Potter and Taylor 1996, Thomas 1994). International environmental organizations such as Greenpeace, the World Wildlife Fund, and The Nature Conservancy increasingly claim to represent global environmental interests. These international institutions often share common understandings and views and, as J. Peter Brosius (1999) notes, inscribe certain discourses.

The proliferation of protected areas in the tropics is linked closely to the process of environmental globalization. Tropical parks relate to several global environmental concerns. One is that parks often include trees and forests. Tropical forest conservation has been one of the most important international environmental issues, both as a popular topic attracting widespread public interest and for its role in shaping the way that environmental scientists and groups have approached global environmental issues (Frank et al. 2000, Taylor and Buttel 1992, Yearley 1996). Rain forests have been seen by the global environmental community as particularly important for their role in stabilizing climate and soils, exceptional biodiversity, and potential future benefits to humans through new medicines and crops, as well as particularly endangered because of their rapid loss (Milton 1996, Yearley 1996). Also, the very term "rain forest" draws attention to the forest as an abstract global concept with general properties, rather than to more specific ways local people may refer to forests where they live (Carrier 2004, 6).

Protected areas and tropical forests are also associated with global climate change. Global warming is unambiguously a global environmental issue in the sense that it links people around the globe in cause-and-effect relationships and affects the world as a whole (National Research Council 1999). Yet it also involves important global-local interactions. Michael R. Dove (2003) notes that tropical forests are often referred to as the "lungs of the world," which may be seen as a simple representation of their importance to maintaining the world's climatic conditions but may also be seen as a more strategic usage to focus attention on the tropical countries and perhaps away from environmental problems in temperate zone developed countries. For example, Taylor and Buttel (1992) note that the popularization of global warming was accompanied by a disproportionate focus on Third World sources of greenhouse gases, notably tropical deforestation, as opposed to carbon dioxide emissions in developed countries.

Parks and forest conservation also reflect globalization by protecting habitat for a variety of plants and animals, thereby helping to preserve the world's biodiversity. More than one hundred fifty nations participating in the 1992 Earth Summit acknowledged the importance of biodiversity protection by signing the Biodiversity Convention. "Biodiversity," like "rain forest," is also a globalizing term in that it generalizes local concerns about the loss of particular species as a global concern (Yearley 1996). Conservationists' avowed concern with all species may be counter to local people's focus on more useful species and may interfere with their property rights and their desire to reach full productive use of their land (Gerritsen and Wiersum 2005, Theodossopoulos 2004). In other cases, local people may feel that conservationists focus on their land use practices when the more important causes of species decline may be industrial or tourism development (Carrier 2004, Paolisso and Maloney 2000b).

In global environmental protection efforts, tropical areas are regarded as centrally important, and they are assigned important responsibilities in protecting the common good. "In effect," as Yearley (1996, 59) points out, "tropical countries are being asked to conserve their natural resources for the good of the international community." It is not clear, however, whether purportedly global environmental interests, such as the preservation of tropical forests and biodiversity, are inherently universal. These interests are created through the interaction of various, sometimes competing international organizations, such as environmental NGOs, the United Nations, and the World Bank. Given the constructed nature of these claims to represent the global good, we might expect persons representing particular local needs to challenge representations of universal environmental interests (Lipschutz and Conca 1993, Yearley 1996).

Conservation Discourses and Global-Local Interactions

There have recently been increasing numbers of books and articles focusing on conservation discourse, many of which analyze generalized social discourses of conservationists and local people (e.g., Carrier 2004, Greenough and Tsing 2003, Selin 2003). These works show clearly that environmental understandings and discourse matter and have complex connections to material factors (Gezon 2005, Heyman 2004). A substantial portion of this literature addresses the global-versus-local issues in environmental discourse, including the historical and current ways that tropical nature (and culture) has been viewed and defined by naturalists, scientists, and the public in Western or developed countries and the role of this discourse in the imposition of new national and global conservation and resource use regimes on local people (Greenough and Tsing 2003, Grove 1995, Slater 2003). James G. Carrier's (2004) book is notable among these for including cases that show how people can be both losers and beneficiaries. When harmed, they tend to resist global environmental practices like forest conservation and protected areas. When they stand to benefit, they often embrace global discourses and conservation practices.

In fact, globally driven forest conservation efforts have had very different results in different places. In some cases, forest conservation and protected area regimes have been seen as impositions by outside forces, sometimes to enable core regions to extract resources or exploit them through tourism, sometimes as a way of expanding power of the nation-state and/or international organizations in remote regions. Sometimes these entities promote conservation interests of core regions over local livelihood needs (Brandon et al. 1998, Brechin et al. 2003, Carrier 2004, Haenn 1999, Peluso 1992). In some cases, there has been open conflict (Neumann 2001); more commonly, there have been subtle forms of everyday resistance, such as illegal hunting, grazing trespass, and fuelwood theft (Little 1999, Neumann 1995, Pfeffer et al. 2001). In other cases, there has been common ground between conservation programs and local people's desires to defend the resources they have traditionally used from new, externally driven extractive use schemes (Fisher 1994, Heyman 2004, Western and Wright 1994). In many cases, the rhetoric of sustainable development has served to mask conflict by allowing all parties to talk of the need for community development and conservation, even when they have radically different perspectives on what these are (Campbell 2002, Neumann 1995, Nygren 1998). This can ultimately lead to conflict as these differing agendas are asserted but can also enable diverse groups of people to come together to manage difficult problems (Tsing 2005).

Conflicts are not always stark, and the resulting cultural forms produced by global-local interactions are not simply limited to adoption of either global conservation or oppositional discourses. Luis A. Vivanco (2001) discusses how a dairy farmer turned nature reserve maintenance worker enacted the ecotourist experience, taking pictures of waterfalls and wildlife, in the same encounter in which he expressed a desire to use the forests of the reserve for hunting and collecting products for food and home construction. Just as we have seen for other global issues, the interaction of the global and the local often has complex results in which new cultural forms result that reflect some global environmentalist themes but also adapt them in new ways to unique local conditions. In fact, when diverse and changing global environmental discourse and conservation regimes meet diverse and changing local culture and land use practices, complex interactions and dynamic processes ensue.

Dove et al. (2003) and David John Frank et al. (2000) note that environmental concepts do not travel on their own and impose themselves on people without agency. Simply contrasting global versus local discourses can be misleading. Paul Robbins (2000) highlights the importance of an empirical analysis that shows the roles of individual agents; Frank et al. (2000) emphasize the importance of organizational networks; and Lisa Gezon (2005) and Charles Zerner (1994) discuss the importance of addressing scale by using multiple levels of analysis while focusing on the empirical connections among people and places. Conservation concepts become powerful in new settings through complex processes of integration, reinterpretation, translation, and hybridization of ideas (Carrier 2004, Dove et al. 2003).

Finally, it should be mentioned that park and protected areas themselves enter into local communities not only in connection with abstract global ideas but also in very real (and unique) manifestations of the particular organizations and people that implement them. The specific laws, policies, incentives, and sanctions, as well as the ideology, that these actors bring to their work have real implications for local people's practices and ideology. For example, Paige West and Dan Brockington (2006) provide several examples where policies providing accommodations for certain indigenous groups in protected area policies play a role in redefining identities and resource use practices.

Environmentalism and Forest-Related Behavior

Ultimately, it is important to return to the question of whether the rise of global environmentalism makes any difference in terms of the way that people living in and adjacent to protected areas treat tropical forests on private lands and in reserves. The literature on the social determinants of land and natural resources is vast, and we only cover a few highlights here in order to develop a framework for analysis.

Forests and trees provide a wide range of products for subsistence use and sale. While these products can be harvested at unsustainable rates, resulting in forest loss or degradation, there are tree and forest management systems that result in relatively stable tree and forest cover. These range from extensive forest management, to the extraction of timber and nontimber forest products, to intensively managed forest patches, such as complex agroforestry systems, shade-grown crops, tree plantations, and woodlots (Arnold and Dewees 1995, Schelhas and Greenberg 1996, Schroth et al. 2004).

In some cases, forestland uses are competitive with agriculture in returns to land and labor. They can also provide fallback resources for food and cash income in times of crop failure and economic need. Because households often combine high-return/high-labor/high-risk options with low-return/low-labor/low-risk options, forests may be important components in economic systems beyond their immediate economic returns (Schelhas 1996a). Forest land uses may also become economically attractive to older people or those engaged in off-farm employment, because, once planted, they increase in value and provide periodic returns with relatively low labor investments (Schelhas 1996b). Largely for this reason, research suggests that agricultural intensification, off-farm employment, and urbanization can all lead to increases in forest land uses (Schelhas 1996b). The forest transition theory posits that this adds up to a general pattern; as a country goes through economic development, urbanization, and industrialization, forest cover, after initial declines, begins to recover (Rudel et al. 2005).

Forests can also be a component of land speculation (Smith et al. 1997, Wear and Newman 2004). John Schelhas (2001b) suggests that, through the 1980s, cattle production was the land use of choice for land speculation in Central America, but, at least in Costa Rica, forests began to play the same role in the 1990s. Trees and forests may also be planted largely for symbolic purposes, as a demonstration of environmental concern (Cary 1993).

Forests also provide environmental services to landholders that are generally not assigned monetary value. These services include soil and water conservation, restoration of soil fertility, and facilitation of pollination and pest control for some agricultural crops (Alcorn 1990, Clinnick 1984, Daily 1997, Power 1996). Some studies suggest that environmental services may be at least as important to landholders as forest products (Thacher et al. 1997). For example, rural people may attach great importance to the role of forest in the abundance and safety of their water supply (Jantzi et al. 1999, Thacher et al. 1997). Although some of the environmental services from forests may be widely recognized by rural people, we know relatively little about how these influence their land and resource use decisions.

Recent literature on the human dimensions of biodiversity conservation has placed greater emphasis on economic determinants of land use choice and natural resource use than on cultural or attitudinal factors under the assumption that poorer people are motivated by immediate livelihood concerns (Brechin and Kempton 1994, Schmink 1994). Yet the few studies that have addressed attitudes find a more complex picture. There are cases where the cultural value of forests for indigenous people has led to the retention of forests, even when economic pressure for forest clearing have been very high (Alcorn 1996, Lebbie and Freudenberger 1996). But perhaps more significant to our study are the attitudes toward conservation that have been found among a wide range of people in many lesser developed countries. William D. Newmark et al. (1993) found positive attitudes toward protected areas and conservation (but not toward protected area employees) among people living adjacent to five protected areas in Tanzania. B. K. Hartup (1994) found that landholders participating in a voluntary community conservation program overwhelmingly favored the protection of black howler monkeys in Belize for predominantly noneconomic reasons. Nora Haenn (2005) finds that, as for environmentalism in general, protected areas, as one of the most significant state presences in many rural regions, can become the focal point for a broader range of social issues.

Direct ways that culture and attitudes drive land use and forest cover changes cannot be easily identified, but many indirect relationships exist through attitudes toward population growth, settlement patterns, demand and consumption patterns, social movements, and politics (Arizpe et al. 1996, Rockwell 1994). A wider variety of social and economic factors influence the extent and way that environmental values are carried into behaviors. For this reason, it is more appropriate to look at socially situated environmental knowledge and values in seeking to understand the link to behavior. For example, Atran et al. (1999, 2002) found that different ethnic groups in Guatemala had different forest cognitions, social networks, and behaviors, which ultimately resulted in different levels of forest degradation. Also, forest values can change over time. Changing values are one way that humans, as adaptive agents, anticipate and respond to changes in their environment (Turner et al. 1995). Changing environmental values may directly catalyze changes in individual land use choices or catalyze land use change by stimulating new forms of community organization and political action.

Relatively little is known about the effect of environmental globalization on behavior. Much of the research on environmental globalization has focused on the distribution of attitudes and opinions across countries (Abrahamson 1997, Brechin and Kempton 1994, Dunlap et al. 1993, Inglehart 1995, Kidd and Lee 1997), but their impact on conservation behavior has not often been examined. Past research has not demonstrated clear links between general environmental attitudes and specific environmental behaviors (Pfeffer and Stycos 2002, Shanahan et al. 1999). It is difficult to gauge the material impacts of environmental globalization without an understanding of the influence of ideas on behaviors.

Concepts for Understanding Environmental Values

Environmental values are widely discussed as a key ingredient in successful natural resource management and policy, sustainability, and biodiversity conservation (Dietz et al. 2005, Leopold 1966, Norton 2003). Social psychology approaches to understanding the values that people hold[3] tend to focus on values as a set of basic, slow-changing concepts or beliefs about the desirable end state of behaviors that influence attitudes, beliefs, norms, and behaviors (Dietz et al. 2005, Fransson and Gärling 1999, Satterfield and Kalof 2005). Through surveys, this research seeks to measure the nature and degree of environmental value orientations that people have (for example, self-interest, concern for welfare of others, and concern for the biosphere) and to determine how these values are associated with environmentally related behaviors (Stern et al. 1993).

Our approach is different in that we see values as dynamic and more deeply embedded and entwined in mental and social life. Rather than seeking static indicators of individuals' values, we endeavor to study the way values are socially constructed through dynamic processes. Our approach emphasizes the social construction of values. For us, values are artifacts grounded in social interaction. We do not conceive of values as essential and unchanging; nor do we consider values to be freely created by individuals. Instead, we are interested in how various forms of social organization foster the systematic development of a logically interconnected set of values. Certainly individuals articulate certain values and often orient their behaviors based on priorities established with reference to values, but we see these values as received. Organizations not only foster the construction of these values, but they also serve as social carriers that disseminate interconnected sets of values across the social landscape (Kalberg 1994, Pfeffer et al. 2001). We refer to these sets of values as cultural models. Such models exist for different dimensions of social life (e.g., conservation, religion, science, education) and may complement or contradict one another. Likewise, different social carriers (e.g., churches, conservation organizations, universities) may represent one or more of these models.

Cultural models incorporate both beliefs and values, with beliefs referring to what people think the world is like and values referring to what they think is moral, desirable, or just (Kempton et al. 1995, 12). Cultural models are made of smaller units, called schema, which are more bounded, distinct, and unitary (D'Andrade 1995). Schema theory sees culture as partly individual and partly shared, resulting from the interaction of individuals with other people and stored knowledge and ideas (Strauss and Quinn 1997). The mental models by which individuals orient personal behaviors are informed by cultural models that represent widely held beliefs and values. Schemas, networks of strongly connected cognitive elements that are largely built up through human experience, provide an organized framework for objects and relations and thereby mediate many of the cognitive processes of individuals (D'Andrade 1995, Strauss and Quinn 1997). Schemas are fundamental to people's understanding of their experiences and the meanings they attach to them (Holland and Quinn 1987, Strauss and Quinn 1997). Schemas are closely associated with discourse but can also include representations of sensations, action, and events (DiMaggio 2002, Strauss and Quinn 1997). Because the activation of schemas is based on weights or the strength of connections, rather than formal rules, schemas are very sensitive to small changes in context and highly variable across individuals (Strauss and Quinn 1997). However, when people have common and recurring experiences, they come to share schemas. Claudia Strauss and Naomi Quinn (1997) thus conceive of each person as a junction point for many different, partially overlapping cultures, some of which are more widely shared than others. Individuals do not have exact copies of schemas in their head, but many schemas are shared, and cultural meanings are created in the interaction between the individual and interpersonal realms (D'Andrade 1995, Strauss and Quinn 1997).

Schema theory and cultural models thus provide a basis for the empirical study of environmental beliefs and values as socially constructed, complex, dynamic, contextually specific, and resulting in a wide range of behaviors worldwide. Environmental schemas and models can be identified through discourse analysis of transcripts of individual interviews, and variations in them can be assessed through qualitative analysis and by quantitative analysis of survey results (Kempton et al. 1995, Paolisso 2002). Recent advances in schema theory suggest several lines of analysis particularly useful in the study of environmental values: shared cultural models, differences in cultural models by social groups, motivation, and social discourses and the mediation of competing discourses.

One important approach is identifying the cultural models shared by individuals (Quinn 2005b). Schemas can be thought of as a generic version of some part of the world that is built up from experience and stored in a person's memory (Quinn 2005a). While schemas can change, when they result from similar, repeated experience they become relatively stable and are used to interpret later experiences, undergoing little change in the process. To the extent that people share experiences, they share schemas and hence cultures or subcultures. Research on cultural models looks for patterns across interviewees and passages that indicate that shared and stable understandings exist (Quinn 2005b). Quinn's approach is to focus on key words, metaphors, or reasoning that tend to be governed by schemas operating on an unconscious level as people express themselves (Quinn 2005b). Strauss (2005), suggesting that deep assumptions are often left unsaid, suggests focusing on people's assumptions; underlying assumptions support the evidence they assume can be trusted, how they connect two topics, how they describe sequences of events, or the implied point of stories they relate. The goal of research on cultural models is to reconstruct people's implicit assumptions and, by finding common underlying assumptions, identify shared understandings (Quinn 2005b). Quinn (2005b) suggests that even if people tailor their responses to the interview situation in some way, these underlying assumptions continue to operate. A principal objective of our research is to understand the underlying structure of people's environmental values.

Bradd Shore (1996) notes that recent research questions the degree to which people share cultural models when they live in communities made up of different interest groups and politically positioned individuals. In accord with this observation, Strauss (2005) goes beyond cultural models to consider how they may differ, both in meaning and significance, by social subgroup. Differences in the content and structure of cultural models can be expected to be found among social subgroups, such as those distinguished by class, race/ethnicity, or gender. Other research has also focused on how similar schemas may have different levels of motivating force for individuals and thus different levels of influence on behavior (D'Andrade and Strauss 1992, Strauss and Quinn 1997). Motivating force has been found to depend both on factors internal to the individual (e.g., emotional saliency) and the context in which the individual acts (e.g., social discourses and institutions) (Shore 1996, Strauss and Quinn 1997). Strauss (1997) finds that models can also have "lip-service" motivation, where people have internalized a widely available or dominant model without its leading to corresponding action.

Another line of analysis is Strauss's (2005) work on how people internalize public culture. Strauss suggests that social discourses[4] are different from cultural models in that they are made explicit amid a general awareness that there are competing belief systems. Social discourses are extensively developed by ideologists and disseminated to the public, which tends to absorb these in at least fragmentary form (Strauss 2005). Environmentalism, as developed and spread by environmental thinkers, educators, and activists, clearly has associated social discourses. Strauss suggests that social discourses can be recognized in people's talk by the presence of ideas, jargon, and phraseology typical of that discourse. When social discourses become common opinion, they may be indicated by formulaic language, which Strauss calls verbal molecules, indicated by repetition of the same verbatim bits of discourse by speakers. Although social discourses can become dominant and emanate from powerful forces, Shore (1996) notes that alternatives to the dominant model can emerge and calls these counter-hegemonic discourses.

If individuals are exposed to competing discourses or hold conflicting models, Strauss (2005) suggests that they organize them in three different ways. One, ideas can be compartmentalized, or held in largely unconnected cognitive schemas with individuals being generally unaware of the conflict between them. Two, they can be ambivalent—aware that they seem to hold inconsistent ideas and show signs of being bothered by this without any reconciliation. Three, they can integrate the ideas by drawing selectively from multiple discourses and blending these elements into a new idea that is consistent and makes sense for them, even if it differs from more widely shared public ideas. While people can keep these ideas compartmentalized, it is generally believed that people make ongoing efforts to create coherence in their ideas and life stories (Quinn 2005b). When conflicting schemas are brought together, a wide range of outcomes is possible, but often new unifying or mediating models or discourses arise that help to sort out the conflict and subsequent behavior (Strauss and Quinn 1997).

These concepts (shared schemas, differences in schema by social position, motivation, mediating models) help us to understand variations in environmental values, their operation, and their influence on behavior under different conditions. Together, they enable us to develop descriptions of cultural models and environmental values that have great depth and to understand the dynamic processes in which they are embedded. A cultural model approach sees environmental beliefs and values as cultural artifacts available to individuals. Under this conceptualization, environmentalism is shared but subject to change as individuals mold it based on their personal experiences. The most common method in empirical studies of environmental values is to identify a set of environmental values (often from environmental literature), phrase these as statements for respondents to react to, and measure the extent to which people have adopted or not adopted these values (e.g., Dunlap 1991, Holl et al. 1995). A cultural model approach differs from many other approaches that work with fixed notions of environmentalism and environmental values. The cultural model approach recognizes multiple environmentalisms and seeks to understand their content and construction.

Cultural models have been used by several other researchers in environmental research. Kempton et al. (1995) used cultural models in a study of environmental values in the United States that sought to understand the underlying structure of environmental beliefs and values. They found that environmentalism in the United States had become integrated with core values, such as parental responsibility, obligation to descendants, and traditional religious teachings, and that biocentric values are important for many people. The sample was designed to compare extreme social groups (e.g., radical environmentalists and loggers). The results indicated that opponents of environmental laws had environmental values similar to environmentalists but that these were overridden by competing models (e.g., political concerns or other values, such as opposition to human suffering or unemployment). Disagreements tended to be in the relative rankings of values, rather than in the values themselves.

Michael Paolisso and colleagues carried out an extensive study of the cultural models of different stakeholder groups in environmental conflicts around the Chesapeake Bay in the eastern United States, including pollution, harmful algae, and fisheries declines. The results indicated that different stakeholder groups had different interpretations of what it meant to be an environmentalist and had complex cultural models of nature that were closely tied to their group identity and livelihoods (Paolisso 2002, Paolisso and Chambers 2001, Paolisso and Maloney 2000a, 2000b). Farmers and fishermen distrusted science and felt that, because they were politically weak, environmentalists and politicians shifted blame to them, rather than regulating other sources of nonpoint pollution (Paolisso 1999, Paolisso and Chambers 2001, Paolisso and Maloney 2000a, 2000b). Rural people sometimes framed these conflicts along rural-urban lines, seeing themselves as the real environmentalists opposing the morally bankrupt, pollution-generating urban centers that they felt were the source of misguided environmental protection efforts (Paolisso and Maloney 2000b).

Niels Einarrson (1993, 1990) has used cultural models to study conflicts between environmentalists and Icelandic fishermen over whaling and seals. Regarding whaling, environmentalists have come to see whales as an important symbol of the human relationship to the environment and what has gone wrong with it, while fishermen see them as competitors for fish and economic resources that enable their survival and the possibility to continue village life (Einarrson 1993). Inequalities in power and the realities of international conservation politics result in outside ways of thinking about whales being forced on local people (Einarrson 1993). In the case of seals, fishermen quickly went from neutral to negative feelings. Einarrson sees this shift as due to practical reasons—because seals were lost as an income source due to antisealing protests and because seals also negatively impact fisheries—and symbolic ones, with fishermen attacking the seals as representations of environmentalists who are beyond their reach or influence (Einarrson 1990).

What emerges in all these studies, as well as others (e.g., Marvin 2000, Song 2000), is differences and conflicts in cultural models between the local people who make their living from these natural resources and outside environmentalists who promote their conservation with little consideration of local economic needs or worldviews. Rural people find themselves with little power relative to urban interests and environmentalists, and in some cases, polarization and counterhegemonic discourses arise and become associated with an active antienvironmentalism. As a result, environmental conflicts become mapped onto, or intertwined with, other social conflicts.

In another study of theoretical relevance, Lourdes Arizpe et al. (1996), while not explicitly using cultural models or schemas, studied the social perception of forests in the Lacandona forest in Mexico. Rural farmers tended toward deistic views of nature, while urban professionals emphasized ecological justifications. Outside pressure and influences had changed over the previous decades from clearing forests for development to efforts to stop deforestation and promote conservation. Deforestation was mentioned by local people more in places where workshops and meetings on sustainable agriculture and rain forest conservation had been held, suggesting that these programs changed the way people talked about the forest. There was a tendency for each group (small farmers, cattle rangers, urban residents, government, and indigenous people) to blame other groups for the deforestation and for social discourses to crystallize along existing, unequal social relationships. Arizpe et al. (1996) believed that norms related to deforestation were in the process of being created and that their research could only map out emerging perceptions of environmental change.

Methods for Capturing and Distilling the Local Environmental Discourse

To accomplish our goals, we examined transcriptions of interviews with rural residents residing in communities adjacent to the La Amistad International Park (LAIP) in Costa Rica and residents of communities in the buffer zone of the Cerro Azul Meambar National Park (CAMNP) in Honduras. We sought to identify common beliefs and values (cultural models), as well as individual and divergent socially constructed beliefs and values. We analyzed the content of individual transcripts in view of (1) the individual environmental experiences and social locations of our respondents, and (2) the national and international social and political discourse, material and structural relationships, and power dynamics within which local people lived.

Our approach to studying cultural models of forests in Costa Rica and Honduras involved analysis of transcribed interviews and questionnaire data to accomplish several main objectives:

1. To identify cultural models related to forests and their conservation by identifying common ways that people talk about forests
2. To identify traces of the international conservation discourse in the talk of rural people and local park rangers (as intermediaries between conservation and local people)
3. To look for evidence of the motivating force of expressed forest values and to examine the ways that people mediate between forest conservation values and their livelihood needs
4. To look for indications of forest-related behaviors in interviews and questionnaire data
5. To compare and contrast the above for the Costa Rica and Honduras cases, with particular attention to difference due to (a) levels of economic development, (b) exposure to conservation messages, and (c) different park management approaches (strict protectionist versus parks-and-people approaches)

The cultural model approach suggests that the context in which a discourse takes place influences its content, and it is important to address the specific context in which the narratives we analyzed were generated. Leach and Fairhead (2002) discuss how, due to unequal power relationships, rural inhabitants interacting with outsiders may talk about the environment differently than they do in everyday discourse, for example by adopting outsider terms or saying what they think outsiders want to hear. However, Strauss and Quinn (1997, 241), in discussing the way that discourses are constructed between researchers and interviewees, find that, while what people say cannot always be taken at face value, what people choose to say or leave unsaid in the interview process is itself very revealing. In our research, because many environmental messages in Costa Rica and Honduras have originated from North American scientists and conservationists, it is very likely that a research project of North American origin asking questions about forests and the environment would elicit responses favoring environmental conservation, some of which may be hollow or reflect values unlikely to influence behavior. We were aware of this potential problem when we designed and carried out the research and addressed it in several ways: (1) intentionally bringing up ideas that prior research and experience had suggested compete with or contradict environmental schema (e.g., livelihood issues) as a way trying to push people beyond simplistic responses, (2) probing deeper with questions about problems with conservation, and (3) engaging in lengthy interviews to get beyond initial responses and reactions. Strauss and Quinn (1997) note that an interview reveals what people think is worth mentioning in that context, which is in itself important. Detailed interviews help to elicit responses that go beyond simply trying to say what the respondent thinks the researcher wants to hear.

But these concerns highlight the importance of being explicit about how the research was carried out and of conducting careful and in-depth interviews. We visited communities and community leaders prior to beginning the interviews. Semistructured interviews were carried out by two male and two female North American researchers who spent several weeks living in the communities. In all cases, researchers sought to solicit and understand local attitudes and values and to take great care not to suggest or give preference to certain values or conceptualizations.

We conducted a set of semistructured qualitative interviews with fifty-four individuals in five villages within Cerro Azul Meambar National Park (completed in 1999) and sixty-seven persons in five villages within five kilometers of the La Amistad International Park's southern perimeter (completed in 2000). The villages we selected were geographically dispersed. We selected respondents purposefully, typically making initial contacts in the villages through park guards or other local informants targeting community leaders for interviews. About half of the interviews resulted from cold calls that initiated contacts with individuals we felt were missed in the introductions provided by park guards or informants. We engaged respondents in semistructured interviews of between one and two hours' duration. Our questioning was based on an interview guide consisting of a variety of open-ended questions about attitudes and behaviors related to forests and the park. Specifically, we asked respondents (1) to discuss forests in general in the region and on their own land, including ways in which they might be beneficial and detrimental, how forests had changed over the years, and who had been responsible for these changes, and (2) to discuss the national park, including what they thought the benefits of the park were, who benefited from the park, if they felt the distribution of benefits was fair, and if they thought there were any problems associated with the park. The responses were open-ended and allowed us to capture the respondents' sentiments in their own words.

Our analysis of the qualitative data began with a simple reading of field notes and interview transcripts. This allowed us to identify a set of important themes in the discourse. We then used *Nvivo* to code sections of the transcripts and field notes according to these themes, developing a finer focus for themes and at times creating new themes as we worked. With the transcripts and field notes coded, we extracted sections of text with the same codes and looked for patterns of responses to our questioning. In our analysis, we frequently moved back and forth between the extracts and the original transcripts so that the context of statements was not lost. For the purposes of this book, we focused on a subset of the patterns or themes related to forests and the park and looked for consistency and differences in responses across the interviews. We present selected quotations to support and elaborate the findings of our qualitative analysis.

In 1999, with the assistance of students and faculty at the Honduran National Forestry School, we interviewed 601 randomly selected household heads living in eight communities in or near CAMNP. In 2000 we conducted a similar survey of 523 randomly selected households in eight villages within five kilometers of the southern border of LAIP with the assistance of faculty and students from the National Autonomous University of Costa Rica. The communities were purposefully selected to provide a complete geographic coverage within the CAMNP buffer zone and along the southern boundary of the LAIP. In both cases, our sampling frames were complete lists of all households in our selected communities. We targeted household heads after discovering in earlier qualitative interviewing that they were much more informed about land use decisions than other household members. When household heads were not available, we interviewed their spouses. Thirty-eight percent of our Honduran and 36 percent of our Costa Rican respondents were female.

The wide-ranging survey interviews included questions about attitudes toward natural resources, especially forests and the park; land use, including agricultural production and de- and reforestation; sources of information about forests and the environment; expected benefits from the park; and a variety of sociodemographic characteristics like income, income sources, age, education, and household composition. Copies of our qualitative and quantitative instruments can be found in Appendixes B–D.

We use these different data in the following chapters as we attempt to understand the evolving local environmental discourse in the two Central American parks.

Looking Forward

In the remainder of this book, we will use the conceptual framework outlined in this chapter to guide our empirical analysis. In this chapter, we have outlined our point of departure: national parks and protected areas, in their role in conserving tropical forest and biodiversity, are a phenomenon of globalization. Their establishment and management are carried out by national governments with support and guidance from international organizations. Because of unequal power relationships, they often have been imposed on local people without their consent or input. Although the ideology of national parks, biodiversity, and tropical forest conservation is globalized, over the past few decades significant efforts have been made to adapt both messages and practices to on-the-ground realities in lesser developed countries. One result of this is that there is a number of international conservation approaches, ranging from conventional protected areas to various parks-and-people approaches. In addition to different approaches, actual park management practice introduces even more variation as managers seek to adapt received models to local realities. In the end, unique local forms of environmentalism emerge. Local environmentalisms are structured to a significant extent by interactive processes between global environmental ideology and local livelihood needs (which themselves have important material, as well as ideological, determinants), mediated by the formal and informal conservation practices and policies that are in play at a particular locale. The results of this process determine, to a significant extent, local people's environmental values and forest-related conservation behaviors. To begin our examination of the formation of these values and behaviors, in the following chapter we describe the history and social structure of the two parks in our study.

Notes

1. There is some evidence for tropical forest transitions, where forest cover returns with development, industrialization, and urbanization, although most clear examples of forest transitions to date have been in the temperate regions of North America and Europe (Rudel 2005).

2. A political cartoon by Scott Willis from the late 1980s succinctly made this point by showing a large man sticking his head out of a big, pollution-spewing car saying to a *campesino* (with a burro) who is about to fell a tree, "Yo! Amigo!! We need that tree to protect us from the greenhouse effect" (1989 San Jose Mercury News/Copely News Service).

3. Economic approaches to value are fundamentally different in nature, focusing on assigning prices to environmental goods and services rather than investigating the values that people hold (see Satterfield and Kalof 2005).

4. "Social discourses" in this case refers to discourses in the Foucauldian sense as "a way of talking and a set of associated practices, forms of subjectivity, and power relationships that together constitute a body of knowledge identified with members of some subgroup of society" (Quinn 2005a, 5).

Protected Areas in Central America

FOREST CONSERVATION HAS BEEN a topic of increasing concern in recent decades. This concern has spread around the world and has been especially evident in Central America. Concerns about deforestation were especially pronounced in the 1980s as large swaths of forest were transformed into pasture and for other land uses (Bilsborrow and Carr 2001, Kaimowitz 1997, Rudel 2005, Rudel et al. 2002). Deforestation became a global concern, and international organizations became actively engaged in promoting a variety of measures intended to arrest tropical deforestation. In this way, local problems with global consequences were addressed with global solutions applied at the local level.

Our case studies illustrate this phenomenon of environmental globalization. Although both Costa Rica and Honduras had some history of forest conservation, their efforts had historically only been sporadic. The attention to forest conservation grew in both countries in the 1980s, and worldwide attention turned to the region and the pronounced land use changes underway there. Certainly, there was a distinct national flavor to some of the forest conservation measures adopted in Costa Rica and Honduras, but it is also striking that forest conservation is framed in the respective countries in much the same way that it is around the world. Not only is forest conservation organized in similar ways, but a variety of different people in distinctive settings talk about it in ways that are uncanny in their similarity.

A number of scholars have observed this globalization of environmental concern (Frank 2002, Frank et al. 2000, Milton 1996, Pfeffer et al. 2001, 2006, Schelhas and Pfeffer 2005). These observations raise the question of how similar forms of social organization and expression of concerns and values appear in very different contexts (Frank et al. 2000, Pfeffer et al. 2006). In considering this question one cannot ignore the organizations that serve as "social carriers" of ideas and values and that structure social interaction and environmental behaviors in ways that lead to a striking degree of uniformity (Kalberg 1990, 1994, 2004; Pfeffer et al. 2006). Our study sites offer interesting illustrations of such organizational intervention. Both sites were the locus of forest conversion and resource extraction typical of frontier areas. Almost all of the inhabitants of our study sites were poor people who came there in search of resources they could claim for the purposes of subsistence production. In both areas, settlers began to rapidly deforest the landscape to lay claim to the land.

Observers worldwide witnessed this deforestation, and it became an issue of global concern. One widely implemented solution to such rapid environmental change was the creation of protected areas. The protected areas created in our study sites are the focal points of our attention. In Costa Rica, La Amistad International Park (LAIP), and in Honduras, Cerro Azul Meambar National Park (CAMNP), established new frameworks that conditioned how people thought about nature and how they used forests and other natural resources. But by the time these protected areas were established, some people had already populated the areas and had transformed parts of the landscape. This chapter provides an overview of the parks and the context within which they were established. We briefly review forest conservation policies in Costa Rica and Honduras, the basic features of the organization of the respective protected areas, the established pattern of land use, and some of the characteristics and behaviors of the inhabitants of communities closely linked with the protected areas.

Land Use Change and Forest Conservation

Forests in our two study sites are situated within a mosaic of land use.[1] The current configuration of land use has changed, especially in about the last forty years. During this time, the areas went from being almost entirely uninhabited and heavily forested to having significant populations that claimed lands that by 1999 were 23 and 30 percent forested in our Costa Rican and Honduran study sites, respectively.[2] Although some current residents inhabited the areas as early as 1938 in Costa Rica and 1918 in Honduras, rapid population growth did not take place until the latter half of the twentieth century. Both study sites represented the agricultural frontier in the 1960s. Figure 2.1 shows that substantial growth of the working-age population in the two areas began in the early 1960s.[3] In Costa Rica new arrivals from other places dominated this population growth. In Honduras, natural increase of the local population rose rapidly from the early 1960s to the early 1980s. In the mid-1980s, new arrivals became the most rapidly increasing component of the working-age population.

This growth in the working-age population created demand for land and led to deforestation as residents cleared land for subsistence agricultural production. In

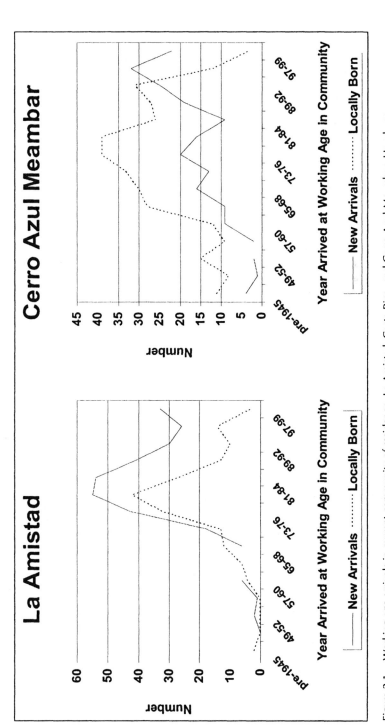

Figure 2.1. Working-age arrivals in current community of residence, La Amistad, Costa Rica, and Cerro Azul Meambar, Honduras.

both areas, trees were typically felled and then burned in swidden agricultural systems. Initially land was cleared for maize and bean production, or *milpa*, and pasture for cattle production. Pasture-based cattle production was especially important in Costa Rica during the 1970s and 1980s (Angelson and Kaimowitz 1999, Kaimowitz 1997, Rudel et al. 2000, Schelhas 1996a, 2001b). But beginning in the 1980s, growth in demand for coffee led to additional forest clearing. While it is hard to document the extent of this change, especially the increase in coffee plantations, for our Honduras site we estimated, based on extensive on-site observations, that land in coffee grew about 7 percent in the 1993–1998 period, at the expense of cropland (–1.7%), forest (–0.3%), and especially fallow land (–3.2%) (Pfeffer et al. 2005).[4] As a result, the configuration of land use on occupied land in the area was approximately as summarized in table 2.1.

Occupied lands in Costa Rica were dominated by pasture. A third of all the land occupied by the persons we surveyed was in pasture. Accounts of forest change in Costa Rica indicate the strong influence of clearing land for pasture beginning in the 1970s (Schelhas 1996a, 2001b). As shown in figure 2.1, the rush into our study area began in the early 1970s. As indicated above, this land was used for grazing cattle, but it also served as fallow for agricultural production. One-fifth of the land was dedicated to coffee production. Much of the land for coffee came from converted pasture and, as a result, did not have as marked an impact on forests as might have been the case if the land needed to be cleared. The fairly large proportions of the land dedicated to coffee production and cattle grazing indicate that there was an active cash economy in the area. Nevertheless, residents of the area continued to produce maize and beans mostly for home consumption.

Table 2.1.   Reported Land Use on Occupied Land, La Amistad, Costa Rica, and Cerro Azul Meambar, Honduras

Land Use	La Amistad	Cerro Azul Meambar
	Percentage Distribution	
Agriculture:	11.3	19.2
Corn/Beans	11.2	18.6
Horticulture	0.1	0.6
Coffee	20.9	16.1
Forest	23.0	30.4
Fallow:	43.1	31.0
Brush	9.7	22.3
Pasture	33.4	8.7
Other	1.7	3.3
TOTAL	100.0	100.0
Total Hectares Reported	7,714	3,063

Land use in Honduras was dominated by forest and forest fallow, followed by cropland and then coffee (see table 2.1). Until the recent growth in coffee production in the area, there was little production of cash crops. Maize and beans were produced mainly for subsistence production, and a small amount of horticultural production was mostly garden production for home consumption. However, this pattern changed in the 1980s and 1990s with the growth of coffee production. The introduction of coffee as a cash crop led to the start of a gradual transition away from a largely subsistence economy. The growth of coffee production is the most important factor leading to the increase of arrivals from other communities. As indicated in figure 2.1, this trend began in the early 1980s.

Forest Conservation Policies

In both areas, rapid population growth and associated land use change contributed to concern about conservation of the natural resource base of the areas. This concern coincided with efforts around the world and in both countries to create conservation areas as means of limiting the destruction of tropical forests (Brandon et al. 1998, Daily 1997, McNeely et al. 1994). In our study sites, the respective national governments established protected areas, or parks, to limit direct use of natural resources. In both study sites, the parks were to achieve conservation goals like forest, watershed, and biodiversity protection. These goals are widely held by globally oriented conservation organizations, as well as the governments of Costa Rica and Honduras.

Forest Conservation in Costa Rica

Costa Rican conservation history encompasses rapid deforestation associated with frontier colonization followed by a multipronged government response. Forestlands in Costa Rica were long viewed as unused land open to settlement by anyone willing to convert forest to agriculture (Brockett and Gottfried 2002). Deforestation proceeded slowly until the 1950s, increasing rapidly in the 1970s when the humid lowlands were opened up for banana plantations, cattle pasture, and frontier settlement (Carrière 1990, Evans 1999). Rapid deforestation continued through the 1980s and was driven by a demand for land and not for timber, with the majority of the timber cut, burned, or left to rot (Brockett and Gottfried 2002). While agriculture and pasture were a part of the frontier dynamic, the rapid rate of deforestation was driven more by a preference for investment in land in a highly inflationary economy and related land speculation than by a need or desire to establish productive land uses (Schelhas 1996a, 2001b). Motivated in part by laws that favored cleared land over forests in claiming and titling land, as well as to discourage squatters, landholders of all sizes converted forests to agriculture and, most frequently, pasture (Schelhas 1996a, 2001b).

Significant conservation efforts began in Costa Rica in the 1960s. The 1969 Forestry Law and subsequent revisions required permits for any tree cutting, and a technical study showing that cleared land could be used sustainably after forest clearing (Brockett and Gottfried 2002, Watson et al. 1998). Although this regulatory approach looked good on paper, in practice underfunded agencies could not enforce the laws, seldom got out into the field, and had a record of bureaucratic delays and corruption (Brockett and Gottfried 2002). At the same time, the difficulty in acquiring permits meant that landowners often had to rely on loggers who had the necessary connections (and sometimes paid bribes) to get permits. Loggers often paid low prices and high-graded timber (Brockett and Gottfried 2002).

A second policy approach was to provide incentives for forest conservation. Government fiscal incentives for reforestation began in 1979, incentives for forest management began in the early 1990s, and payments for environmental services from intact forest (e.g., carbon sequestration and watershed protection) began in 1996 (Brockett and Gottfried 2002, Watson et al. 1998). Many of these incentives favored large landowners and those possessing title to their land, although several programs have sought to make these incentives more widely available to the many small landowners who possess legal rights to land but not title (Thacher et al. 1997, Utting 1994, Watson et al. 1998).

Creation of national parks and other protected areas is a third important way that forest conservation has been implemented in Costa Rica. Parks and protected areas in Costa Rica date back at least to 1945, but significant establishment and management of parks and reserves began in the 1970s, when a few key individuals led a very successful effort that generated internal political support in Costa Rica at the highest levels, international support from conservation nongovernmental organizations (NGOs) and international aid agencies, and widespread public promotion of the parks both within and outside of Costa Rica (Boza 1993, Brandon et al. 1998, Evans 1999). By the mid-1990s, 11 percent of the country was in national parks and an additional 13 percent in biological reserves, national forests, national monuments, and national wildlife refuges.

Costa Rica's national park system was initiated in the 1970s and rapidly became one of the premier park systems in Latin America, both in terms of the percentage of national land designated as parks (World Resources Institute 1994) and the effective level of protection provided by the country's national park service (Boza 1993, Evans 1999, Gamez and Ugalde 1988, Schelhas and Pfeffer 2005). While the park system traditionally focused on park boundary protection and environmental education, recent reorganization of the country's parks and protected areas into conservation units sought to promote buffer zones and corridors around parks to compensate for the inadequate size of some parks (Boza 1993). Thus, there has been active engagement in conservation efforts of residents living in communities near parks.

The Costa Rican section of La Amistad International Park was created in 1982. The park protects 207,298 hectares in Costa Rica and is supplemented by a similar sized park in Panama and several other contiguous parks and reserves, making up the largest area of continuous protected forest in Central America. The park encompasses the higher reaches of the Talamanca Mountains in southern Costa Rica and largely includes only lands over two thousand meters in elevation. While the park is exceptionally large, seasonal altitudinal migrations of birds and butterflies are significant phenomena in Costa Rica, making management of lands adjacent to the park a key issue. In the Coto Brus area, where we concentrated our Costa Rican research effort, buffer zone management activities have been carried out by the National Park Service (emphasizing protection with some sustainable development activities), the Organization for Tropical Studies Environmental Dialogue Program (emphasizing participatory community development), the grassroots nongovernmental organization Agroecological Foundation of Coto Brus (organizing an "ecological committee" and promoting sustainable agriculture and forestry), and the local nature conservation organization *Asociación Preservacionista de Coto Brus* (emphasizing environmental education).

Figure 2.1 shows that creation of the park halted further population growth in the communities bordering the park. After 1982 there was sharp drop in the number of persons arriving at working age in the park. This reduction certainly had an impact on land use change. We observed numerous abandoned dwellings at the park's edge. Persons who continued to live nearest the park boundary complained that they were left with insufficient land when the park was created. They and others who have since left had planned to clear forest inside the boundaries of what was to become park land in 1982. The clear cessation of further incursions into the forest indicates the effectiveness of the park in halting deforestation inside the park boundaries.

Forest Conservation in Honduras

Until recently, forest conservation in Honduras has been intermittent and has only occasionally been successful. Forest conservation was virtually nonexistent in the colonial era. Colonists did plant trees in some instances, but typically to establish landownership, not for conservation. For example, in the sixteenth century, colonists were required to plant trees or cultivate crops within three months of receiving a land grant or risk forfeiting it (Barton 2001, Stokes 1947, Vallejo 1911). After independence in 1821 until the 1950s, the Honduran government enacted few forest conservation laws. Policy in the postindependence period continued to emphasize the occupation of wildlands through forest clearing for crop cultivation (Barton 2001, Mariñas Otero 1962, Merrill 1995). Even land reserves established in the early twentieth century were intended to be a stock of land that could be used to facilitate land reform by offering opportunities for the colonization of new lands. However, these early reserves served as a foundation for subsequent conservation efforts, especially the creation of protected areas (Barton 2001).

The Honduran Congress enacted one of the nation's first conservation laws, the Forests Law (*Ley de Bosques*), in 1939. This legislation provided for watershed protection, reforestation, and regulation of cutting and burning. For example, it prohibited the felling of trees in sensitive areas (e.g., along stream banks) and required individuals to obtain permits to cut trees or burn forests. Although this law was striking for its foresight regarding conservation measures, the Honduran government lacked the administrative capacity to effectively enforce it. The Honduran government established forest management agencies for the first time during the 1950s. The 1955 Forestry Law created the Forestry Service (*Servicio Forestal*). In 1961, the nation's conservation apparatus was extended with the creation of the State Forestry Administration (*Administración Forestal del Estado*, or *AFE*) that was charged with the enforcement of regulations. But the most significant development for forestry management came in the 1970s with the creation of the Honduran Forestry Development Corporation (*Corporación Hondureño de Desarollo Forestal*, or *COHDEFOR*). *COHDEFOR* was a parastatal agency that had management responsibility for, and control over, the management of the nation's forests. It gained importance and power because it was able to generate funds by selling timber harvested from the nation's forests (Barton 2001).

Between 1954 and 1982, the Honduran government also established thirteen protected areas. In 1961, legislation created the first Honduran national park, but the law was only briefly and sporadically implemented by conservation-oriented administrations that were in control for very short periods between 1961 and 1980. Military regimes dominated Honduras during the 1960s and the 1970s and were most responsive to populist demands for land reform, which were often seen as being at odds with forest conservation. However, at the end of military rule in 1980, additional protected areas were created to protect Tegucigalpa's watershed and to preserve the national patrimony in the Mosquitia region (the La Tigra National Park and the Río Plátano Biosphere Reserve, respectively). Since the early 1980s, the Honduran government has created a large number of protected areas. By 1996 there were one hundred parks and other protected areas in Honduras, and an additional fifty-six areas were proposed for protection. Different international agencies estimated that by the late 1990s between 10 and 25 percent of the national land base was under some sort of protected status. However, more sites were created than could effectively be managed (Barton 2001).

In 1987, Law 87-87 declared all lands over eighteen hundred meters in altitude protected areas. The rapid expansion of this protected area system created a number of management problems, including conflicts between environmental protection and the economic needs of people living in and near the parks. Honduras remains one of the poorest countries in the Western Hemisphere, second only to Haiti in poverty. Not only is literacy very low, but most rural areas have no access to electricity, only poor transportation infrastructure, and very little exposure to mass media (Barton 2001, Pfeffer et al. 2001, 2005).

Cerro Azul Meambar National Park was created by the Honduran government in 1987 with the expansion of the protected area system. The park includes all of Cerro Azul Meambar mountain above 1,800 meters to the peak of 2,047 meters. CAMNP covers about thirty-two thousand hectares. Initial responsibility for management of the park was assigned to COHDEFOR, but this agency never mounted any significant management program.

In 1992, *Aldea Global*, a nongovernmental organization, entered into a park management agreement with COHDEFOR. This contract assigned responsibility for management of CAMNP to *Aldea Global* for an initial five-year period, and this contract was subsequently renewed. *Aldea Global* continues to manage CAMNP on behalf of COHDEFOR. *Aldea Global* proposed a set of fixed boundaries that were officially adopted in 1994. The boundaries established three zones: (1) a core zone of 890 hectares, or about 3 percent of the park; (2) a 9,129 hectare special-use zone; and (3) a buffer zone covering 21,357 hectares, or about 68 percent of the park area (*COHDEFOR–Administración Forestal del Estado* 1994). Settlement is not allowed in the core or special-use zones, but there are forty-two communities in the buffer zone. In 1994, these communities were home to about 19,600 inhabitants altogether and between 490 and 949 inhabitants each, and their economies are oriented to small-scale coffee and subsistence maize and bean production. Efforts to regulate land use in the park led to several conflicts with ongoing economic activities. Regulations that impinged on existing economic behavior included restrictions on cattle grazing, tree harvesting, use of pesticides and fertilizers, and burning ground cover (Barton 2001, Pfeffer et al. 2001, 2005). The creation of the park did not stop newcomers from arriving until about the mid-1990s, as indicated in figure 2.1. Since active management of the park did not begin until 1992, there were no barriers to continued settlement and forest clearing. Increases in the locally born working-age population stopped in the early 1980s before the park was created, then leveled off for a few years. With active management of the park, the number of locally born individuals arriving at working age dropped off, suggesting that these young people are leaving the park for other areas.

Contrasting Park Management Models

Maps 1 and 2 show the locations of the communities in our study, the respective park boundaries, and land use patterns in the two study sites. Map 1 (figure 2.2) shows LAIP, Costa Rica, a conventional park. No settlement or resource extraction is allowed inside the park boundaries, as is true of many parks initially established in lesser developed countries (Campbell 2002, Pfeffer et al. 2006, West 1991). This model emphasizes biodiversity conservation, defined as the sanctity of "scientific and ethical values of biological species regardless of utility for humans" (Kramer et al. 1997, 4). It implies the need for protected areas unaltered by humans, and it inherently conflicts with extractive uses that have an impact on biological resources. This model requires strict enforcement of regulations within its boundaries and can be coupled with regulation of ecological hazards outside park boundaries (Wells and Brandon 1992). These "conventional" parks, based on the U.S. national park model, set aside large tracts of land where significant natural features, landscapes, ecosystems, and wildlife would thereafter be altered minimally by human intervention.

In contrast, map 2 (figure 2.3) shows that the CAMNP in Honduras is a much different model. As indicated above, it is a zoned park that allows settlement and limited, controlled resource access in the park buffer zones. The special-use zone can be used for scientific purposes, but the core zone is to be left untouched. The zoned park model is based on a philosophy of local participation and stewardship. It typically includes a core zone where use is restricted to scientific, educational, and tourism activities; a special-use zone which also has restricted use; and a buffer zone where resource use and habitation is allowed, usually regulated through land title and permit systems (McNeely 1990, Price 1996). Zoned parks are politically appealing alternatives to conventional ones because they attempt to protect biodiversity *and* provide for human needs. The belief among zoned park supporters that rural people make the best stewards due to presumed historical relationships with the land has led to increased community participation in conservation projects. The potential positive results include increased local control over resources, greater autonomy, and higher income for park residents (West and Brechin 1991, Wilhusen et al. 2002).

Characteristics of Park Residents

The success of parks as a forest conservation strategy depends on interactions between the park's organization, including the regulation of resource use, the natural resource endowment of the area, and the local population. We are most concerned with the latter. Generally speaking, the residents in the communities included in our study came from humble beginnings. Their characteristics are similar to peasants in many parts of the world. For example, in both study sites, educational attainment was limited to about three or four years of primary school (see table 2.2). It was somewhat surprising that, in both study sites, those who were born locally had an additional year of schooling. This observation

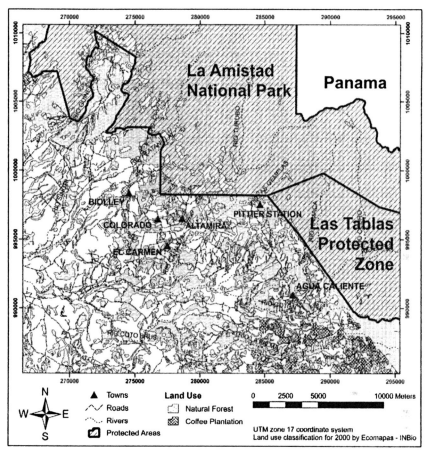

Figure 2.2.   Land use map of La Amistad International Park, Costa Rica, and surrounding communities.

suggests that newcomers were poorer people who had grown up in areas with even more limited educational opportunities than in our study sites. Newcomers also had slightly larger families than the locally born. Newcomers had a significant presence in the Costa Rican site, making up about 64 percent of the population in the communities included in our study. For newcomers in Costa Rica, the number of children per family was about five compared with three for the locally born. The family size of the locally born was about the same for Costa Rica nationally. In 2000, the average number of children per family nationwide was 2.8. Family size was slightly larger in Honduras, with the average family reporting five children. In the Honduran communities, newcomers made up about 40 percent of the population. The number of children per family was slightly higher for newcomers, but fertility of all families in our study site

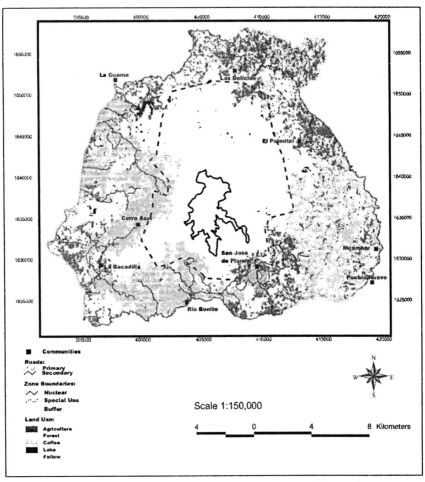

Figure 2.3.   Land use map of Cerro Azul Meambar National Park, Honduras, with communities and park zoning.

was higher than the national level in Honduras (4.3) (United Nations 2001). Thus, higher fertility, especially among newcomers in our study sites, without corresponding out-migration from the area presents potential future pressure on the natural resource base. On the other hand, newcomers were older than locally born residents in both Costa Rica and Honduras and tending past the childbearing years. In Costa Rica, the locally born were twenty-nine years old on average, but newcomers were about forty-six years of age. The female newcomers were about forty-three years old. In Honduras, the average locally born person was thirty-nine years old, but the newcomers, forty-eight. The average of women newcomers in Honduras was forty-four years.[5] Although there were some differences in religious affiliation, our analysis indicates that religion was not related to fertility levels in either study site. The religious affiliation of newcomers and the locally born was about the same in the Costa Rican communities. Three-fourths of those interviewed identified themselves as Catholic. Evangelical churches were much more active in the Honduran study site, and the locally born were more likely to be active in them. Newcomers were more likely to identify themselves as Catholics.

We classified individuals as newcomers if they were at least seventeen years of age when they arrived in the community. As indicated in table 2.2, newcomers had lived in the Costa Rican study site for an average of about fourteen years and in the Honduran site for about sixteen years. On average, in both study sites the newcomers had been in the area about the same number of years as the locally born have been of working age. For example, the average age in Costa Rica was about twenty-nine years, indicating that they had been of working age about twelve years if we assume that individuals reach working age at seventeen. In terms of years at work in the area, newcomers and the locally born were quite close in Costa Rica (fourteen versus twelve years). In the Honduran site, the locally born were little older and had a slight advantage in terms of years at work in the area. The locally born would have been at work an average of about twenty-two years, and the newcomers about sixteen years. Nevertheless, in Honduras, as in Costa Rica, newcomers reported incomes about the same as the locally born.

Table 2.2. Characteristics of Persons Living in Park Communities, La Amistad, Costa Rica, and Cerro Azul Meambar, Honduras

Respondent Characteristics	La Amistad			Cerro Azul Meambar		
	Place of Birth		Total	Place of Birth		Total
	Local	Newcomer		Local	Newcomer	
Male (%)	60	65	63	63	60	61
Mean Years of Schooling:						
Primary	5	4	4	4	3	3
Secondary	0.6	0.4	0.5	0.2	0.1	0.2
Mean Household Size	5	5	5	6	6	6
Mean Number of Children	3	5	4	5	6	5
Mean Years of Age	29	46	42	39	48	39
Mean Number of Years Living in Community	29	14	17	39	16	29
Mean Annual Income (US$)	2,471	2,449	2,458	1,102	974	1,053
Religion:						
Catholic (%)	72	75	75	44	57	48
Evangelical (%)	15	17	16	42	27	38
Number of Respondents	198	325	523	393	208	601

Figure 2.4.   Park boundary near Altamira, La Amistad National Park, Costa Rica.

Figure 2.5.   Park (background) and adjacent lands near Pittier, La Amistad International Park, Costa Rica.

The Demand for Land

As mentioned above, both study sites are frontier areas that were occupied in the past half-century. Most of the residents moving to these areas were people of modest means. Typically, they survived by sustaining themselves with staple production. As already mentioned, over time this staple production was supplemented with cash income from cattle and/or coffee production. By the late 1990s, 85 percent or more of the residents of our study communities in both Costa Rica and Honduras had access to some land (85% and 92%, respectively). Access to land was clearly associated with economic well-being, even in more subsistence-oriented portions of the Honduras study site. In Honduras, the landless reported a cash income about half that of landholders. In Costa Rica, even with its more active market economy, the landless earned only about one-fourth as much as landholders. In both study sites, most of the landless worked as wage workers, especially picking coffee. About two-thirds of the landless were concentrated between the ages of twenty-five and fifty.

In Costa Rica, many of the original settlers came to the area to work for a large farm near the village of Colorado. The village was established in 1973 after the five hundred hectare coffee farm went broke. Many of the farm's workers were due wages when the farm failed and many of them occupied land they felt entitled to as payment for wages. They began to farm this land for subsistence. Initially, they abandoned coffee production because there was no way to get it to market efficiently. Roads in and out of the area were very poor. In fact, the large coffee farm had shipped coffee out of the area by airplane.

Others steadily arrived in the area until LAIP was created in 1982. Until that time, settlers laid claim to land by clearing it for pasture, coffee, or staple production. As indicated in table 2.3, by the late 1990s, about one-third of those interviewed claimed control of some forestland. This land could have been primary or secondary forest, most likely the latter, given rampant land clearing by settlers in the 1970s and 1980s. On average, those who reported having forested land reported having about ten hectares. A larger proportion (44%) reported occupying forest fallow, or *tacotal*. This land is used as part of the system of shifting cultivation mentioned above. Perhaps most distinctive about our Costa Rican study sites is the extent to which producers are engaged in production for markets. Forty percent of the individuals in our study communities had land in pasture, and half had land in coffee. The mean size of coffee holdings was about four hectares, and that for pasture was fourteen hectares. About one-third cultivated maize and beans. The latter proportion is fairly low and reflects the importance of cattle and coffee production as sources of cash income. Nevertheless, this is an area of smallholders. Landholders occupied an average of about sixteen hectares, and 90 percent had less than forty hectares. Two large farms in our sample occupied about five hundred hectares, but they were exceptional in this area dominated by smallholders.

Figure 2.6.   Core area, Cerro Azul Meambar National Park, Honduras.

Figure 2.7.   Buffer zone, Cerro Azul Meambar National Park, Honduras.

In our Honduran site, an increasing number of newcomers continued to arrive until the early 1990s. By the late 1990s, about one-third occupied forested land (see table 2.3). As was true in Costa Rica, most of this forest was secondary growth given the heavy deforestation completed by the initial settlers. On average, farmers had more land in forest (about two hectares) than in any other land use. Forty percent of the persons surveyed had land in forest fallow, or *guamiles*, and those who had land in this category had about one hectare. A relatively small proportion of the population (18 percent) had land dedicated to pasture in the Honduran site, and most of that was concentrated in the southwest portion of the buffer zone (see figure 2.3). A majority (58 percent) of the population depended on staple production. This production is small scale and clearly geared to household production. Those who had land in maize and bean production had less than one hectare dedicated to this use. But coffee production strongly took hold in the area in the 1990s. About half the persons we interviewed had land in coffee, but these were typically very small parcels. It is important to note that these data do not reflect several very large coffee plantations that are not included in our sample because they are operated by absentee landowners. These plantations had the effect of bringing coffee production to the area. Many of the smallholders got into coffee production only after the larger plantations were established. Often the smallholders work on the large plantations, especially during the coffee harvest. People who occupy land have an average of about six hectares. Ninety percent of the landholders have less than twenty hectares. There are a few large landholders who reside locally. The largest had 290 hectares, but, as was true in Costa Rica, the resident population of the area consists of smallholders.[6]

Table 2.3. Mean Number of Hectares Occupied by Land Use and Place of Birth, La Amistad, Costa Rica, and Cerro Azul Meambar, Honduras

Land Use		La Amistad				Cerro Azul Meambar			
		Mean Hectares				Mean Hectares			
		Place of Birth				Place of Birth			
	Percentage Who Have	Local	Newcomer	Total		Percentage Who Have	Local	Newcomer	Total
Agriculture:									
Corn/Beans	31	1.5	2.3	2.0		58	0.8	0.8	0.8
Horticulture	8	0.2	0.2	0.2		8	0.3	0.4	0.3
Coffee	52	3.6	3.1	3.3		51	0.9	0.7	0.8
Forest	33	5.8	2.4	3.7		34	1.7	2.0	1.8
Fallow:									
Brush	44	1.8	1.6	1.7		42	1.3	1.2	1.3
Pasture	41	5.6	5.9	5.8		18	0.5	0.5	0.5
Other	14	0.6	0.6	0.9		17	0.3	0.4	0.1
TOTAL	85	19.1	16.1	17.6		92	5.6	5.5	5.6

Differences in landholding between the locally born and newcomers were fairly slight. In Costa Rica, the average amount of land occupied was about three hectares less for newcomers than for the locally born. Newcomers averaged about fifteen hectares compared with about nineteen hectares for the locally born (see table 2.3). The biggest difference was in the amount of forested land claimed. Newcomers occupied less than half as much forested land as their locally born counterparts. The absence of income differences between newcomers and the locally born suggests that income from the commercial exploitation of resources on forested land was not significant. In Honduras, there were almost no differences in the average amount of land occupied by newcomers and the locally born. The small proportions of individuals who were landless (15 percent in Costa Rica and 8 percent in Honduras) were much more likely to be newcomers. About 60 percent of the landless in both study sites were newcomers.

Nevertheless, newcomers were a sizeable group and controlled a significant proportion of the occupied land in both study sites. In Costa Rica, 64 percent of the population were newcomers, and almost 60 percent of them moved to the area after the LAIP was established. They occupied 57 percent of the land in our study sites. Overall, compared with those born locally, newcomers had more land in pasture than in forest (see table 2.4). This difference reflects that little forested land was available to be claimed by newcomers arriving after LAIP was established in 1982. Often, newcomers purchased land that had already been cleared. Otherwise, the allocation of land to different uses is almost identical for the locally born and newcomers.

In Honduras, the newcomers made up about 40 percent of the population in the communities studied, and nearly one-half of them arrived after CAMNP was established in 1987. They accounted for about one-third of the occupied land. The allocation of land to most uses is fairly similar for the locally born and newcomers. In contrast to Costa Rica, newcomers in Honduras tended to have more of their occupied land allocated to forest than did the locally born. Consequently, as indicated in table 2.4, the newcomers had a slightly lower portion of their land in coffee and pasture than did their locally born counterparts. The newcomers lived in the park's buffer zone, and this fact posed some significant constraints on their behavior. Although newcomers may have claimed forested land, after 1987 it was subject to restrictions on further forest clearing. Thus, they had to make do with land already available if they wished to enter into more intensive uses like coffee production.

Land Use across the Life Cycle

The establishment of the two parks in our study sites restricted the supply of land. With the supply of land limited, demands for available land intensified. The

Table 2.4.   Reported Land Use on Occupied Land by Place of Birth, La Amistad, Costa Rica, and Cerro Azul Meambar, Honduras

Land Use	La Amistad		Cerro Azul Meambar	
		Place of Birth		
	Local	Newcomer	Local	Newcomer
Agriculture:				
Corn/Beans	7.2	13.7	14.4	14.1
Horticulture	0.1	0.1	0.5	0.7
Coffee	19.2	20.8	17.1	12.9
Forest	30.7	15.6	31.8	39.1
Fallow:				
Brush	8.8	9.8	23.7	20.8
Pasture	27.6	36.9	8.9	9.8
Other	6.3	3.9	1.5	2.5
TOTAL	100.0	100.0	100.0	100.0
Total Hectares Reported	3,429	4,509	1,693	909

growth of individual farms was not an important source of increased demand for land. There was no strong accumulation of property within our study sites. As was indicated above, in both of our study sites, landholding was not highly stratified or concentrated. Differences in the amount of land occupied and socioeconomic status more generally were not large. While the growth of farms operated by local farmers was not an important source of increased demand for land, demand did grow and change over time. In our study sites, the age structure of the population and the family life cycle are important determinants of the demand for land in our study sites.

Figure 2.8 shows that the age structure of the populations of both study sites was skewed to the younger ages. The population in our Costa Rican site was concentrated between the ages of twenty and forty. The Hondurans were concentrated in the twenty-five-to-fifty age range. Population pressure eased somewhat with the exodus of young people born in the areas, as indicated in figure 2.1. But the effect of out-migration was offset somewhat by the arrival of new residents. This population redistribution does little to alter the age distribution in the two areas. As indicated in figure 2.9, the proportion of householders born locally was higher in the younger age groups, especially in Costa Rica. This structure makes sense given the relatively high fertility levels, especially in Honduras. But newcomers were also an important addition to the numbers of householders in the younger age categories, especially in Honduras.

The demand for land and other resources was concentrated in householders aged about twenty-five to fifty. Householders in this age range had the largest households, as shown in figure 2.10. These householders were in the peak child-

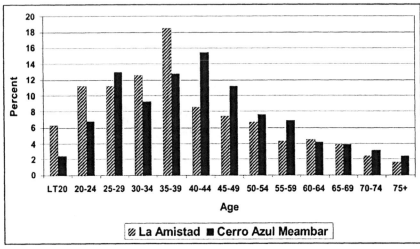

Figure 2.8.   Survey respondents by age, La Amistad, Costa Rica, and Cerro Azul Meambar, Honduras.

rearing stage and also took on responsibilities for other dependents, like elderly parents. The land occupied by households tracks very closely with the age structure of the population in Costa Rica, as indicated in figure 2.11. In Costa Rica, there appears to be some conversion of forest into other uses between about the ages of thirty-five and forty-five. When demand lessens among those in their late forties, it may be allowed to revert to forest before being turned over to children who are establishing their own households. All the other land uses (coffee, pasture, maize and beans, or *milpa*) all tracked closely with total land across the age distribution of householders in our Costa Rican site.

In Honduras, land appears to be disproportionately in the hands of persons between the ages of forty and seventy. Forested land especially appears to have been occupied by householders in this age range. Younger people dealt with this relative lack of land in different ways. As was mentioned above, some young people leave the area when they reach working age. Others intensify production. Younger households can do this because they have more workers available. In our Honduran study site, younger households disproportionately concentrated on coffee production. Households with householders less than forty-five years of age occupied a disproportionate share of the land dedicated to coffee production (see figure 2.12). Householders passing beyond the peak child-rearing years have more land in forest and forest fallow, indicating a less intensive use of the land. The combination of agriculture with other sources of income was not age-related in either of our study sites.

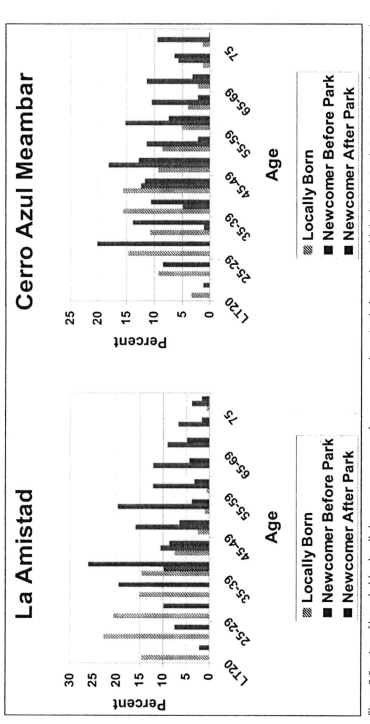

Figure 2.9. Age of householder, locally born, newcomers, and newcomers who arrived after parks established, La Amistad, Costa Rica, and Cerro Azul Meambar, Honduras.

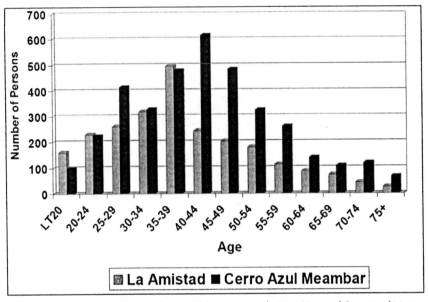

Figure 2.10.   Population by age of householder, La Amistad, Costa Rica, and Cerro Azul Meambar, Honduras.

Park Creation and the Demand for Land and Other Resources

As indicated above, in both our study sites, creation of the respective parks reduced the supply of land and forest resources available. Earlier, both areas had been frontier areas that provided resource-poor migrants opportunities to clear forest and claim land. That changed in 1982 with the creation of LAIP in Costa Rica and in 1987 with the birth of CAMNP in Honduras. Yet, as we have shown above, new residents continued to arrive in the two sites after the parks were created. The establishment of the parks clearly had some impact on the ability of new settlers to gain access to land. Figure 2.13 shows persons who had settled in either of the areas and reached working age (seventeen) before creation of the parks on average occupied more land. In Costa Rica, workers who reached working age before establishment of the park occupied an average of about six hectares more than more recent arrivals. This advantage spread across the various land uses, but differences were most pronounced in the amount of forest and pasture occupied.

In the Honduran site, the differences were not as large. Workers who reached working age before the park was created only occupied a little more than one hectare more than those who arrived after creation of CAMNP. Prepark workers had slightly more land in all uses except for pasture, which was the least common land use in Honduras. The difference in the amount of land occupied was con-

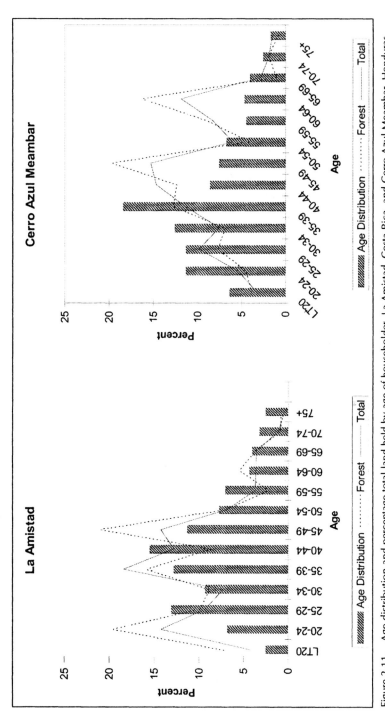

Figure 2.11. Age distribution and percentage total land held by age of householder, La Amistad, Costa Rica, and Cerro Azul Meambar, Honduras.

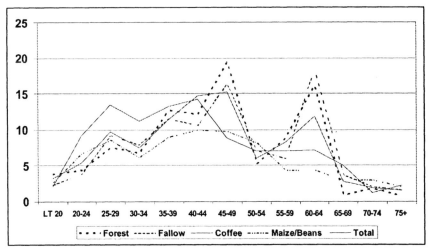

Figure 2.12.   Share of occupied land in principal uses by age, Cerro Azul Meambar, Honduras.

centrated in forested land. Prepark workers had almost one hectare more forested land than those who arrived at working age after creation of the park. Prepark workers also occupied slightly more land dedicated to the production of maize and beans.

Of course, the parks were created to conserve forest. In doing so, they restricted access to forested land and the use of forest resources. The parks appear to have had an impact on the behaviors of persons living in the two study sites. In both cases, persons who reached working age (seventeen years) after establishment of the parks were less likely to have cut trees on their own land (see table 2.5). This pattern was true for both locally born persons and newcomers. Overall, individuals in our Costa Rican site were less likely than Hondurans to have cut trees. Also, the establishment of the park appears to have had the greatest behavioral impact in Costa Rica. A smaller percentage of persons who reached working age after the park was established reported that they had cut trees on their own property. In fact, only about one-third reported that they had cut trees on their own land. They were about 15 percent less likely than prepark workers to have done so. In Honduras, the park had a less obvious effect on tree cutting. Persons who arrived after the park was established were less likely to report that they had cut trees on their land. But they were only about 5 percent less likely to have cut trees compared with prepark workers. About half of all those who arrived after the park was established cut trees on their own land.

Individuals reported different reasons for cutting trees. In both Costa Rica and Honduras, the most important reasons for cutting trees were to clear land for crops, to harvest timber for the construction of their own house, and for firewood. In

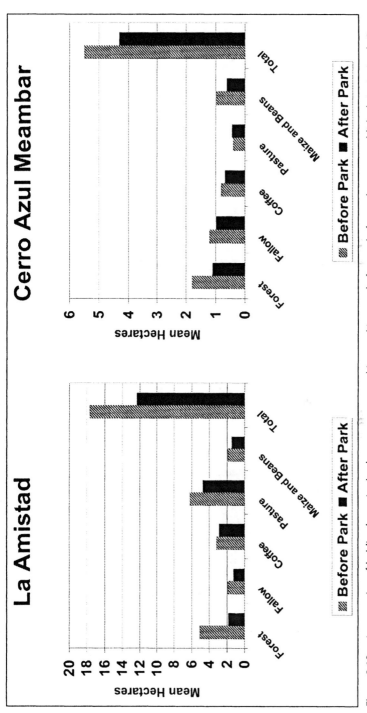

Figure 2.13. Average size of holding by major land uses, persons reaching working age before and after parks were established, La Amistad, Costa Rica, and Cerro Azul Meambar, Honduras.

Table 2.5. Tree-Cutting Behavior on Own Land by Place of Birth before and after Park Established, La Amistad, Costa Rica, and Cerro Azul Meambar, Honduras

Tree Cutting and Reasons for It	La Amistad Place of Birth		Cerro Azul Meambar	
	Local	Other Community	Local	Other Community
	Persons Who Reached Working Age after Park Established			
Have Cut Trees	28.4	33.9	56.1	51.6
Reasons for Cutting:				
To Clear Land for Crops	83.3	88.9	64.9	47.9
To Build Own House	52.9	88.2	62.2	70.8
For Timber Sale	25.0	28.8	0	4.2
For Firewood	66.7	63.3	59.5	70.8
To Claim Land	6.7	24.4	5.4	6.3
	Persons Who Reached Working Age before Park Established			
Have Cut Trees	44.1	48.5	62.0	55.2
Reasons for Cutting:				
To Clear Land for Crops	85.7	91.4	53.2	48.3
To Build Own House	73.8	91.4	58.2	60.3
For Timber Sale	34.6	27.9	6.3	5.2
For Firewood	81.4	83.6	71.5	72.4
To Claim Land	21.4	31.8	6.3	8.6

both sites, newcomers were substantially more likely to have cut trees for timber for the construction of their own house. Understandably, this difference is most pronounced for those who arrived after creation of the parks. Being new to the area, they could not occupy a home passed down from their parents. But there are also some interesting differences between the two sites. In Costa Rica, individuals were more likely to have cleared forest to claim land, and newcomers were most likely to have cut trees for this purpose. Newcomers who had arrived most recently were less likely to have cut trees for this purpose compared with newcomers who had arrived earlier. Nevertheless, almost one-fourth of the most recent newcomers in Costa Rica reported having cut trees for this purpose.

Cutting trees for the sale of timber is more common in Costa Rica. Overall, about 30 percent of the individuals interviewed had cut trees for sale. As indicated in table 2.5, cutting trees for sale is fairly rare in our Honduran site, especially since the park was established. In Honduras, until 1992 tree felling for private timber sales required special permits because all trees were property of the state, and their harvesting for sale required special permission. Aspects of this provision date back to policies adopted in 1851. In 1992, the Agricultural Modernization and Development Law (*Ley para la Modernización del Sector Agrícola*) gave landholders ownership rights to trees on their own lands (Barton 2001, Hernández-Mora 1995). But the CAMNP management plan prohibited commercial sales of timber from anywhere in the park, including the buffer zone. Our data indicate that park restrictions on the felling of timber, especially for commercial sale, were effective, especially among those who arrived after the park was established (see table 2.5). This effect is all the more impressive given that the management plan has been implemented by *Aldea Global* but never officially recognized by the Honduran government (Chet Thomas, personal communication 2006, Barton 2001). Thus, compliance is entirely voluntary given that no legal prohibition has been adopted.

Conclusion

LAIP and CAMNP are the central features of forest conservation in our two study sites. The establishment of these protected areas has transformed both areas from frontiers where poor settlers attempted to transform forested land into cropland and to lay claim to land that could provide them with a modest livelihood. Now the areas are part of the national heritage, officially protected by legislation that attempts to restrict natural resource extraction and, most importantly, to arrest deforestation. People who continue to live in, or adjacent to, these areas must manage to eke out an existence from the existing resource base, and they must husband the remaining resource base both for their own survival and to protect the national patrimony.

Establishment of the parks limited the growth of the working population and reduced the consumption of forest in the two areas. But the remaining populations will continue to place demands on the natural resource base, and their decisions on how to husband these resources will determine the degree to which parks are effective in resource conservation. For this reason, park managers in both our study sites invested much of their limited management resources in education efforts. They attempted to educate people to think about the use of natural resources in terms of broader resource conservation objectives. As mentioned above, these objectives are shared by conservationists throughout the world, and park managers are often the social carriers of conservation ideas. In the following chapters, we consider how individuals living in or near the parks think about conservation and how their thinking was shaped by their interactions with natural resource managers and other influences associated with the parks.

Notes

1. Data in this chapter come from two main sources. One source is surveys of random samples of the populations of selected communities in or near LAIP and CAMNP. In Costa Rica we surveyed 523 individuals and in Honduras, 601. In addition, the land use maps we present below are based on Landsat Thematic Mapper satellite images. The maps represent a supervised classification of land use. A more detailed description of these data is found in Appendix A.

2. These percentages exclude forest fallow, or young (i.e., less than about ten years) forest regrowth. About 43 and 22 percent of the occupied land in the Costa Rican and Honduran study sites could be classified as forest fallow (*tacotal* or *guamil*, respectively). In both sites forest fallow is used in rotation with other lands as part of a system of shifting cultivation.

3. Figure 2.1 shows the number of persons surveyed who were age seventeen or older by the year they moved to communities in or around the respective parks. It also shows the number of persons born in the communities reaching age seventeen by year.

4. Details about our land use change estimation procedures can be found in Pfeffer et al. 2005 and Appendix A.

5. We limited our interviews to household heads. In some cases, women were the heads of households. When we could not locate the household head, we interviewed the available spouse. As a result, about 37 percent of our respondents in Costa Rica, and 39 percent in Honduras, were female.

6. These data pertain to persons living in the communities included in our study. The largest coffee plantations in the area were operated by absentee landowners, most of whom lived in San Pedro Sula or Tegucigalpa. Since most of the area is occupied by smallholders who reside in the park buffer zone, our study is limited to them.

Diverse Cultural Models to Manage Competing Interests in Natural Resource Use in Costa Rica

3

A S WE DESCRIBED IN CHAPTER 2, Costa Rican conservation history encompasses rapid deforestation associated with frontier colonization, followed by a multipronged government response. Motivated in part by laws that favored cleared land over forests in claiming and titling land, as well as to discourage squatters, landholders of all sizes converted forests to agriculture and, most frequently, pasture. Significant conservation efforts began in Costa Rica in the 1960s, and by the 1970s the Costa Rican park system became one front in the effort to arrest forest loss. Costa Rica's national park system became one of the premier park systems in Latin America. In managing this park system, officials have actively engaged residents living near parks to gain support for environmental conservation and to educate them about the benefits of living near a park. Forest-clearing and tree-felling laws outside the park were also enforced by the park guards at the time of our study. The Costa Rican section of La Amistad International Park (LAIP) was created in 1982, and management of the park and its surroundings is representative of Costa Rica's approach to natural resource conservation.

Our qualitative interviewing was designed to elicit responses related to forest and park values, social contexts and relationships, conflicts between forest conservation and livelihoods, and forest-related behaviors in a park context. We have structured our discussion of the results of our interviews to first look at forest values and their strength at both individual and community levels. We then look at a number of more specific issues related to conservation laws and policies, such as forestry regulations and the national park. Following this, we consider the extent to which people attribute forest conservation awareness and actions to regulations, community action, or individual values. We then briefly look at responses related to the national park and hunting, which are closely related to, but distinct from, forests. After this, we turn our attention to conflicts between livelihood needs and forest conservation, examining the discourse and identifying mediating models that show the way people come to terms with this conflict. Finally, we turn our attention to local notions of desirable landscapes and, ultimately, forest-related behaviors in order to address the fundamental questions of people's land use preferences and how forest-related values impact behavior. Throughout this section, we give priority to quotes from our interviews in order to give voice to local people and in an effort to show the full complexity in the way people discuss forest and conservation. We generally emphasize shared cultural models, while at times pointing out alternate views.

General Cultural Models of Forests

As we indicated in chapter 1, cultural models incorporate both beliefs and values about what is moral, desirable, or just. Cultural models are made of smaller units, called schema, which are more bounded, distinct, and unitary. Schemas, networks of strongly connected cognitive elements that are largely built up through human experience, provide an organized framework for objects and relations and thereby mediate many of the cognitive processes of individuals. Schemas are fundamental to people's understanding of their experiences and the meanings they attach to them. To uncover the schema and cultural models constructed by people to make sense of their relationship to natural resources, we began our interviews by asking a very general question about the first thing that came to mind when trees or forest were mentioned. We attempted to determine the cornerstones of people's thinking about forest and trees. From there, we probed deeper on these responses, and later asked more specific questions about trees, forest conservation, and the national park. This approach allowed us to uncover common themes about air, water, and wildlife. Many of the responses were automatic, and there was a great deal of similarity among different respondents in both the themes covered and the words used to express them. These striking patterns indicate that there is a shared underlying structure to forest values.

Common Values

Pure air and oxygen. One of the most frequently repeated comments about forests was their importance for purifying air and producing oxygen, often comparing the forest or the park to a lung.

(1) The park for me is something that produces pure air. . . . As you know, the forest maintains our oxygen. (CR16)

(2) When I think about trees and forests, we think about the necessity of natural oxygen, I think this is one of the fundamental parts—if there weren't [forests] we would have problems. (CR21)

Figure 3.1. Sign along Inter-American Highway in Southern Costa Rica: *Produzcamos Oxígeno, Cuidemos Nuestras Montañas, Ulatina*. Translation: Produce Oxygen, Take Care of Our Forests, *Ulatina* (*Universidad Latina de Costa Rica*)

(3)   If there aren't trees, there's no air purification. . . . I think that this park is a lung, not just for this zone; I think it is a lung for the world. That's why it's so big. (CR18)

The persons we surveyed were nearly unanimous in agreeing with the statement "Without forests, we would not have sufficient oxygen to breathe" (98% agreed).

Water. A second major theme was the role of forests in maintaining rainfall and water for human use. A common expression was that, without the forest in the region, it would be a desert. Examples include:

(4)   It is through trees that we see the part about water; the water has completely dried up, there's not any water anymore and that means that it is through trees that water is maintained. (CR1)

(5)   INTER   And what do you think would happen if the park and its forests were eliminated?
RESP   This would surely become a desert. (CR2)

(6)   The cutting of the forests and all this, the deforestation by the people and all this, the region has become much drier, too dry, because right now we have long dry seasons, before, no . . . the whole wet season has changed and thereby the way of life. And more dry weather with the cutting of trees. More dry weather; the region has totally dried out. (CR10)

In the survey, there was almost no disagreement with the statement "Without forests, our community would not have sufficient water" (97% agreed). Nine out of ten of the persons surveyed also agreed that "The forests in our community are a source of water for people who live in other parts of the country."[1]

Wildlife for future generations. A third very common theme related to wildlife, in particular the importance of the forest as a source of food for wildlife and concern that future generations would not be able to see or experience wildlife species that were once common in the region.

(7) [In the forest] there are a lot of animals. . . . The trees are providing food for many animals, it's a relationship, an unending chain. (CR25)

(8) People aren't going to recognize the animals, they aren't going to recognize a peccary, nor a toucan, nor the fauna. I, on the other hand, recognize all of these but those in the future, our children, grandchildren and others, these people won't know them if we destroy all this—where will the animals go to? (CR14)

A park guard made the most explicit statement of the value of the forest as habitat for wildlife for the benefit of the wildlife itself and how this benefit was distinct from the benefits that people receive.

(9) The benefits that [trees] bring, due to the trees . . . having trees, there are wild animals, there is food, it's their habitat. Definitely, if there weren't forests, the poor animals . . . the majority of them wouldn't be able to live without the forest. For example, the jaguar is one of the animals that needs the jungle the most to be able to live. They only leave their habitat when people get close . . . there are a lot of animals that are completely of the jungle, the forest. If they leave it, it is because people have cleared land and taken away some of the space they need. But that's their home. Now, thinking like a human, outside of the forest, in a certain way, being very careful and regulating things, economically, there are also advantages for the *campesino,* because lumber, if you harvest it with a management plan the way it should be done, I think it can provide a lot of economic benefits. (CR11)

Among the 518 individuals we surveyed, there was virtually no disagreement with the following statements:

- "It is very important that our children have the opportunity to enjoy the forests and wild animals" (98% agreed).
- "We should think about future generations when we make decisions with respect to the use of our forests" (97% agreed).
- "Our children are the ones who benefit from the trees and forests we protect" (99% agreed).
- "All living things, including the animals, birds, and trees, also have a right to live" (99% agreed).

Verbal molecules. Thus, among the most frequently repeated comments about forests were (1) their importance for purifying air and producing oxygen (often comparing the forest or the park to a lung), (2) their role in maintaining rainfall and water for human use (often that, without forests, the region would be a desert), (3) the importance of the forest as a source of food for wildlife, and (4) the importance of forests for future generations (e.g., children would not be able to recognize or experience wildlife species that were once common in the region). We consider these responses to reflect cultural models that are widely available in the media, in environmental education programs, and in contacts with professionals, thus explaining their wide use by rural people in talking about the forest and the environment. Claudia Strauss has used the term "verbal molecules" for this type of concise terminology that is often repeated (Strauss 1992, 1997, Strauss and Quinn 1997), for example "the forest is a lung," "without forests this would be a desert," "without forests future generations won't be able to recognize wildlife." Strauss defines verbal molecules as frequently heard and expressed ideas that become internalized in fixed or frozen terms, that are very likely to be indices of common opinion, and that, within individuals, may not be connected to other schema and not be particularly motivating (Strauss 1992, 1997, 2005, Strauss and Quinn 1997).

Expressions like these recurred both within and throughout the interviews, and we believe that these are powerful general models of how people think about forests. This appears to be true regardless of whether these widely available models have motivating force or are merely lip-service models. Supporting our claim that these represent general and widely available cultural models, we note that very similar terms were used by people who opposed forest conservation or the park. For example, the following statements from two interviews with people who expressed strong opposition to the park or forest conservation show the use of water, air, and wildlife themes in statements of opposition to the park:

(10)   People say that it is important to not cut trees because they create oxygen, but that is not a problem here, we have plenty of oxygen. (CR27)

(11)   Costa Rica is not a desert without forest, like they say. Actually there is more forest than cultivated land. People are living under bridges and stealing; land should be made available to them. (CR26)

(12)   I have always said that we have studied in books about the value that nature has, and we see that it is a shame that [all this deforestation happened]. . . . But we were talking in a meeting, and they said that birds have to eat and do their "work" and it's true, but as we say, we aren't caterpillars that can eat the leaves off the trees, right? . . . We're not caterpillars, our children aren't caterpillars that can survive on leaves, and therefore it is necessary to eliminate some forest to plant something productive like coffee. (CR7)

Other Values

Forest utility. There were many other responses about the importance of forests that include many details and variations. Some of these responses reflected utilitarian ways of looking at forests.

(13) We need to get forests back, so there is wood. Because otherwise we will have to build with cement, and, really, you can't . . . wood is needed for a lot of things. (CR5)

(14) I think that trees are important because they give us wood to build houses and all this. (CR15)

(15) We also have to take care for our land because, definitely, we depend on nature. You can see land that doesn't have any life, because we have burned it, we have put a lot of agrochemicals on it—there are little things that that give life to the soil, this soil that we share. [The ground] gets hard. We go out to plant something, a cassava, something to eat, and it's no good. On the other hand, forest protects the earth, the leaves and all give life to the soil, and later, if we want to plant a crop, the soil will be fertile, have life. But if we don't have forest, if we don't take care of our soil, we will die. (CR4)

Table 3.1 shows the proportion of persons surveyed who agreed with various statements describing a utilitarian orientation toward forests. People we surveyed were most likely to agree with the statement "Before we can worry about saving the forest, we need food and income" (58%). A much smaller proportion of those surveyed were likely to agree with such statements if they focused exclusively on money or income, rather than if the comments referred to food production. For example, only about 17 percent agreed with the statement "The most important thing concerning trees is to make money from them." The group of people standing out as being most likely to agree with the utilitarian statements comprises persons who were born elsewhere and reached working age before the park was created. These persons were drawn to the area by the prospect of clearing forest and claiming land. They were also older than the others (fifty-four years on average compared with thirty-two years for all the others) and held more traditional views about the legitimacy of exploiting natural resources.[2]

Some people suggested that forest conservation and the national park might help attract tourists and economic benefits. For example,

(16) I say that a forest, one that looks like virgin forest, the important thing is to conserve it for animals, and in the future it can be useful, perhaps a tour group or something like this [will come]. Many people from other countries come to walk around, look at birds and big trees, and they pay. This is a help. (CR15)

Table 3.1. Proportion of Survey Respondents Who Agreed with Utilitarian Statements, La Amistad, Costa Rica

Place of Birth and Time When Reached Working Age	Percentage Who Agreed
"Before we can worry about saving the forest, we need food and income."	
Newcomer who came of working age before park	64.4
Newcomer who came of working age after park	56.0
Locally born who came of working age before park	55.0
Locally born who came of working age after park	53.7
Total	57.7
"It's better to use the land to produce food than to leave it in forest."	
Newcomer who came of working age before park	56.8
Newcomer who came of working age after park	38.0
Locally born who came of working age before park	39.4
Locally born who came of working age after park	41.8
Total	43.9
"If we were to conserve forest here, we would have fewer opportunities to earn money."	
Newcomer who came of working age before park	48.5
Newcomer who came of working age after park	35.5
Locally born who came of working age before park	38.7
Locally born who came of working age after park	26.9
Total	38.5
"More than for any other reason, the forest exists to give us firewood and lumber."	
Newcomer who came of working age before park	41.7
Newcomer who came of working age after park	34.8
Locally born who came of working age before park	20.7
Locally born who came of working age after park	23.9
Total	32.0
"The most important thing concerning trees is to make money from them."	
Newcomer who came of working age before park	22.7
Newcomer who came of working age after park	15.2
Locally born who came of working age before park	16.2
Locally born who came of working age after park	9.0
Total	16.6
Number of respondents	
Newcomer who came of working age before park	132
Newcomer who came of working age after park	184
Locally born who came of working age before park	111
Locally born who came of working age after park	67

Almost everyone agreed with the statement "We have to protect our forests if we want tourism to grow and bring us income" (97%). Likewise, almost everyone considered the park important to promote tourism (56% very important, 40% important) and to promote community development (51% very important, 41% important).

Coolness. It was common to mention that good general climatic conditions are often associated with forests, including coolness and fresh air.

(17)   INTER   Why would you like to have more forest?
RESP   A lot more, a lot more, because of the coolness. Now it is hotter. There has been a big change. (CR5)

Concerns about the forest's role in climate maintenance were pervasive. The individuals surveyed were virtually unanimous (98%) in agreeing that forests were essential for maintaining sufficient supplies of oxygen and a cool and pleasant climate.

General forest values were important. Almost everyone we surveyed indicated that they thought the park was important to protect forest and trees (59% very important, 40% important) and to reduce impacts on the environment (58% very important, 35% important).

Projecting the social onto the natural. Interestingly, good climatic resources are sometimes described in opposition to the polluted air, crime, and other negative characteristics of the city. These seem to be an example of what others have described as projecting social values and conflicts onto natural features, species, or environments, where elements of the environment are used as symbols of social concerns or divisions (Knight 2000, Milton 2000, Song 2000). For example,

(18)   [*talking about the park*] It's important. It's good for the health. We hear, one hears, on the news about how little oxygen there is, how many cars, how many factories, and how much smoke there is. It is deteriorating the ozone layer, and one goes to San José, the parks there in the city, they are little parks with a few trees, the air you breath, if one goes by a repair shop or walks down Central Avenue, it's all smoke, all the smell of diesel fumes, all gasoline. (CR9)

(19)   To go to this park [Amistad] or to go to San Jose, I'd prefer to go into this park even on foot. This would benefit me. On the other hand if I go to San José, I walk around scared there, afraid of the people and fleeing from them. (CR3)

Nature appreciation. In other cases, comments reflected recreational use of forests, pleasure in visiting the forest because of its beauty, or appreciation for the beauty of forest in general. A number of individuals expressed these sentiments.

(20)   When I think about forests I imagine going into those mountains over there, I have been there and it is beautiful, it is something that fills one with the spirit of life, to see the tremendous amount of beauty that is there. (CR6)

(21)   I think it is pretty, it adds to the way a place looks, to see it all covered in trees and not stripped bare. (CR8)

(22) For me it is beautiful to see forest, to see animals. I am not capable of harming an animal, and it bothers me to see people destroying forests around streams or burning. I am not capable of doing it. (CR13)

Such sentiments were almost unanimous as indicated when the people surveyed agreed with the statement "We should have lots of forest around here because it is so beautiful" (97%).

Sometimes, people made very general comments that showed affection for the forest or a desire to live in harmony with the forest. For example,

(23) I am in love with this forest. . . . I repeat, I have always been a lover of nature. . . . I am a protector of nature. (CR3)

(24) What comes to my mind when we talk about trees and forest is to live in harmony; by harmony I refer to not destroying any more than we already have. (CR6)

A spiritual basis for environmentalism. Willett Kempton et al. (1995) find that religious and spiritual values often serve as the foundation of environmental values and morally acceptable behavior toward the environment. Similarly, our interviewees often talked about the forests and forest destruction in religious terms, often mentioning many of the values discussed above (e.g., beauty, environmental services, a productive earth), while also talking about human responsibility for conservation in religious terms.

(25) INTER When you think about trees and forests, what is the first thing that comes to your mind?
RESP That it's part of nature, part of our nature. I think about the beautiful things that God has created. (CR23)

(26) Well, when I think about forest the first thing I think about is how marvelous God's creation is. And that we share the same creation. There's all the biodiversity—birds, insects, and all that. It is marvelous. One sees the forests and the great creation of God for humanity. . . . I have worked a lot in the Catholic religion, and they have showed us that we have to take care of what God has given us. Frankly, God has given the forest to humanity, and we have to conserve it, not degrade it. (CR18)

(27) We should help He who made this earth without help. Thanks to Him. I am referring to God, who made heaven and earth, and left a perfect nature, only for man to destroy it. (CR21)

(28) INTER Who do you think has the responsibility to care for the trees and forests here?
RESP I think that the biggest responsibility is for those of us that really know and appreciate the forest. We know and appreciate nature, and we want to care for it. We have to care for it. I have some books about the

earth, mother earth. Mother earth is what supports us all, it gives us everything, everything we need. The animals and everything ... everything. What a wonderful mother we have, and we live under the roof. We live under heaven. Earth is a dome [bóveda], a dome. And we all live within this dome. And this dome gives us all food. And it is what feeds us with the help of the powerful hand of God. And we haven't known how to appreciate the great love of God, that God gave us as a wonderful house. There are so many things. First, I work in the parish. There we are taken care of. It is the Christian thing to take care of what God has given us, to promote taking care of what God has put in our hands. We've never responded, never done what we should have done. Now we're starting to think about what we have to do for God. (CR7)

In some cases, people saw a relationship between the way people treated the environment and their ethics toward other people, seeing a relationship between respect for the environment and respect for other people.

(29)   If I don't mind destroying what God gave us, which is nature, then later I can begin to not care if I destroy a brother, and later I can get to the point where I could do anything—a crime, drug trafficking, anything. Why? Because I don't respect myself, I don't start by respecting myself and doing what nature has taught me. That's why I say, if we appreciate and admire nature, it will teach us. It gives life to everything. (CR3)

A large majority of those surveyed agreed with the statement "Because God created the forests, it is wrong to abuse them" (83%). There was no difference in the likelihood of agreeing with this statement based on religious affiliation, age, or place of birth.

Forest Values

In summary, we found that people value forests for many different reasons. There was a noticeable number of people who cited the importance of products and environmental services, such as timber and water. Wildlife was often regarded as important in our interviews, but more for appreciation than consumption. The values associated with forests included the utilitarian but went well beyond this to include recreational uses, beauty, and broad appreciation of nature. Furthermore, forest values were often discussed in religious terms emphasizing the responsibility of society for the environment. Figure 3.2 shows the level of agreement with a variety of statements. In general, the people we surveyed were relatively unlikely to express agreement with statements expressing utilitarian sentiments like "The most important thing to do with trees is make money" (16%). In contrast, those surveyed were nearly unanimous in expressing agreement with statements that expressed

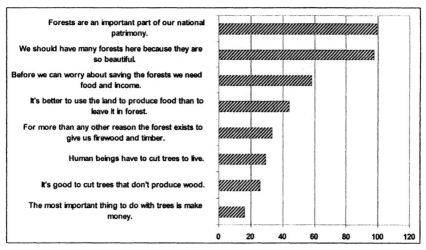

Figure 3.2.   Proportion who agreed with selected statements about forests, La Amistad, Costa Rica

aesthetic or spiritual sentiments, like "We should have many forests because they are so beautiful" (97%).

Stories of Forest Change

Although our interviewees ranged from recent arrivals to people who had lived in the region for more than thirty years, an important backdrop for many of the discussions was the fact that the region had once been forested, followed by descriptions of what it was like in those times. Many of the descriptions talked about the earlier conditions of the frontier, including the extensive forests and abundant wildlife, as well as the lack of development and difficulties of frontier life. Some also talked about the efforts and hard work that went into developing the region. These dramatic changes in land use and forest cover through the actions of early colonists, along with what were considered to be associated changes in climatic and social conditions, shaped the complex and often conflicted way many people looked at relationships between forests and people.

On the one hand, people often coupled descriptions of what the forests and wildlife had been like before with tales of their efforts to open up roads and build communities.

(30)   This was forest when I arrived, all this was forest. . . . There were only a few clearings: where the school is, and here at this store—although at that time it was a sawmill. All the rest was forest, and there was biodiversity—peccaries, tapirs, and pacas passed through and were abundant in

the region. Over time, people cleared forest and all this began to disappear; the animals went away. And the same people hunted them for sport, and thus to me it seems that it has been a big change, very drastic, to get to where we're at now. (CR18)

(31)   When I came here, this was pure forest, big trees—*amarillón* and *zapatero* and *guilcano* and *roble* and up a little higher *maria*. These were the trees that there were a lot of. And there weren't any roads and thus, down below, there was a trail that was rough to get through on horse because there were big muddy places. And I arrived poor, for certain, to this place. I only brought a mule, a machete—a mule, a machete, and thirty *colones* [roughly US$3.00 at the time]—and I started to live down there below the Platanillal River. . . .

When I came here there were a lot of paca, and down in that low spot I killed a cat, I think the last one that came here for sure. After that they built a school down there below in Los Naranjos, and there was this school—and later one here above in Biolley. I went to talk to the Jimenez family, and we rented a bulldozer and we were able to open up a road by charging all the neighbors a fee. And after we opened this road, this bulldozer was there the first year—and higher the second year—taking out a lot of *amarillones*. The timber cutters came and bought wood very cheaply. We sold it for about thirty *colones* per tree. Mostly they helped open the road. (CR14)

Yet, in spite of the efforts to clear forests to develop farms and communities, often the people we interviewed also described this earlier forest destruction as something people did out of ignorance. In many cases, people expressed guilt about what had happened and described it as "destruction." They described forests as something that were destroyed out of ignorance and need by humans, although they also mentioned that now people know more and are trying to reconstruct what was lost with forest clearing.

The following statements are typical of the particularly common attribution of earlier deforestation to ignorance:

(32)   I think that, out of ignorance, we cut everything down flat, no one thought that we needed to protect the places where there was water, the springs and such, and thus, now there are consequences. All anyone wanted to do was clear more land, only fell trees, and nobody thought about the consequences this might bring later. . . . I think we did it out of ignorance, to grow crops, because that was the way we made money to live, to plant more crops, and to have food, and we would sell the rest to buy other things. But these were the only successes this provided. We cleared to grow crops but unjustly they knocked down forests in places that should have been left in forest. (CR18)

(33) INTER   Why do you think the forest has changed so much here?
RESP   Mostly because of the ignorance of humans, the ignorance that we have. We don't think of the future; we don't think about the consequences we could bring if we destroy the forest. Because twenty years ago, I remember there was a lot of water, we would see streams and springs everywhere. Now they have disappeared, and the cause is precisely this—destruction of forests. And now, the climate is not the same. Years ago the climate was very cold, very cold, and now it is a totally different climate. Before you didn't feel heat like we have now, never. And all this is our fault because we didn't take care of the forest. (CR13)

Ignorance was also combined with a sense that people earlier did what they had to do in order to survive, often with the encouragement of the government, as indicated in the following statements:

(34) INTER   A question: You told me at the beginning that when you came here twenty-four years ago, you didn't know anything about protection.
RESP   It didn't exist. Nobody talked about it.
INTER   No? So what were people thinking about when they came here?
RESP   Like I was just saying, the people that came in here, they were thinking about making farms, not taking care of forest. Everyone that came here, came to make a farm, not to care for the forest. Up there in the hills, people were clearing forest. People were hungry for work, had great needs. (CR7)

(35) An institution called *IDA* [*Instituto de Desarollo Agrario*] came. Before it was called something else. It was a government institution. They came here to give land away to people who didn't have any land. This was unsettled land. So they did this to give people some land. But it was all forest, right? Forest; and one did what he had to do to survive, clear forest, the same government permitted it. (CR22)

Yet, now the earlier forest clearing is generally seen as having been very destructive as the following statements demonstrate:

(36) We've burnt a lot of land, pastures, farms. Sometimes to burn just a little piece of land we set fire to a whole lot of hectares. We've felt the weight of great destruction. That's why I think that we need to care for what little forest we have left, even *tacotales* or secondary forest. (CR8)

(37) They can't stand any more, the forest can't stand any more destruction, not any more. (CR10)

Yet, this destruction is generally viewed as something of the past and an outlook and a way of life that has been replaced by better treatment of the forest. For example,

(38)   In the beginning, quite a few years ago, we didn't think about things the way we think about them now—the forests. We were destroyers, in those days all we did was work and destroy; destroy the forests. We never thought about the future. But today, it's different; for the new generations it's very different. They conserve and also reforest, creating new forests. (CR24)

(39)   What a great sin was committed with the forests! And with the animals. Now people are beginning to conserve. Here we have a gentleman who is conserving a small forest. The community has united to not permit hunting. Because of this, things are in the process of being repaired. (CR18)

The quotes above clearly show a sense of deforestation being associated with destruction and guilt for this. Even when clearing, often promoted by the government, was done a long time ago to grow crops, people felt that more had been cleared than was necessary. Seventy percent of the persons surveyed agreed with the statement "Young people should be angry with earlier generations for the damage they had done to the forest around here." Persons who came of working age before the park was created during the years of rampant forest destruction were more likely to agree with this statement that others (78% versus 62%).

Ethics of Tree Felling and Forest Clearing

We were interested in learning about social norms related to tree felling and forest clearing. We asked people to talk about the circumstances under which it was acceptable or unacceptable to fell trees or clear forests. Many people's values included utilitarian views of forests that valued trees in terms of their usefulness to people and thereby legitimized removal of older or dead trees, or of trees that were not useful to people.

(40)   INTER   Do you think that sometimes it is alright to cut a tree?
       RESP   It depends. If the tree is dead, it is alright; it is not wasted. But if the tree is growing, if it is not yet big, it is a shame to cut it.
       INTER   In terms of cutting down a tree, do you think there are times when it is good to cut one?
       RESP   Yes. Because when trees get to a certain age, they start to deteriorate. (CR12)

People made very clear distinctions by type of trees, conserving those that had important human uses while often seeing little need to conserve those that they did not have uses for.

(41) INTER   On that land that you work, have you cut trees during the last
      ten years?
      RESP   Good trees, no. Big trees, no. I've cut a few little trees like
      guarumo and little trees that don't give wood, and perhaps a few that give
      a little wood, like *balsa*, *guarumo*, and *capulina*. (CR1)
(42) I leave all the trees [in my coffee], it looks pretty with them overhead,
      the trees that are big and good. What I remove are ones like *mayos*, all
      the species of trees that aren't good for timber, of bad quality. Here we
      always cut those. But they say that you can't cut any kind of tree, even
      if they're not good for anything. But I think that is hurting people. You
      have to get rid of the bad ones and keep the good ones. And in other
      places I plant trees—along the fence lines and where it is sparse—I plant
      trees—nice trees like *amarillones*, because in the future who knows what
      we're going to need. (CR15)

On the other hand, wasting trees by felling them but not using them, as was
often done during the early period of colonization, was generally considered unacceptable.

(43) Well, if it's unnecessary, it's not good. Because if it is necessary to cut
      them because they are causing harm or you're going to use them, it's fine
      because you need to do it. But if you cut them just to do damage, just
      to fell them, that's not good. (CR15)
(44) It's bad if you [fell trees] without needing to. (CR23)
(45) INTER   Do you think it is alright to cut trees sometimes?
      RESP   I don't think so; not cutting just to cut.
      INTER   Do people do that?
      RESP   Not any more. But earlier I was talking with my children about
      this, and I told them that if the politicians had told us, say around 1950,
      that they were thinking about stopping forest clearing like they did just
      a few years ago, it would have been good because Costa Rica would still
      have all its forests. (CR23)

Streamside forests were considered important by everyone we talked to, and
no one suggested that cutting them was acceptable. This is consistent with the
strong ties that most people see between forests and the presence of water in the
streams.

(46) Along the edge of streams it is bad to cut trees. Definitely. Even if it is
      dead because when a tree falls it knocks over another. (CR2)
(47) If a tree is in a certain place, I think that there may not be any time that
      you should cut it. Because it is not right if a tree is near a spring of water,
      and we know that that spring is there because of the tree that is there.

This is not just something that I have heard, but something that I know from experience, because I have seen things, I have lived, and had experiences. So I know you should never cut that tree. It is better to look for another one somewhere else. (CR3)

But in many ways, trees are seen as renewable resources, and it is acceptable to cut one if you also planted some trees. This view is articulated in the following statements:

(48)   RESP   When you are thinking about cutting down a tree, [you should] plant, or replace what you cut. So you cut one, but you replant another. Then you are more or less not destroying as you go along.
INTER   So you cut one, you plant one?
RESP   Plant more, if possible; it could be more. (CR1)

(49)   If you fell a tree, you should try to plant a tree. If you fell one, you should at least replant the same area. Or if you really need that land, at least, in that little corner there along the stream, you could plant a tree. (CR4)

In the survey, a relatively small proportion (21%) of the individuals surveyed agreed with the statement "For lack of employment, it's sometimes necessary to clear-cut forest." On the other hand, persons were much more likely to find cutting individual trees acceptable under specific conditions. For example, slightly more than half of those surveyed agreed that "For lack of employment it's sometimes necessary to trim or cut trees down." People surveyed were more likely to agree with statements that expressed practices that allowed for the replacement of old trees with new ones. For example, 80 percent of the surveyed agreed that "It's alright to cut a tree if you plant a new one." Streamside forests were considered particularly important. Ninety-six percent of the persons surveyed agreed with the statement "The trees that grow along the edges of rivers and streams should never be cut" (see figure 3.3).

Newcomers, or migrants into the community, were more likely than those born in the community of residence to agree that cutting trees or clearing forest was acceptable, regardless of the circumstances (see figure 3.4). This observation is especially true of newcomers who arrived before the park was established and when people typically settled in the area with the aim of clearing forest and staking a claim to the land. This expectation changed as new regulations and ideas favoring forest conservation were introduced by government officials and private conservation organizations. Newcomers arriving after the park was created were socialized into the new conservation regime. The locally born did not face the same pressures to clear land as newcomers. They were born to households that already had access to land cleared of forest. Unlike newcomers,

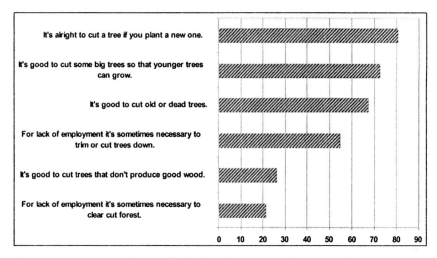

Figure 3.3.   Proportion who agreed with selected statements about appropriate circumstances for cutting trees, La Amistad, Costa Rica

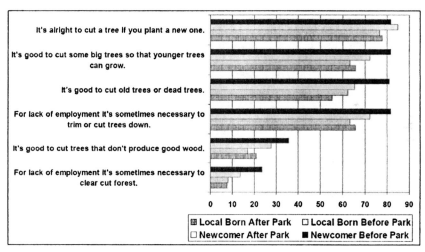

Figure 3.4.   Proportion who agreed with selected statements about appropriate circumstances for cutting trees by place of birth and time when reached working age, La Amistad, Costa Rica

they had less need to justify actions that were demanded to eke out an existence on the land.

People generally felt that clearing in Costa Rica and in the region had been so extensive that it was no longer acceptable to clear forest or that giving permission to fell trees only led to greater abuses. For example, when asked, "Do you think that sometimes it is fine to clear forests?" respondents said,

(50)   Well, now with the situation we're in, I think that all the forests that we have in Costa Rica should be conserved because there already has been a lot of forests cleared to grow crops. There are big farms with only one owner, we could use some of the areas that are already cleared. My idea is that it's not good to clear big areas of forest right now. Improve the farms that are already made, these big farms that are abandoned. We should restore them and leave the forests for environmental conservation. (CR18)

(51)   Well, I think that at these altitudes you shouldn't clear forest. You shouldn't clear forest because there isn't any left. You can see that all that is left is the park . . . here above . . . the park . . . the La Amistad International Park . . . and down below there aren't any trees left, very few. Really, more should be planted. (CR14)

A few people had near total opposition to tree felling and forest clearing.

(52)   RESP   Well, I don't think that it is good from any point of view. Why is it necessary to cut a tree for firewood? No, that would be a mistake. Not for lumber, either, because there are other materials, that would be better, too, that will make a better building than wood. I don't know why we cut trees. We do it out of ignorance.
INTER   And when it is bad to cut trees?
RESP   Well, all the time. . . . Because we're causing damage, it always causes damage. (CR22)

(53)   I have always thought that it is not good [to fell trees], and now I am even more sure of it. When we went up there, on this side of the mountain, you go through this area of giant trees, they could be one hundred years old, or one hundred and fifty years. Pretty trees. And they're not here anymore. All there is, is pasture. Sometimes people cut down trees and make a pasture, and two years later they don't want cows anymore and so they don't use the pasture. And the forest is gone. I'm not in agreement with felling trees. If they cut them they should at least plant some more. Because the forest is very pretty, it is very beautiful to be there in the forest. Some people think that it is good to sell trees, that they are making money. But I don't think that it is ever good. Definitely I don't think it is good. Because there were so many trees here, and now there's only half as many, and in another fifteen years there will be yet half as many again. Until this place looks like Guanacaste—which is a place that is way too flat, that doesn't have any trees, and where the heat is tremendous. Here we have a beautiful climate and now it is hotter than it was when we came here, and in another fifteen years if people keep cutting down trees. . . . That's why I don't think it is acceptable. It is beautiful and we should conserve it. We could reforest many places that don't now have trees. Some people are reforesting little by little. (CR20)

Commercial versus Household Timber Consumption

Most commonly, people opposed commercial logging but felt that it was acceptable to cut trees for personal use. There were a number of strong statements opposing selling trees to loggers.

(54) INTER So you only used them for your own use. And when you came here and cleared forest for crops, what were the results of this, were they positive?
RESP I no longer remember how it was, but we needed the crops to live, so to grow crops we had to clear forest. But never to sell lumber, to exploit wood—never! (CR5)

(55) INTER Can you tell me if you think it is good to cut trees?
RESP Perhaps in this situation, the way I see it, I will talk from my own point of view. I am never going to talk in favor of any commercial use, never. Commercial use, I am completely against. I don't agree with commercializing wood. I am talking mostly about that which is done with bulldozers and trucks, because they have their own interests—good economic earnings. (CR21)

As this person continues talking, it becomes clear that the opposition is more a belief that commercial loggers are harvesting at unsustainable rates and taking the lumber and profits out of the community than opposition to timber harvesting to meet community needs for timber.

(56) INTER So you are completely against commercial use, but the way you are going to use the trees is alright?
RESP Yes. It seems to me that, for example, this forest that we have in front, if the community would organize itself and take advantage of management plans, with wood that is milled right here we could solve the need for housing. With just what we have here in the community, without destroying the roads, without eliminating the forests, there would be less misery.
INTER So you think that commercial use is bad, but local use with a management plan is more correct?
RESP It is more correct. Why? Because management plans take into account the watersheds, the species. . . . Management plans, for me, are very regulated, very regulated. There's not so much messing up of the roads or other things because of the style. It is harder to take out the trees, and logically it is more profitable because the wood will last longer—there's many things, many advantages. I want to tell you something, capital is necessary, but if we advance and if I supply my needs but destroy your property, then we are meeting a need but destroying something that is more important, to maintain the forests. There should

be another way, perhaps there is, to solve the needs in the urban areas and to maintain the forested areas that supply us with so much. (CR21)

In the survey, there was almost universal agreement that commercial logging companies were destructive of the forest and that this destruction exceeded anything wrought by the local population. More than nine out of ten persons surveyed agreed with the statement "Timber companies destroy more forest than the people who live in this community." People were in somewhat less agreement about the acceptability of commercial forest exploitation by local residents. About one in five agreed with the statement "The most important thing about trees is to make money from them." The material needs of the household figure into the likelihood that people place importance on trees as a source of cash. Figure 3.5 shows that households with more children were more likely to agree that trees were for making money. But this sentiment also appears to be most widely held by people who came to the area before the park was created. More recent arrivals and the locally born are less likely to see trees primarily for their cash value (figure 3.6).

Sometimes clearing forest and felling trees were judged with regard to their broader moral implications, particularly if these were done without true need or seriousness. The following statement exemplifies a moral outlook:

(57)   Nature can teach us a lot—honesty, respect—that's what's been missing, respect. We have lost respect, respect for nature. To see it, to adore it, to see a little bit of nature, the only time we see is when we're destroying it. Let me tell you, it is something to see a person walking with a chainsaw

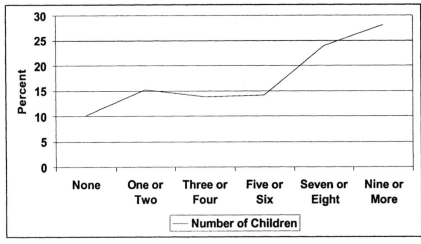

Figure 3.5.   Proportion who agreed that "the most important thing to do with trees is to make money," La Amistad, Costa Rica

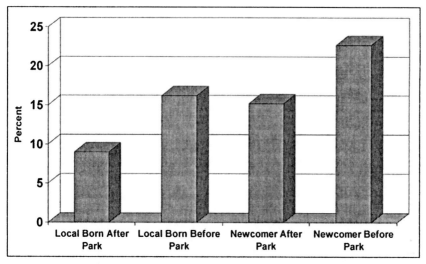

Figure 3.6.   Proportion who agreed, "the most important thing to do with trees is to make money," by place of birth and time when reached working age, La Amistad, Costa Rica

on their shoulder, because they're going to the park or because they're going to stop at any tree along the stream bank. And they treat it like a party, like a good thing. Well, I say, Blessed Lord, what could be in the minds of these people. This is just a bad way to do things, a way of doing things that is totally wrong. (CR3)

Changing Values

As is indicated in the quotes above, many people noted that significant changes had taken place in recent years in people's attitudes toward trees and wildlife. People see themselves and their neighbors as now generally not clearing forests. There is no single reason given for this change; rather, it is attributed to several factors. Some of these factors are external, including enforcement of environmental laws and the arrival of park environmental education programs. But a number of people took pains to point out that people had reached these conclusions based on their own experience seeing deterioration in the forest and environment.

(58)   INTER   And why do you think it has changed, from seeing the effects or from . . . ?
RESP   Because people have come to see that the only ones it hurts is ourselves, those that work in the countryside, from true awareness in each person. And also because people aren't just going to go and cut down a tree anywhere, because *MINAE* [*Ministerio de Ambiente y Energía*, or the Environment and Energy Ministry] will see them. (CR22)

(59) INTER   Then this change is due to the laws?
RESP   Well, also because people have recognized that we're in the middle of a big mistake, from what I know, to clear so much forest that we don't have to clear.
INTER   Then from experience?
RESP   Exactly, experience is bringing an awareness that you shouldn't do this, it's the future, the children's future. (CR8)

In the survey, more than nine out of ten persons we surveyed agreed with the statement "Nowadays people in this community are more careful with the forest than before."

People also talked about past waste and suggested that now they should only clear the amount of forest that they really need. In this sense, they grounded their current mental models of forest conservation in prior experience or, in this case, the repudiation of the way things had been done in the past. In some ways, this is a general statement against wasteful forest destruction, but it also reflects the view that past waste has led to government restrictions on their activities.

(60) This happened a long time ago, when these trees were felled. But I say that a person should only work what they need. What you don't need should be left in forest, because perhaps someday it will be useful to someone. This is what has been happening here in this country. Before, everyone came here and the banks even gave them money for clearing forests, planting pasture. But now we are left with very little wood, now they don't even let us work where we need to work. (CR15)

Forest in Social Relationships

We believe that the forest values of individuals are strongly shaped by those individuals' social relationships, for example where they learn about forests, forest-related messages disseminated by governmental and nongovernmental organizations, and whom in their communities they talk with about forests. We asked people where they learned about the forest, and people gave a diversity of responses. People mentioned family and relatives, environmental education programs put on by park guards, environmental programs on television, and church. The most common source of knowledge, however, was that they had learned "naturally," or from living and working in the forest or countryside. Many people strongly expressed that their experiences and the things they had seen had taught them a lot, even while recognizing that they had also learned from environmental messages.

(61) This [knowledge of forests] I didn't learn. It was born in me from being raised in the forest, I became familiar with the forest, I knew and know

how beautiful it can be; that which is natural. I was raised in the forest and I remember sitting at the base of a big fig tree and seeing a whole lot of birds, seeing a lot of things. All this has been planted in me since infancy. . . .

[*later*] For example, on Channel 13 we almost daily see programs about things; where they teach a lot. You can see a lot of things about nature, trees and forest, rivers and all these things. And the things about places where there are fights to conserve something and all this. I, whenever I can, this I try not to miss it because I enjoy it. (CR3)

(62) INTER   Where did you learn what you know about trees and forests?

RESP   From my father, who saw this great deforestation and concluded that we had to conserve. And from my brother-in-law, who likes all this, too. Because he likes the forest so much, he's always learning about it. From this a base was formed. (CR8)

(63) INTER   And where did you learn what you know about trees and forest, from whom or where did you learn about trees and forests and all this?

RESP   Experience and wisdom, because it's not necessary for people to tell you things if you have already seen it. By seeing the situation and through your lived experiences you see things. (CR10)

(64) INTER   And where did you learn what you know about trees and forest?

RESP   Because one lives. Well, there's a lot on television, a lot comes in from there. And also because one has lived in the countryside, for example if you are familiar with a forest and later come back and it's not there and the climate has changed, a radical change in these things, then you say, yes, there's been a change. That's how one knows that experience is worth a lot. (CR16)

Among those surveyed, working in the forest was the most important way to learn about it (91%), followed by television (85%), radio (86%), the park guards (72%), and schools (61%) (figure 3.7).

Learning through Organizations

Many people indicated that various governmental and nongovernmental organizations (NGOs) working in the community had played a key role in their knowledge and values about forest. *MINAE*, the government agency that manages the national park and the logging permit programs, was often mentioned, along with various extension programs and local NGOs. These groups were not generally discussed as outside intrusions, but rather as groups that had called local people's attention to important issues by working with them and educating them.

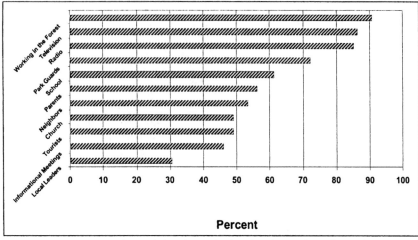

Figure 3.7.   Proportion who said they learned what they know about forests by source of information, La Amistad, Costa Rica

(65)   INTER   And why do you think things have changed the mentality of …?

RESP   Well, the change came over time, people are learning new things. We are getting educated. Before we didn't think like this, about the future and all that, the wood and all that. But now we do, because of the programs of *MINAE*, all that they have done to educate us, we now have a new mentality about these things. (CR24)

(66)   INTER   And do you think the people still think the same about the environment, nature, the forests? Has there been a change in the awareness of the people, or not?

RESP   Yes, there's been a huge change. Look, about four years ago *MINAE* organized meetings making us see this, the necessity of conservation, of not cutting trees just to cut them, including making us aware about water. … I think so, yes, a lot, the people have responded, responded a lot. (CR23)

(67)   INTER   And who puts on these field days?

RESP   The foresters. They meet with a few people in the countryside, wherever—a farm, a forest, a river. In whatever place is related to the themes they are covering. I don't know, but since I was a child I have always liked the forest a lot. When I was very little, when they would give talks and teach people to want to conserve. That's what they talk about in the schools, about the flora, the fauna, and that we need to protect it because it needs to be protected, all these things. And I went on growing and observing and concluded that it is bad to destroy because of what I saw. I have lived here a lot of years, and it is from living through this; from seeing thousands of hectares being cleared and the springs disappearing.

So nobody needs to be told whether it is bad or good to destroy forests, because one can see that it is bad. And on land that was sabotaged and burned, what happens is that big landslides happen, which was caused by this. How many times have we been cut off because a landslide took out a bridge or a road? This erosion, is caused by the same destruction. (CR13)

Local organizations advocating nature conservation have also been formed, often with the assistance of outside environmental organizations, as explained in the following comments:

(68)   RESP   So to see that the animals that are becoming extinct, they train people and call meetings in each school, where an organization called *MINAE* gives talks. And we became very interested in this. . . . There are [other organizations], besides *MINAE* . . . there's a local organization that is involved in this, the conservation of forests and some animals that is called *APRENABRUS* [*Asociación Preservacionista de Coto Brus*].
INTER   Is it Costa Rican?
RESP   Yes, but I think it is financed by international organizations. They give it a subsidy, so that they can take these lessons to various communities. And with this people began to see the great necessity of conserving, and now we have fresh tracks of peccaries, here, we have pacas, and the biodiversity has started to grow again. Thank God. (CR18)

(69)   INTER   You say that a [tourism] board was recently created. How many people are working on it now?
RESP   We have five on the committee; from five to seven. There are a lot of people associated. Some already have cabins, they are building cabins and are interested.
INTER   And how did the board get started?
RESP   There was an Italian who came here to work and promote this; he just left and returned to his country, but the board is truly functioning.
INTER   And this was his initiative or the community's?
RESP   It was his. He worked with a man from San Luis, they started to give workshops about tourism and all this, and people started to get excited. But most of the initiative was from [a local man]. (CR20)

Talking about Trees with Others

We also asked people with whom they discussed trees and forests. The ways and extent to which people talk about trees and forests with other people is an important indicator of the extent to which environmental concern has become integrated into local mental and cultural models and can provide indicators of the extent to which social norms related to forest use and conservation have developed. Some interviewees indicated that they talked about trees and forests with the agencies and organizations working on forest conservation. Others talked about it more broadly and more actively, with some indicating that they would call people's attention to environmentally destructive practices. On the other hand, a number of people indicated that they talked mostly about trees and forests with family and friends and were reluctant to take the risk of social conflict or retaliation by getting involved in other people's affairs.

For many people, trees and forest were something they only talked about in specialized venues, with forest professionals and other like-minded people. When asked if they discussed trees with other people in the community, respondents said,

(70)   Do I discuss this? No. I learn about it. I have met with these people who come here to present courses like the management of trees. How to prune them and how to fertilize them; how to make nurseries and all this. I know about the tools that that you use to prune, and the long pole saws, and shears and saws and all this. I more or less know how to take care of a tree plantation. I have been at their meetings. (CR14)

(71)   Well, I haven't talked much about these, neither with the people nor with *MINAE* or anybody. Because, no . . . I try not to get involved in these problems of tree cutting. But if I would talk about this with someone, it would be with the people from *MINAE*. (CR15)

(72)   Yes, sometimes with people from the tourism board, we talk about nature. There are some people, mostly those working with this in the park or on the board, that are protecting something to see if tourists will come here in the future. (CR20)

In other cases, people indicated that they would speak out in the community about the value of forest conservation and call attention to practices that were environmentally destructive. Often, this was done mostly with family and friends, with much greater reluctance to talk about forests in the broader community. Again, when asked if they discussed trees and forests with other people in the community, respondents said,

(73)   Yes, of course. Mostly with my brother-in-law, who is a great lover of forest. He likes to go a lot, for days, into the forest, exploring. So, more than anything I talk with him. We say, what a great time this would be to go to the forest, to see that ridge, the mountains. We sometimes pass a little time like this. We have some maps where you can see the great expanses—here we have the Amistad International Park. It's an area you can talk about a lot. A little while back, we went on a long walk there. (CR17)

(74)   Well, with friends from around here, because there are people. . . . There
        are people that are pretty young who think like mature people, right? I
        am older, but I think that . . . that other older people need to leave some-
        thing for the youth. I have been talking to people for many years, since
        we started to plant trees. With older people like me, and we talk about
        and think about . . . there's just a few of us . . . there are people who don't
        think about and plant trees. So there are always people opposing us. I talk
        to them and say, look, in twenty years there's not going to be any wood.
        You have a child. They say they need to think about the cows, which
        eat grass, instead of planting trees. They drive me crazy. They plant cof-
        fee but not trees. Not me, I plant trees. It's that I have noticed that there
        are people who have this mentality, that it's better to make pastures and
        have a few cows than to plant trees. Only some of us think differently.
        . . . There are young people, I have talked to young people who like to
        hear it. They have a mature mentality, they agree with me about what I
        tell them about needing to take care of trees. Because the trees of a forest,
        of a good forest, we can see . . . we have heard about other places; other
        places in other countries where the air is not good to breathe. So I think
        we need to think about the forests, and about the beauty that we have,
        the beauty of the earth. (CR8)

(75)   Yes, sometimes a comment to friends, right? The damage that is done by
        felling trees. . . . Whenever there's an opportunity I comment about these
        things. . . . [Like] when I am in the store, I start to talk to people about this.
        We talk a lot about hunting, because there are a lot of us that are against
        it. This comes up a lot, and almost everyone is against it. (CR22)

(76)   Yes, when I see . . . mostly when I see something that I don't like, like
        a fire, for example, which is one of the things that I am most against;
        burning the land.
        INTER   So you talk to someone who is burning?
        RESP   Yes, yes. Not directly with the people, but at least with friends,
        that to see such a thing, how bad it looks to me. About not doing it, if
        the neighbor sees someone clearing forest or burning the land, and you
        know that this causes damage. They can do it but it hurts us all. I repeat:
        if we're going to pollute our own air, put smoke in the air, it is everyone's
        air and this earth that he is burning today belongs to him today. But
        someday it will belong to another. But the other will be the recipient of
        the bad conditions without being responsible. (CR13)

Other people talk about trees and forest more widely in the community, sometimes to the point of getting involved in what happens on other people's land and
provoking conflict. Some expressed a sense of frustration or futility in accomplish-
ing anything through this. When asked if they sometimes discuss trees and forests
with other people, respondents said:

(77)   I talk about it to everyone, sometimes they don't like it. I know they
don't like it, but sometimes I talk about it. Everywhere I talk about it.
I am a protector of nature. What happens, though, is that one can't do
anything just by oneself. What can I do? . . . [But] all my life I have done
this. It is a profession of mine for my whole life, like something that
comes natural to me. (CR3)

(78)   Yes, yes, one talks about this, and with certain people. About the situation, the situation of the destruction of trees and all this. There are people
who agree with me, and people who do not. . . . There are some people
who don't agree and some who do. . . . There are more people without
money than with money, do you see? And the one who has money wants
more, and wants more power—these are the ones that destroy everything, do you see? To some of them, I talk and talk and talk, and it's just
talking for talking's sake because nobody listens or pays attention. Some
people see what is happening and don't do anything, because there are
bigger people, who have money and pay to do what they want. This is
exactly the problem we have. (CR10)

(79)   About the need to conserve? Yes, sometimes we have some conversations
about this. . . . I talk with my neighbors about the need to protect, including to turn people in so these things don't happen. But after talking
about it for a little while, the difficulties become apparent and in the end
one is left with one's hands tied and can't do anything. (CR6)

Regulations

While many people talked about the degree to which attitudes had changed in response to noticeable changes in local environmental conditions, it was also evident
that people attributed a lot of the changes in people's behaviors to government
agencies (*MINAE*) and forestry regulations. People viewed the laws as effective in
changing people's behaviors and, often, as the only way that people would change
their behaviors.

(80)   INTER   Today are there fewer fires?
RESP   Now there aren't any. People are scared that they'll be hauled off
before the judge in San Isidro; people are a little scared. Nobody wants
to burn anymore, and we don't want to burn because we have seen the
damage that it causes; burning the land. It causes damage to the soil.
(CR14)

(81)   INTER   So the rules and laws that say you can't cut a tree have an
important impact on people?
RESP   Yes, directly. Perhaps you don't like it, but there are consequences. (CR2)

(82) INTER   And why do you think that the mentality of the people here has changed, why don't they burn anymore, why aren't they clearing forest as much?

RESP   Are they cutting trees, clearing, you say? Yes, but very little, very little because of the laws. A human is very stubborn. They won't obey the law until they are fined. But yes, it has a lot to do with the law, it has affected the *campesinos*, because otherwise this would all have been destroyed.

INTER   So you think that the change is due to the laws?

RESP   Well, also people have recognized that it was a big mistake, to cut so much, to be cutting so much that we really don't need to cut, clearing it. (CR8)

A park guard grounds his discussion of the importance of the law in his own experience, noting that many people historically violated forestry laws out of ignorance and stressing the importance (and effectiveness over time) of efforts to educate people about the law and, ultimately, the enduring need for law enforcement:

(83) INTER   Many people have said that about eight or ten years ago things changed—less hunting, less clearing of forests, and all this. How do you explain these changes?

RESP   This is due to the laws, a little from the law and because the park is here, when they declared the park. That is to say, people ignored many parts of the law, if you ask me. Right now I am following the law. Before I didn't know it was prohibited to collect palm hearts from the open forest, and one time the park guards caught me. Two hundred palm hearts, but ignorantly, ignorant because I didn't know. A guy who was the owner of this farm told me, go get some palm hearts. . . . I didn't know that it was prohibited. Really, people do these things ignorant of the law. They didn't know that it was prohibited to burn at the edge of the forest, so people did it. The burned a lot, they hunted a lot, and nobody told them it was prohibited. Until the park came, and they closed the park. So it started little by little. People have been changing, and have noticed that clearing forest is not permitted, even on private farms, clearing forest is prohibited . . . sometimes I see people beginning to clear forests. So I tell them it is prohibited, but it seems they do it anyway. We turn them in, and they don't do it because of the law. (CR11)

In the survey, more than nine out of ten persons surveyed agreed that without legal restrictions there would be fewer trees because people would not limit their tree felling ("If we did not have laws to protect the forests, we would have far fewer trees." "If people were permitted to cut all the trees they wanted, they would not know when to stop."). About three-fourths also agreed with the statement "People do not burn land for cultivation because they are afraid of the government."

In many ways, people saw a synergistic role for some combination of community and government action. Some felt that they could turn to the authorities for support when they wanted to stop some environmental damage in the community and saw the government as an important ally in their own conservation efforts by being able to intervene in ways that were difficult for community members.

(84)   We like to take care of things, and therefore we have benefited [from the park] because now if we see someone hunting we don't have to confront them directly. The park [guards] can be summoned; you go to the park and tell them, and they go and look for whoever was hunting to arrest them, and they will be punished by the law. It is apparent that we have benefited from the park, and for me this is why we have benefited. And besides, who is harmed by the park? Only the hunters, who now can't freely enter the park because they will be caught and have problems with the law. We haven't been harmed at all. (CR10)

On the other hand, as some of the quotes above begin to indicate, people saw a number of problems with the regulations in terms of making life more difficult for them in some fundamental ways, such as not allowing them to plant crops or thin shade in coffee, or due to a perceived unfairness that commercial loggers are able to get permits to cut trees when it is very difficult for the average landowner to do so, even to cut one or two trees for personal use. Others express support for forest conservation but say that they cannot afford to do it unless they get some financial assistance from the government. There are, however, some people with a strong interest in conservation who feel that too many people get permits, often objecting to commercial loggers but also to individual landowners' getting a permit and using it as cover to cut more trees than they were authorized to do.

(85)   INTER   And are there times that you can use these [fallen] trees?
RESP   Well, it depends. . . . If it doesn't fall along a stream and isn't green. If it's dead and not along a stream, you can use it for your house, but not sell it.
INTER   And do you need a permit?
RESP   Yes. . . . For everything, even if it's for a house, you need a permit.
INTER   So if a tree fell in the wind, and you didn't do anything, it just fell in the wind, could you use it without a permit?
RESP   Without permission, no.
INTER   And what's it like to get a permit, is it hard?

RESP   Yes, very. The hard part is that you use your resources to go to town, and perhaps have to pay something like eight thousand pesos [about US$28 at the time] for just one permit to use a tree here, wood for a house. We're talking about a house, right? For a house, nothing more. You have to pay perhaps eight thousand pesos for a permit and have to go to town and waste money. Perhaps you don't have much money. (CR1)

A majority of the persons we surveyed felt that restrictions should not apply to local residents who use timber to construct homes. About 60 percent agreed with the statement "People should be allowed without any government restrictions to cut trees to build their house." Tree felling for timber for home construction seemed to be a privileged use of wood in the minds of the local residents. Much smaller proportions agreed with statements that opposed government restrictions on other uses of trees. For example, only about one-fourth of the respondents agreed with the statement "People should be allowed to thin or clear forest without any government restrictions to cultivate or plant coffee." An even smaller proportion (14%) agreed with the statement "People should be allowed to sell trees that are on their own land without any government restrictions."

Many of the statements that people made when talking about forestry regulations are interesting because of the rationalizations that are given for needing to cut trees (e.g., too much time had passed, they were diseased, it was worthless secondary forest, there was a great need), as well as the extreme examples, or even exaggerations, of the possible consequences (e.g., confiscation of land). They also reflect the conflict that is sometimes generated and the ways that the community at times pushes back against the conservation laws when they seem too strict.

(86)   RESP   I was thinning out some shade, and I only left the best trees, and a little while later after about a month they came and said that they were going to report it to the fiscal agency to see what they would do about this. But this was after some time, I thinned the shade in June, it's already been six months. . . . [The park guards] came here after about a month. I think that's too late.
INTER   And when you thinned out the trees, could you describe what you cut? Big ones, little ones, what were they like?
RESP   Small, some about six inches, others three, all sizes. And some big ones, but trees that weren't useful. . . . They were big, but they had termites, they weren't any good.
INTER   So you weren't cutting them for lumber?
RESP   Well maybe a little piece, up there, but the rest was bad. I want to see if I can get a permit, to see if I can have the right to harvest a little piece of forest that I could use.

INTER But when you were doing this thinning, did you have permission to cut them, or weren't you able to get permission?

RESP I didn't want to get permission because I thought that if I asked for it and they didn't give it to me, I would have been slowed down. And this was in a coffee plantation, and if I had waited disease would have ruined the coffee. . . . Trees are important because they give us wood to make our houses and things, but apart from this, we also need to work growing crops like coffee. So I at least like to leave the biggest and nicest trees, and those with good wood. But I think that, for trees that aren't useful, it is best to get rid of them so they don't bother us.

INTER What happened?

RESP I was convicted of cutting trees, and spent twenty-two days in jail. I was sentenced for a year, I got out on appeal and later they gave the order to capture me and gave me two years. I was in jail for twenty-two days and then got out.

INTER And what kind of tree felling were you doing? Were you cutting trees to sell them?

RESP No, it was to work, to plant corn, rice.

INTER And what kind of an area was it? Was it in a forest or something like *tacotal*?

RESP Well, you could almost say it was primary forest.

INTER Oh, primary forest. Was that why they didn't like it?

RESP Yes that's why they didn't like it. They arrested me for felling trees. Thus, they felled me.

INTER Tell me then, we were talking, you were cutting recently in your coffee, a few more or less big trees but you said they weren't good trees, not for lumber. But what did *MINAE* say? Do they think that these are good trees? How did they answer you?

RESP I think that for them all trees are the same, whether they're good for timber or bad; to them it's all the same. What they want is forest. But I don't consider something good just because it is a tree, one that after six years will be eaten by termites.

INTER Very interesting. But let me change the subject a little and talk a little bit about forests. Do you think that sometimes it is good to clear forest?

RESP Well, I think that perhaps it is not good, but, if it is necessary, you have to do it. Perhaps you have to do it because you have, let's say, an area of forest and don't have any place to work. We would have to rent some land from people where there wasn't forest, even though we had this land that we couldn't use for anything. And nobody is paying us to conserve, and we have the need to work. We don't have a job or any way to survive. So we need to clear forest, to work the land. Many times the forests are secondary, as they say, and the loggers won't come here to take bad wood, they only come for good lumber.

INTER   So they only come for primary forest, and secondary forests aren't of interest to the loggers?

RESP   No. They're not any good.

INTER   So when you are thinking about clearing forest for crops in a place with secondary forest, it doesn't bother you too much.

RESP   Right, but here, some of what they call forest [montaña] is secondary, and they say you can't clear it. (CR15)

(87)   INTER   Do people here in the community sometimes cut trees?

RESP   Here, no. What they do, perhaps, is look for a fallen tree to get some lumber. But even for this fallen wood you need a permit; even though it is on the ground. Even though it is rotting, they don't let you have it.

INTER   And if someone cuts trees, what happens?

RESP   They'll come and confiscate their saw. . . . They almost always come when they hear the sound of saws. . . . That's their job. They pass by here, down and up, and up and down, looking.

INTER   And how would the community react if . . . ?

RESP   Like I was saying, the community, here we have had various meetings, and they have been told this. Now it appears that things are calming down a little. Because they have been told it is good, they have been told in the meetings to remember that animals live on the leaves and all this, but people can't eat wood. They can eat chicken. It doesn't work for the children that the government doesn't have enough money to say, "We're going to subsidize people." So people got mad and told the "parkies" [parquistas] that if they kept being so strict they would set the park on fire. (CR7)

(88)   INTER   And you mentioned the system of permits to cut trees. What happens if someone cuts without a permit?

RESP   First you lose your land, if they see me out there working, they'll confiscate my land. I have to defend myself before the law, and if it was a big violation—three little trees wouldn't be one—they'll fine me, or confiscate the land so I recognize that I did something wrong. But like I said, they put one man in jail. I heard he was sentenced for cutting a tree for a neighbor without a permit. It wasn't even a tree. It wasn't in the forest, but just a trunk there on the edge of the coffee. . . . It was because of planting beans, he was going to fell some trees that created shade. It was just tacotal, it wasn't forest, and they arrested him and put him in jail. And the whole town was really mad, and the people said that if they didn't let him out they would cause a big scandal, a protest [huelga] there at the court. (CR9)

These difficulties are recognized by some park guards, who indicate that they try account for people's subsistence needs when enforcing regulations. One park guard explained this approach.

(89) Our neighbors complain a lot, and on certain points they are right. There are things that aren't permitted. . . . It's certain that in terms of farming, it is unjust. . . . I have seen some of my fellow guards, there are people that, say, bring in some poor guy for cutting a downed tree. I say why did you bring this guy in. You need to help people. Poor guy, he's trying to keep it from going to waste. Not everyone has a salary like I do, they need to survive from their farm. Some park guards earn one hundred fifty thousand pesos or two hundred thousand [about US$525 to US$700] and think that everyone else does, too. I say, the people have to live like us, and we shouldn't go around bothering our neighbors. I have always tried to help people a little. Let's say they have to cut some lumber. Here, the laws aren't good. You have a fallen tree, and sometimes they require so many things before they will give you a permit. Are you going to pay five thousand or ten thousand pesos [about US$17 to US$35] for a permit, for a special paper or a lawyer? Someone who has nothing to do with your tree? They're just taking money from the poor person. I always say, I don't have any reason to send a poor *campesino* to jail for not having permission from a lawyer, it's a technicality.
INTER So for the process of getting a permit, I need an attorney to get the papers together?
RESP Well, it's a lot of trouble. Well, it's that it's not easy. . . . It's fine if it's a big permit, if it's commercial, to sell the wood, it's good that they ask for a few things because these people are earning some money. But if it's just a little permit for two trees to make a house, why not go and do an inspection? If it's fine, if it's not along the edge of a stream, there's no problem. They're ready to go. But no, there are some who say, bring me this and this and this, here there are more than a few people who don't have title to their land, and they ask them for their title.
INTER If you're going to give permission for . . . ?
RESP For five or ten trees, for a house. And they tell them if they don't have a title, they can't do it. How can they say they can't do it? It's not their fault. It's the fault of the committee for titling land that people don't have titles. It shouldn't be like that. So people like to do it undercover. Instead of spending all that time getting a permit and everything, they figure they can find a way to get away with it. But what you have to do. . . . People try to find dead trees so they don't have problems. You go with them, and if it's not near a stream, it's nothing. Really, it's unjust. They need it to make a repair on a house. (CR11)

Not everyone complains about enforcement, however. Some people expressed a feeling that the laws are inadequately enforced, at least with regard to commercial loggers.

(90) RESP What comes to my mind when we talk about trees and forest is to live in harmony. By in harmony, I refer to not destroying more than we've already destroyed. For crops, use what we've already cleared, and take care of what is left. But things happen, contradictory things, like what happens in *MINAE*. They talk about protection and then give out permits to cut lumber. I don't understand this, even right next to the park. They're contradictory things.
INTER That they give permits to people?
RESP *MINAE*, the same organization that protects, gives permits, too. The wood that can be used, I think it should be used, but sensibly. It should no longer be taken out of here. It should be used here in this community. . . . They pretend to take care of the trees, while other trees are taken out on the road by those that have political power, or something like that. But it's our community that should be taking care of the trees. Here we have a guard station, but people get away with a lot. (CR6)

(91) If a businessman pays for the permit, he has the right to go and destroy the forest. They don't worry, if they stop them on the roads, the people who make the roads and who make the bridges want to stop them, they say that what they are doing is legal and it doesn't matter to them if they wreck something. (CR21)

(92) I think that these people that are working for the park up there, they give permission to people to fell trees, and I don't think it should be like that. Because they give permission to cut one tree and they cut a bunch. (CR3)

There is similar resentment about participation in government incentive programs, such as the payments for environmental services of standing forest, and some people feel that these are not equally accessible to all landowners.

(93) What I have been seeing, for example, when *MINAE* had these meetings that I told you about before, when they called meetings, there were a lot of people from the bigger farms, right? Areas that . . . with an incentive to conserve, there are people ready if they pay them an incentive. They had conserved forests, primary and secondary, and they said they had because they had. But I went to San Isidro, because I was one of the ones interested, I wanted them to pay me to conserve the secondary forests that I have. But no, there wasn't anything, and later everything went to the northern zone, everything the government had was sent to the north of Costa Rica. (CR23)

Responsibility

Another way we sought to learn about the social context and motivating force
for forest conservation was by asking who had the responsibility of taking care of
the forest. In this, we were particularly looking to understand, given that a lot of
the ideas related to conservation come from outside the community, the extent to
which local people felt that forest conservation was their responsibility, as opposed
to the responsibility of the government agencies or international conservation organizations. In general, while an important role for the government was acknowledged, most people indicated that caring for the forest was the responsibility of
landowners and community members.

(94) INTER   Who has the responsibility to take care of the forest?
      RESP   Well, I don't know, but I think it is the state or the government,
      because they have *MINAE* and things like this that are watching out for
      tree cutting. But also, it should be each person, because we know that in
      the future we're going to need it. Well.... We have to leave some, and not
      clear everything, because what has happened here on some farms makes
      me sad. They wanted agriculture so they cleared it all, but then they gave
      up on agriculture. The land is abandoned and now there's not even forest,
      because they cleared it. It would have been better to have left it, for now
      they could use the wood; the wood that they wasted. That's why I think
      it is good to take care of the forest. (CR15)

(95) INTER   Who has responsibility for taking care of the forests?
      RESP   I think that everyone [does]; all the people; not just the govern-
      ment. Because we're all responsible. . . . All the citizens. Everyone has to
      take care of our heritage, our health. (CR22)

(96) INTER   And who do you think has the responsibility to take care of
      the forests?
      RESP   The people or the government, is that the question? . . . Both,
      but mostly it is us, the *campesinos* that have the responsibility to care for
      the forests. . . . Because we're the ones living here in the forest, and if we
      don't, what will happen? (CR5)

(97) INTER   Who is it that you think has the responsibility to take care of
      the forests?
      RESP   We do, definitely, to be aware and think. It's not the law that
      should teach us not to destroy, but we ourselves that have to take care of
      it. Why would we destroy what is ours? I don't think anyone should have
      to tell us that we have to take care of the forests, and not to burn and to
      protect the animals and all this. I think this is each person's responsibility,
      those of us who live here. (CR13)

In the survey, about four out of five persons we interviewed felt that the main
responsibility for protecting trees was with the government. But the persons inter-

viewed were quick to add that the government could not be expected to succeed without the active support of the populace. Almost all (98%) of the people we surveyed agreed with the statement "The government by itself cannot care for the trees and forests; community members should help, too."

A number of people's comments showed sophisticated reasoning about the complex relationship between government policies, communities, and landowners in terms of responsibility for forests.

(98)   I think that we all have the responsibility, but principally the politicians, because they make the policies that can make this happen. . . . The politicians have the most responsibility, because they have their policies. For example . . . well . . . this is hard to say in just a few words. A long time ago in Costa Rica there was an institution that was called *IDA*; well, before it was *ITCO* [*Instituto de Tierras y Colonización*, or the Land and Colonization Institute], many years ago. And the help that the government gave people was to give them land, right? They gave them land, when all this was forest, and all these forests, this land, was for people to grow crops. Through this a lot of forests disappeared. Not now, because there are laws that don't permit this, but years ago these were forests. Not all the land that *IDA* gave out was forest, but a lot of it was. (CR23)

Others express frustration with what they are able to do or the lack of coordination between the people and enforcement agencies.

(99)   Well, the responsibility belongs to everyone, because deforestation hurts everyone. It begins with the laws of the government. There are the foresters—they get a salary. They receive money. They get money and everything, but they don't take care of anything. The owners of the farm are only interested in "*Don Dinero*," and the rest doesn't matter. This is the problem. But in terms of preventing deforestation, it's everyone. I think it's like protecting wildlife. Some take care of it while others destroy it. And everyone, actually, should be taking care of it, because it's disappearing. This is happening, too, with the trees, through the years. Our great-grandchildren aren't going to be able to see anything; not trees, not what we call wildlife. This is the bad situation we have. Because if you protect wildlife, you make enemies and then there are problems. Because everyone is looking to destroy, there are terrible things that are coming to be in Costa Rica, like the deforestation and the destruction of wildlife. They are terrible. (CR10)

(100) The community itself [has responsibility], but they don't let us take care of it. Our hands are tied. There are four or five that have the law in their hands and they don't let us do anything. One tries to care for it, and the others don't help them; those who have political power. Political power

or something like this. But we should take care of these things. We're the neighbors in the community. Here we have a park guard station, but undercover people do a lot of crazy things. But that's it, hand in hand with the community these people can do it, too, the park guards. But they have a lot of limitations—lack of resources, of vehicles, firearms, and people—almost everything. All they have is the guard station, they don't have the personnel, they have very few people. (CR6)

What Happens When Someone Cuts a Tree or Clears Forest?

Yet another way we sought to gauge the content and strength of norms related to conservation was to ask people what would happen if someone in the community cut a tree or cleared forest. Many people quickly noted that this was now restricted by law and that people could get fined or jailed for doing this, indicating that the threat of law enforcement and punishment was real.

(101) INTER   And if someone would start to cut trees here in the community, what would happen to them?
RESP   You can't do it, because it is controlled by *MINAE*. To cut trees you need to get a permit from *MINAE*. I need to go and ask for a permit, and *MINAE* comes and says, this tree you can cut, this one you can't. And I have to do it like this.
INTER   If you have a permit, it's alright. But if you don't have a permit, what happens?
RESP   They fine you. (CR16)

(102) INTER   And what would happen if someone cut trees here in the community?
RESP   It's hard to get away with, because we have enough laws now that they can stop us. Thirty years ago, nobody paid any attention. You could do whatever you wanted. But not now, because now nobody can cut down trees because one's companions will say, "Don't do it, because you'll get in trouble with the law and go to jail." So nobody does it, people have stopped doing it because it's punished, or because a friend says not to do it. You can't do it. (CR8)

There was little doubt that the word had gotten out about laws against forest clearing and that there had been some cases of enforcement. Among the individuals we surveyed, there was almost unanimous agreement (90%) that clearing forest was prohibited. However, there was some ambivalence as to whether this was a good thing or not, due to people's need to meet their livelihood needs and perceived inequities in enforcement between *campesinos* and loggers.

(103) INTER What happens if someone here in the community cuts a tree without a permit?
RESP Someone will go and talk to someone outside. And they'll come, and grab you for felling trees. Before, people could fell anything they wanted. But now, no. You now have to have a permit to fell trees. If it's not to get wood to build a house or something like that, you can't get a permit. For example, we wanted to cut some of the forest that we had in our coffee plantations, but definitely not. If park [guards] catch you felling a tree, they'll take you away. Because a neighbor of ours already went to jail for this. To plant beans, he felled and cleared a few little trees that were in the way. And for this they took him away. So you can't touch a tree without a permit. I don't know if this is a good or a bad thing. (CR17)

(104) INTER What do you think would happen if someone cuts a tree without a permit in this community?
RESP Well, here the government of Costa Rica has an organization that is in charge of watching out for this, to control the cutting of trees. This is *MINAE*. And they are the only ones that can give permission for cutting trees. They have certain requirements. . . . People can't cut trees without adequate permission, this part of the government takes care of this. Sometimes it seems very unjust, because a person who needs a tree to build a house can be denied permission under this same law. So they are closing the gate on the person that needs to build a house. I think this situation should be analyzed, but if there is someone regulating the cutting of trees, well, we thank them for having prevented more of what is called deforestation, although it happens everywhere. I don't know if you have gotten into this, but what sometimes happens is that they give permits to big logging companies, and they do a lot of deforestation. Although they say that, with permits they are allowed to cut so many trees. But they are deforesting, they are doing tremendous damage to the forest. This forest will need fifty years to recover from this big deforestation, that they did with a permit. So I think that we are against this, in terms of me, personally, I am against this. That these people give a permit to a logging company to harvest a certain number of trees and at times refuse permission to someone who needs a tree to build his house. People are treated differently under this system. (CR18)

This ambivalence also appeared in the survey results. Ninety percent of the persons we surveyed agreed with the statement "It is easier for rich landowners to get permits to cut trees than it is for common or poor people." Most people surveyed also felt that small, or peasant, farmers (*campesinos*) should be able to get permits to cut trees for their own use. Eighty percent agreed with the statement "It should be easier for a *campesino* in this community to get a permit to cut a tree for home use."

We tried to probe further to ask how people in the community would react if someone were cutting trees, and here the responses were mixed. Some people felt that no one in the community would do anything, either because they didn't care or because they didn't want to risk retribution. Others noted that it had happened, sometimes not through a formal accusation but by informally telling a park guard.

Some people felt that there was at least some chance that someone would get turned in if they felled trees or cleared forest. For example,

(105) INTER   What would happen here if someone in the community started to cut trees?
RESP   Ah! They could even get sent to jail, they could go to jail. If someone really started deforesting. . . . This, it is punished by the law.
INTER   But only if you cut a lot of trees? What if you only cut one tree?
RESP   Well, it depends. Let's say, if I do it in a way that no one notices, nothing happens. But if someone notices or someone turns me in to *MINAE* or something, calls the authorities, it is dangerous because I would have to pay a fine, or something like that. . . . There are people who have had problems for cutting trees.
INTER   But is it because someone in the community turns them in?
RESP   It could be. Well, I don't know about this, but for one reason or another it has happened. (CR2)

(106) INTER   If you are cutting trees, will people complain?
RESP   [*someone who cuts trees for a living*] They will make a complaint, and then I'm lost.
INTER   And has this happened in the community?
RESP   Yes, of course. (CR24)

(107) INTER   So if someone [cuts trees] the park guards come?
RESP   The park guards or the police. There are police, too, that are interested in this; that people don't cut trees and all this.
INTER   And what's it like with neighbors here, if you do this? Do they tell someone if you're clearing *tacotal* or forest?
RESP   Not often, not often. But it happens. It has happened, but not often. (CR1)

Other people did not think that many people in the community cared enough or were willing to create social conflict by reporting someone who was felling trees, as indicated in the following statements:

(108) Surely nothing would happen [if someone was cutting trees] because here nobody would complain. I say that nothing would happen, but it could, because there are laws here. But people don't obey them, that's

why. There are laws, but people don't obey them. But if the law was followed, it would be a crime, it would be a crime to cut a tree like that, without a permit. Not to mention the bad thing that you would be doing, because this is a very bad thing. . . . I want to tell you something. This community is disgraceful. Most of the community has made money from cutting trees. (CR3)

(109) No, people don't worry about [people felling trees]. I already told you about how if they have trees they want to sell them to earn a little money. Perhaps because they don't. . . . The importance and beauty of having nature and these beautiful trees. . . . I want to have a tree like those in the forest, that is one hundred years old, that you can't even get around because they're so immense. But the people that have them want to sell them to get money.

INTER You have said that it is not good to cut trees or clear forest. What happens here if someone cuts trees, what does the community do or what happens to this person?

RESP I don't think the community would do anything. Most of the time they don't want to get involved in the lives of others. If you have your trees and want to sell them, people don't get involved. I don't know, but I don't think anyone would do anything. They don't want problems with the others. (CR20)

Other comments indicated more complexity. There was an indication that some people would like to make a formal complaint if they found someone illegally felling trees but would be reluctant to do it because it may be socially isolating or foster retribution, while at the same time there was uncertainty that the authorities would act or whether wealthy or powerful violators would be prosecuted. Some recognized that these problems could be countered to some extent by organizing grassroots conservation efforts.

(110) INTER I want to ask you something about the community and the care of forests. If someone cuts trees, what happens to this person. . . . What would the community do?

RESP If the man comes with agreement from the law, and I repeat that here in Costa Rica it can be legal to destroy forest—to come in with a bulldozer, a chainsaw, and trucks and take all the wood and leave a big mess—well, it's possible that he does his business and it is good for him. But left behind is this big mess, and a community wounded by ecological, social, and economic damage, sometimes even moral damages. So he gets his benefit at the cost of a lot of damage that surrounds him. (CR21)

(111) INTER Are there people here who have turned other people in?

RESP Here in the community? Up there above some people turned someone in, who now wants to kill them. An association turned in a man up there for clearing forest. . . . They turned him in, and that's where it stands, nothing has happened.

INTER   Is it common for someone to turn someone in?

RESP   It rarely happens. Perhaps once every five years it happens. But nothing ever comes of it. . . . Why turn someone in? Nothing happens. The only thing is you've made an enemy. (CR6)

(112) INTER   And what do you think would happen if someone here in the community started to cut down trees, what would happen?

RESP   Well, in my case I'd turn him in; turn him in for doing something illegal, that really is illegal.

INTER   You respect the law, but if someone was cutting trees, would anyone else turn him in?

RESP   Well, here, no. Because no one has the authority to say don't do it. Perhaps you could give him advice to make him aware of what he's doing. That it's bad for him, too. I was thinking that perhaps we could form a group, what we call a group in support of nature conservation in the community. But how do we get trained by people who know about this? To form a group especially for this, to watch out for things like this in the community? (CR13)

Forest Conservation and the National Park

Our study addressed forests in general, forests on private land, and forest conservation in the national park. Separating forest conservation on private land from park land is important because reference to different contexts can be expected to influence expressions of forest values and the way they are seen to relate to other values. To engage respondents in discussions about the park, we asked them why

Figure 3.8.   Boundary signs, La Amistad International Park, Costa Rica

they thought the park was created, what would the consequences be if the park were eliminated or had not been created, and who they thought benefited from the park.

Why the Park Exists

People generally understood that the park was created for the environmental benefits associated with forests, often citing some of the standard messages about why forests were important, such as pure air, water, and wildlife. It was also very common for people to note that the park was international in nature. Some of this relates to the fact that the park is officially designated as an international park, not a national park, and its connection with Panama (where a contiguous sister park with the same name is located) was noted by some respondents. But it was common for respondents to note that the park received international funds; in some cases, this was carried further to note that these funds were in exchange for environmental services, such as oxygen or pure air. When asked why the park exists, respondents said,

(113) Why? Well, well, I had land rights above . . . this land was within the area [of the park] and they told me they would buy these rights from me because they wanted the conservation of this area for protection under a park. . . . To protect trees, to protect the many plants and vines and wild birds, like toucans and turkeys [*pavas*] and coatis [*pizotes*], the hummingbirds, and . . . and so the quetzal can sing up there above, and those owls, there are owls and other birds. There are so many birds in the forest, they have told me it's to protect the wildlife, right? They told me that this was the purpose of the park, and after that I don't know what they're going to do. It's international and there are various countries involved and I don't know what they're going to do in the future with this. What I do know is that I was one of the ones that got this notice that they gave me [that they were going to take my land]. (CR14)

(114) The way I understand it, there are agreements between some nations of the world that are worried about nature, as we say it, they are buyers of pure air, for that they come to buy in Costa Rica where we have plenty of it. . . . In fact, Costa Rica is not in the position to conserve these lands; they paid many millions of dollars to expropriate people that were there. (CR13)

Most people recognize the conservation goals of the park. They infer its importance from the fact that money—at levels beyond typical levels of public investment in Costa Rica—came from other countries and that the possibility to harvest a large amount of timber was forgone by park creation.

(115) [*asked why the park exists*] I don't know much about this, but I know that the park has an agreement with various countries because Costa Rica doesn't have funds to pay for it, because there are a lot of other things that need to be paid for. Also, we know that it is to conserve nature, the animals and the plants, right? . . . Clearly the park, the park project, I think it is a very important agreement. We're talking about many board feet of timber. Who knows how many millions of trees there are in those mountains? (CR9)

Figure 3.9 shows reasons why the persons we surveyed thought the park was *very* important. People considered the park important for a variety of diverse reasons, but protection of the water supply, soils, and animal and plant diversity were most likely to be considered very important.

If the Park Were Eliminated

In spite of some of this uncertainty about why the park was created, when asked what would happen if the park were eliminated or what would have happened if it had not been established, virtually all the respondents noted that colonists would have settled there, that forests would be cleared, and that to eliminate the park would be a serious setback to the forest and wildlife conservation that had been achieved.

(116) A lot of forest would be lost, and the people would all go there, you can imagine it. It would be deadly, because it has been a lot of work to maintain what there now is, if the park were eliminated it wouldn't only

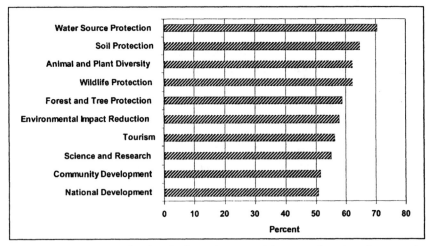

Figure 3.9. Proportion who thought the park was very important for selected reasons, La Amistad, Costa Rica

be the destruction of the forests but also the animals, and we would be left without water, because without forest there is no water. (CR8)

(117) If it weren't for the park, those mountains would be bare. There wouldn't be trees. Without the park, all those mountains would be bare and what happened in this whole region would have happened there. Those that destroyed were destroyed by this park. For that reason and for many others it is good, the authority of the parks. They look out for deforestation, and they look after the wildlife. They like all these things, too, and I think it is good; that the parks are good. (CR10)

(118) I think that due to the perseverance of man and the desire to have his own little piece of land, if the park were eliminated, if it hadn't been declared, let's say, I think that it would be a great disaster because people would begin to cut trees again and eliminate them, and this would be a great mistake for humanity, to start this over again and eliminate the great conservation that we have. (CR18)

Who Benefits from the Park

As the responses thus far make clear, people see many benefits from the park but also see it as an idea and activity that originated from the outside—one that never would have occurred if left up to the people from the region, even though they may have received some benefits from it. The distribution of costs and benefits of parks between the wider national and global interests and local communities has been a key underlying factor for conflicts that have surrounded many national parks. Therefore, we asked people to talk about who they thought benefited from the park. Among the beneficiaries noted were the park guards themselves due to the salary they received, tourists, electric companies (using water from the park), and people from the world at large. Some also complained that local communities had received little from the park in terms of tangible development assistance, such as better roads and jobs, in spite of all the money that was being spent there. Many people also came around to saying that it was important to recognize that local people benefited too, although people were not always sure in what way. Some saw these local benefits as being clean water and air, and wildlife preservation. Others saw the promise of future development and investment in the region associated with the park.

(119) I don't know [who benefits from the park]. But from what I hear it is the government that benefits most. I know they are spending a lot of money to conserve these things in Costa Rica. (CR3)

(120) I really don't know, but I think everyone, I think it is giving something to everyone, we don't know what but it is giving something to everyone. Look, for example, the fact that I am talking with you . . . you wouldn't be here with me spending this time. . . . I think that it helps everyone, in

different ways, but everyone, and those of us who admire it, who truly appreciate it are getting even greater benefits. (CR3)

(121) I think the region, this whole region, benefits from the park. I say the whole region because if these forests were cleared, then this region here would be dry. The park is very big. If they cleared these forests—imagine it.... For this reason I think that not just the employees who benefit, but that we all should care for it, with our own love. Because it is benefiting us all. (CR10)

(122) Mostly the people that live here in the community, they are the primary beneficiaries because the park helps us with roads and protecting the water. And often people are coming here from many countries, there's a lot of tourism. And they can do research and all this can bring us benefits in the future; these research projects that they are doing and what they are learning about.... Every day there is more knowledge, that is why the park is important. (CR13)

The people we surveyed thought that a wide range of groups benefited from the park. Almost three-fourths felt that they benefited from the park personally, but that was less than for any of the other beneficiaries we asked them to comment on. The largest proportions thought that park guards and tourists benefited from the park (see figure 3.10).

In many ways, people had some difficulties stating any benefits that they personally received from the park, even when they generally supported it. Furthermore, personal benefits were usually framed in the same way as global or national benefits and often with the same language.

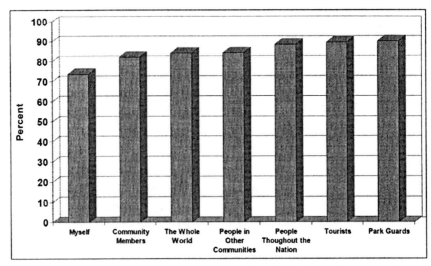

Figure 3.10. Proportion who believe selected groups benefit from the park, La Amistad, Costa Rica

(123) Before I said that people were working and there were many people inside the park with the objective of planting crops and making a life. But now because of the park, personally I can't think of any benefit that I receive. Nevertheless, what I say is that it is something good for the future generations, and I say it is good if it is to benefit the future generations. (CR14)

(124) [Who] benefits? Well, for us, one aspect of the benefits is that it's important to maintain the forest. But in terms of benefits that I see exactly for us, there aren't many. Let me give you an example. You're a worker in the park, and you depend on the park. You feel benefited because they pay you to be there. In this respect we don't depend on it; we depend on our own work. In another respect, the forest maintains more water for us, which is abundant here. More air. In this it is clear that we receive some benefits.

INTER   Is there someone, or some group, that benefits more from the park?

RESP   Yes sir, I think that due to the fact that these parks receive some good money that is shared here, or I see them working. . . . But I don't know. I think that not all this money makes it here. Some is left somewhere else. Because of this, I think we're harmed, according to the way I understand the park. . . . I don't know but I've heard a lot of international aid. And if this money were well invested here in the park, instead of in other places, we wouldn't lack a good road. I'm alright, but a lot of people have left, there's only a few of us left, it's a struggle for us. (CR16)

Others, however, seemed to genuinely believe in the broad global benefits and feel that, in these, there would be opportunities for local people, too.

(125) I think that the park benefits everyone, not just Costa Rica and Panama. I think the whole world. Like I told you before, the big area is like a big lung that is purifying the air. I think we all benefit. If we can increase our tourism, you can build trails and people will come here on the weekend, and I think this will benefit a lot of people. Not just Costa Rica but perhaps those that come here will experience the big change in the air, the environment that is so beautiful, so peaceful. When you breathe, there's no bad odors of cars, and you have no fear of the water. You can drink without fear. I think the whole world benefits from this park. (CR18)

Hunting

Wildlife was a frequently mentioned forest value, with people generally recognizing that wildlife required forest habitats and placing importance on the continuing presence of wildlife, particularly so that their descendants could see them. Although there are still people who hunt in the region, most people felt that there was no longer a real need for anyone to hunt since there were other ways to obtain food.

(126) Before, mostly when people hunted it was for their own food. There weren't bridges; you couldn't go to Buenos Aires, which was the only place there were stores and supermarkets—places where you could go and buy your provisions. That's why people hunted so much, used the animals in the forest for food. But now, everything has changed. We have stores and it is different. People are seeing that it is different than when they came here; all the animals that have been lost—along with the water. (CR4)

(127) [*talking about benefits from the park*] I hope the park is always here. Before, for example, there were a lot of peccaries here, and toucans, and pacas. And people hunted them, and hunted them, and hunted them. Before they came down here real close, but they no longer come down here because people ate them, they hunted and ate them. Thus, the park is very beneficial. Now there are more birds, now there are many more animals that are protected because hunting is prohibited. Thus, it is a benefit not only for us, but also for the generations to come; they will see all these animals. Including me, I see and observe on my land a lot of birds; many, many birds that come down from the park. Thus, it is a benefit, that they are protected and came come down here and go back up. (CR20)

A park guard confirmed that fewer people hunted than before.

(128) I have seen a big change in the ten years or so I have lived here. The park was created in '82, and from '82 on there's been a big change in these very communities, or in the same people that have been living here. They are giving up a lot of things for conservation. . . . And for those that hunt there's been a change in the fauna. There's been a lot of change in the fauna. A few years ago these people were 100 percent hunters, everyone hunted. It was a custom and a lot of people came here to hunt. (CR11)

Although few people needed to hunt for food, about half the people we surveyed in principle still supported hunting if one needed food. Fifty percent agreed with the statement "To hunt or kill wild animals is alright if you need to find food to eat." However, the people we surveyed clearly did not see wildlife as a source of income. Almost nine out of ten of the persons *disagreed* with the statement "To hunt or kill wild animals is alright if you need money."

We were struck by the existence of a strong antihunting norm, with hunting being associated with antisocial behavior and sometimes laziness.

(129) The community has united to the point where they don't permit hunting, and the animals are in the process of recuperation. (CR18)

(130) Sometimes, when I am in the store, I start to talk to people about this. We talk a lot about hunting, because there are a lot of us that are against it. This comes up a lot, and almost everyone is against it. (CR22)

(131) INTER   And why are some people not in favor of the park?

RESP   I think that most of these people like to have fun; on Sundays go into the forest, into the forest, walk and hunt something; they're hunters. Thus, for them it's a big problem. . . . These people are against the park, but I don't know why they don't just stay on their farms and work. They like to be lazy and tramp around [*le gusta un poco la vagabundería*], of course before we had these liberties and it was great, you could go and find an animal and hunt it for your family. (CR24)

Livelihood Conflicts and Resistance to Forest Conservation and the National Park

Conservation, especially when tending toward protectionism, has some incompatibilities with the subsistence and economic demands of rural life. We asked a number of questions about when is it acceptable to cut trees, and when it is not, in an effort to see how people might make trade-offs between environmental values and other values. These questions focused on what is the right or wrong thing to do under certain conditions. The responses reveal that people sometimes make trade-offs between environmental values and livelihood values, illustrated through the mediating cultural models that are used to come to terms with conflicts between incompatible or partially incompatible values. In other cases, people rationalized their actions or assigned blame to other people, such as outsiders and rich people. In still other cases, they adjusted their definitions of forest, trees, and conservation in ways that served their livelihood interests. In all these cases, we see cultural models broadly drawn from Costa Rican public discourse being applied. Here we give six examples of mediating cultural models that have arisen to deal with the contradictions between forest conservation and livelihood needs.

Mediating Model 1: Waste Is Wrong, but People Should Be Able to Cut Trees for Subsistence Needs

People were very clear that trees should not be cut down simply to cut them down; nor should they be wasted. On the other hand, to meet a real need, such as construction of a house, cutting of trees is seen as acceptable as long as reasonable precautions are taken to reduce waste and protect water supplies. Some see this as a necessary evil, something that is painful but must be done. People in general recognize that their livelihood needs, including planting crops and building a house, require some tree felling. There is a general feeling that the negative aspects of this necessary forest clearing and tree felling can be made up for by planting trees.

>(132) It's good to cut trees when they're in a pasture and are damaging the grass, and there's cows down below and the tree is already dying. What's not good is to cut a forest that is virgin, untouched, but if it's in a pasture you have to cut it to maintain it properly. (CR16)

>(133) If there's a danger, it's important to cut a tree. For example if there are some big trees and there's a danger that some branches will fall on a person that is picking coffee, then it is important. But for the pure desire to just clear forest, no. (CR5)

>(134) We know that the forest is something good for the environment, for the air, the purification of the air, but you know there are more and more people in every country every day and we can't all live by studying or by working in factories. (CR9)

>(135) Well, the way we see it, we're *campesinos* who perhaps need to cut a tree to build a small house. But it's bad to cut a tree if you're hurting nature, perhaps if it's from a species in danger of extinction, and we're going to run out of it. But because of the benefit that it brings us, it's a real benefit to cut a tree to build a house. But if we're talking about exploiting timber—we need to stop that. (CR25)

Combined with this utilitarian outlook is a view of forest and trees as a renewable resource that can be replanted and managed, as well as harvested, to get both personal and environmental benefits.

>(136) I say that to cut a tree, to fell trees, is perhaps going to hurt us. But we can also plant other trees, continue planting, go and plant trees, there are good timber trees, any tree that you plant is good, right? Even a fruit tree; whatever tree. The question is to construct, not destroy. To destroy is what is bad. (CR10)

>(137) If I had a good timber tree and I needed a house, and I tried to be as careful as I could to use all of this tree, cut it to the root to not waste anything; if it's somewhere it wouldn't cause harm; if it's not next to a spring, I think, why not [cut a tree]? And hopefully after cutting this tree I take care of the area, and plant more trees; some *amarillones* or something, or perhaps some fruit trees. (CR3)

Mediating Model 2: Because of Our Needs, the Government Should Compensate Us for Conservation

Closely related to the idea that rural residents sometimes need to cut down trees is the idea that if the government wants them to conserve, they should find some way to meet people's needs. Some people, while supporting conservation, feel that they have lost too much in terms of production opportunities. They feel that the government is generally too strict and does not permit people to clear enough land or do the things they need to do to meet their needs, as related in the following statement:

(138) In terms of the park, the park is good. I think if this park hadn't been created, there would be a lot of forest that wouldn't exist anymore. Because just up there around me [where my land was] were eighteen others. More if you count those who were on the land of others—there were at least five of them that I still remember the names of. This hill was really productive, you wouldn't believe how fat the cows got on it because there was a lot of grass. Sure, people were felling trees. To create pasture you have to fell the forest. A tremendous amount of wood was wasted, never used. In the end, it may be useful to have the park for the animals, for the watersheds, to protect. But on the other hand, what about the poor person that had two or three hectares of land that he wanted to grow crops on? Because coffee is one of the most profitable crops . . . and they wanted people who had a hectare or two of land, even if it was barely *tacotal*, to restrain themselves and leave the forest. So there are meetings where they protested this—how is it possible that a person who only has two or three hectares could [conserve forest]. It's fine to leave the stream banks . . . but things should not be so strict. (CR9)

Others argue in favor of direct payment in exchange for conservation or assistance programs to help people develop alternative land uses. They acknowledge that conservation is important but seem to recognize that they are being asked to pay a lot of the cost when the benefits are diffuse or distributed much more broadly. Some of this sentiment might also reflect the fact that Costa Rica has a number of well-known incentive programs for reforestation and conservation of standing forest, but not everyone has been able to participate in these programs.

(139) This farm of mine is twenty-three *manzanas* [about sixteen hectares]. But for me to crop what I need to eat, I could do it in one hectare. Because I would have to destroy the forest, all this forest. This is the awareness that we should learn, to protect part of what we have. Now I am in agreement with what a lot of people say: why should I protect land that's not producing anything, when no one takes my needs into account, and nobody helps me? I respect this, too, because, to be sure, to say this is mine only to look at. . . . And at the same time I hear that in Costa Rica there's a law where the government is paying something, some assistance for this, what we're talking about. For protection, for oxygen, and all this. We should get some of this aid here to help people, that would be a different

thing, at least in my case. Because I don't want to sell forest, I want to buy it, if I were able, but I can't, see? But if there was a way, perhaps some assistance or something like that, I would perhaps be interested. . . . We need to see if there is some way to help. For example, if they come to me and say, "What do you think? I'm thinking about clearing this." And I would tell them, let's talk. Let's see what we can do so that you don't clear this *tacotal*, or whatever. Let's find a way, some way. (CR3)

(140) We should be able to get some assistance for not touching these forests, so that we can survive somehow. That there are a lot of alternatives, but they require money. (CR16)

Others are distrustful of government incentive programs, afraid that if they conserve under them, all their land will get locked up in forest and they won't have any say over how it is managed. Instead, they advocate for diversified farming systems.

(141) There was something, I think in another part of the country. They developed a policy where the government would pay me a determined amount, thousands of *colones*, if I would let my farm recuperate naturally. But at the end of the day they changed the law so that it said that once trees got to a certain diameter they would throw me in jail if I cut a tree on my own farm. So they would give me ninety thousand *colones* [about US$315] per hectare, but three or four years later I couldn't plant anything on my farm. How am I going to live? What is needed is an incentive for the *campesinos* so that they can learn to manage their parcels so that there is diversity, so that there is a little bit of everything. I'm not one of those that is in agreement with a farm that is all coffee. No. There should be fruit trees, there should be vegetables, there should be trees, there should be an area for other crops. (CR21)

Mediating Model 3: *Tacotal, or When a Forest Is Not a Forest*

One of the biggest conflicts is over clearing what was called *tacotal*, or young, brushy second growth. People use this in a slash-mulch bean cultivation system (*frijol tapado*) that is generally considered sustainable both locally and scientifically (Thurston et al. 1994). We found considerable conflict between the forest authorities and community members over when a *tacotal* becomes a forest and when it is acceptable to cut a *tacotal*.

It was clear that many people did not consider *tacotal* to be forest, but rather a fallow stage in an agricultural system.

(142) I don't think it is good to cut trees, but if you need to you can cut one, if not, better to leave it because many animals use it and who knows where

Figure 3.11.   Farmer in beanfield (*frijol tapado*), near La Amistad International Park, Costa Rica

they will be able to go. And burning, they don't give permission to even cut trees much less burn them. But if we're talking about *tacotales* and things like that, these are little sticks that won't be worth anything, then cut them to plant crops. (CR17)

(143) Well, I don't know, in our case we have a way of life here in Costa Rica, that you can see, for example nobody here in the countryside works with machinery. Not because we don't know that this machinery would be helpful but because we can't buy it . . . if we had machinery there would be less need to cut forest . . . but we don't have the economic resources for machinery. But what we know how to do is fell trees, knowing it

harms us. But cut forest? We never cut *tacotal* that has developed into secondary forest. Every year we cover [*tapar*] beans in [*tacotal*]. (CR22)

(144) For example a person has a little forest, what we call a *tacotal*, and they need to clear it to plant that area to have food for their children, for their family, well then I say do it. (CR3)

Enforcement of tree-felling and forest-clearing laws in areas that local people considered to be *tacotal* was a major source of conflict in the region, as the following statements attest:

(145) There are people here in this community who have gone to jail because they were found cutting a tree or because they planted beans in a brushy area that perhaps had a few big trees, perhaps not timber trees. And they think we shouldn't cut timber trees. [They do this to] the same people who have been trying to conserve soil in other places. This is what I think is unjust on the part of the government. (CR4)

(146) Maintain [*tacotal*] low and be very careful, because if we have a timber tree, and it gets too big, you can't [cut it]. (CR24)

(147) They shouldn't be so strict, because they've even taken people to jail. For planting beans! For cutting *tacotal*; not forest but *tacotal*! They gave him three months in jail. (CR9)

A park guard adds a new dimension to this, but suggesting that people call forest *tacotal* in order to justify cutting it down:

(148) Can they clear *tacotales*? Of course they can. But what people call *tacotales* is really forest.... [According to the law], if there's more than seventy trees per hectare, more than fifteen centimeters in diameter, it's not *tacotal*, it's forest. People sometimes say it's *tacotal* when there are big trees there. They call it a little *tacotal* but it's not a little *tacotal*. It's a big *tacotal*. It's a forest. (CR11)

About nine out of ten people we surveyed agreed that when trees on fallow land become large, the area becomes a forest, and about three-fourths accurately agreed that when this growth becomes forest, the government no longer permits this land to be cleared for crop cultivation. But a little more than half (54.2%) of the people surveyed believed that it was permissible to clear fallow land that was not fully grown. A smaller proportion agreed that is was acceptable to burn the growth to clear land for cultivation. Only about 30 percent agreed with the statement "It is fine to burn *tacotal* if one is going to cultivate crops there."

In addition to the dispute over when a forest is a forest, there is some question of what kind of tree counts as having legitimate environmental benefits. Fruit trees are often seen by rural people as being just as good as timber trees.

(149) INTER   Have you planted trees on the land that you work?
RESP   Yes, for example, perhaps not timber trees but if we're talking about fruit trees there are a lot of these. And to plant, for example, a fruit tree is the same or better, since they are dual purpose. They purify the air and also provide a harvest to consume. Yes I've planted trees, of course I have. (CR18)

Eighty percent of the individuals surveyed agreed with the statement "Fruit trees are trees just as much as timber trees."

Mediating Model 4: The Rich and Outsiders Cut Trees but We Can't

A common complaint of rural residents is that it is very difficult for them to cut even one tree when they need to make a house or a piece of furniture, yet they see logging trucks constantly carrying logs out of the community. They interpret and object to this in several ways. First, they describe themselves as being conservationists, being careful not to cut trees around springs and only cutting a tree when they have a true need for lumber, while they see outsiders as not caring at all about where trees are cut and engaging in extractive activities to enrich themselves (and impoverish the community) rather than meeting true needs. Second, they believe that they have to engage in a long and complicated process to get permission to cut

Figure 3.12.   Logging truck, El Carmen, Costa Rica

a tree for their own use, when the loggers can get permission easily because they are making lots of money and perhaps also can afford to pay bribes to facilitate the process of obtaining permits. They fit this into a general model about how things work in Costa Rica, where the poor *campesino* cannot even do what little he needs to do to meet his basic needs, while the rich know how to make things work for them and can do whatever they want. They also assign the responsibility for continuing forest loss to outsiders, seeing themselves as good stewards of the forest.

(150) I have heard people talking: How can it be just and good? I fight that we don't cut a timber tree, but these people are fighting to go and cut them. These are the things I see. For example, to tell you something that is not just talk. I live in the countryside and have no place to get even a little board for myself to build something, but we often see logging trucks coming in here and taking out the last trees that are left.

This is what happened here, the blessed loggers came and destroyed all this. They came and found these people in poverty, and thus, you could say, the people gave them the lumber because they wanted to earn a few cents. They didn't think this lumber was important, and they gave it to them, so what happened was that everything was destroyed—totally. In this region, that is what happened, because the lumber has been taken out, and none of it was invested here. Here you can't find a good house with fine wood, nothing like that; all the good wood from here was taken out. I don't know. This is the fight; to protect everything you can. That's right, protect. (CR3)

(151) [*husband*] For example, if we talk about the timber companies that come into the forest and cut most of the trees, they don't notice that there are streams nearby. They don't notice that when the tree falls it's going to bring down four or five small trees. They don't notice any of this. They only cut and cut, and haul it out with a tractor and a truck.

[*wife*]   They also don't pay what the tree is worth. They pay the minimum.

[*husband*] I say that there, there is the biggest injustice with nature. That for money they give permission—because we know our government and country well. A big businessman can make a lot of millions of pesos from lumber he cuts, so for him sometimes there's permission. On the other hand a *campesino* or a poor person who needs to cut a little tree, let alone try to exploit some forest, to take out that little tree he has to pay for permission. (CR4)

Statements by a park guard lend support to this:

(152) If there's permission to log, there's permission to log; it can't be stopped. Perhaps it should be a little more regulated. There's something wrong

with it . . . because it is unjust, it is unjust and I agree with what people sometimes tell me, that here in Costa Rica the big folks take too much from the small. For example, there are people who are given permits because the logger pays, or I don't know what, but they get permission to fell trees. . . . While a poor *campesino* goes to ask to fell three trees and he can't, they want to prohibit it. They ask for all kinds of things from him, and it is to build a little house. (CR11)

The activities of outside loggers is seen as a sign that the government is corrupt or not genuinely concerned about forest conservation. The following statements express this opinion:

(153) Here in Costa Rica the laws have been stolen, see? Understand? Without money there's nothing. Without money there's nothing . . . this is the problem. *Don Dinero* drives everything. He passes above the law. With *Don Dinero* you pass over the laws. You don't have to comply, see? They make new regulations, and the result is that they pay a bribe because if there's money you don't have to comply with the law, no one does, anymore. (CR10)

(154) The lumbermen are always buying trees. They come and take them away. They buy from people with farms up there near the park, not from the park, but close to it. But if [the government] was really interested in truly not destroying forest they would do something so they definitely couldn't take any more trees, but they're still doing it. (CR20)

In the survey, 90 percent of the persons we interviewed agreed that "It is easier for rich owners of large farms to get permits to cut trees than for common or poor people." The individuals surveyed were almost unanimous (96%) in agreeing with the statement "Timber companies destroy more forest than people who live in this community."

Mediating Model 5: Property Rights

The Environment and Energy Ministry (*MINAE*) is the government agency that has long had responsibility for the national parks. In the mid-1990s, a separate agency that had responsibility for forest on private lands was dissolved (in part due to alleged corruption), and enforcement of the forest laws was transferred to *MINAE*. At the same time, the national parks were reorganized into conservation areas with responsibilities for managing both the parks and private lands adjacent to them in an effort to promote regional conservation approaches that integrated parks with surrounding lands. As a result, government employees working out of the park guard stations are responsible for enforcement of laws and permits for cutting trees on private lands. A number of people who accepted the importance of the national park objected to *MINAE's* enforcing laws against tree cutting on private land. People accepted conservation in the park, on government land, but objected to interference on their own property.

> (155) The park is there to take care of the park. That which is above, but now they try to care for everything. For example here where we live, they caught us felling a tree even though it was on our land. I don't think this is good, because if I, for example, see someone is cutting a tree on the farm next to us, it's alright. It's not on my property. (CR17)
>
> (156) My thought is that—I am always in agreement that the park should be protected, it should be cared for. But farmers that have title to their land shouldn't have to pay money at the municipality to be able to cut a tree. (CR7)
>
> (157) INTER   Why are you and your husband not in favor [of conservation]?
> RESP   He's alright with it, I'm not. I don't like it. Because what you have isn't really yours. The forest that is yours, there will come a day when we won't be able to take out anything, we won't have anything. We'll be like those other countries where they take away from you what you harvest, and I say this is what is going to happen to us. I hope to God that it doesn't. (CR17)

In spite of these nascent property rights sentiments, the majority of people supported government regulations on tree felling and forest clearing on private lands. Ninety percent of the persons we surveyed *disagreed* with the statement "They should let people do whatever they want with the trees on their own land." Surprisingly, they even supported government restrictions on the sale of timber harvested on their own land. Four out of five surveyed *disagreed* with the statement "They should let people sell trees that are on their own land without any government restrictions." Nevertheless, property rights represent a mediating model that people can use to oppose government conservation and justify tree felling or forest clearing on their own land.

Mediating Model 6: Direct Opposition

The above forms of mediating cultural models between private livelihood interests and conservation were by far the most common responses. They indicate an acceptance of conservation as a good thing at some level, but also an effort to reconcile it with other values. This was much more common than outright opposition to conservation, although in a few cases people directly opposed the park and conservation. Those opposed were mostly people who had owned land in the park that was expropriated and for which they did not feel adequately compensated. In these cases, the mere mention of forests or the park stimulated responses voicing this opposition. However, most people expressed agreement with the park but wanted some accommodation for their needs. It was easier to get people to talk about other people's opposition to the park. While it is difficult to be sure what these comments mean, they do seem to indicate some of the things that are talked about in the community.

(158) I think the park is good, I repeat, it's good. What I don't think is good is that before we planted a few crops, and there wasn't so much damage to the corn. The animals didn't come and eat it. Now with the park, there is an overproduction of birds and animals, and these animals cause damage [to our crops], and to protect our crops we have to kill them. They should give us some assistance, some aid, so we could work in something else; so we could protect these animals and still survive and we wouldn't have to go to the city. Because, really, we can't get by because of this problem with the park. (CR16)

(159) INTER   And why are people opposed to the park?
RESP   [*talking about other people*] Because the park perhaps didn't pay them what their farm was worth, or if they paid them what it was worth they still say, I would really be doing well if I still had that farm. Others because "they took away my rifle and they took away my dogs, and threw me in jail; I can't be a hunter like I was before." Some have a little farm and suffer from hunger, and say "if I still had that farm up above I'd have cattle."
INTER   And do you think the park has hurt people?
RESP   Yes, in some places, for example the payments for land have been delayed, for the delays, and for the fraud and all these things. The appraisals is what they call them. They try to value a property with low prices instead of paying what is just. There are things a little wrong with the park. (CR21)

(160) RESP   Are there any other benefits we could get from the park? A thing that a lot of people complain about is that because of the park we'll never be able to really have a town here, to make a community. Roads will never come, the people complain.
INTER   That the park doesn't directly benefit anyone?
RESP   Yes, I think that the park needs to show the people that there are benefits, at least help us a little with roads, at least. Because it's not a problem to be somewhere like this, as long as there are good means of communication, good roads. (CR22)

Expressing personal outright opposition to the park was generally rare, but people often talked about other people being opposed to the park or complaining about it because they had been inadequately compensated for land or because of delays and fraud in compensation, because dogs or rifles had been confiscated when they were caught hunting in the park, or because the park was keeping the community from developing.

Because the park guards were also in charge of enforcing forestry laws, perhaps the most significant conflict centered on the use of secondary growth on fallow agricultural lands. As indicated above, when secondary growth is allowed to grow without disruption for enough time, it is considered forest and can no longer be cut, even on private lands. However, there were conflicts over the classification of secondary growth as forest or not. In the early 1990s, there was conflict over the cultivation of lands that had been left fallow for a considerable time when *MINAE* tried to restrict the use of fallow land with mature secondary growth. In one community, this conflict was resolved when groups of local producers cleared secondary growth from parcels in question. They operated in groups to avoid arrest; officials were reluctant to arrest a whole group of producers. This conflict made producers aware that if they let the secondary growth go, they would lose their right to cultivate the land. The producers began to cut secondary growth to keep it low so that they would not lose the freedom to cultivate the land as they pleased.

Desirable Landscapes

At the end of our interviews, we showed people a series of six photographs of landscapes from Central America that ranged from nearly completely deforested to all forest. We asked people to talk about the photos, telling what they saw, which photo they liked best and why, and which photo they would most like their own land to be like. Their discussions of the photos brought out many of the themes that had come up elsewhere in the interviews but also engaged subjects in talking about landscapes in very concrete ways that provided interesting insights into their land use preferences.

By the time they saw the pictures, all the interviewees were undoubtedly aware of our interest in forests. Most people expressed admiration of the forested pictures or pointed out forest patches in mixed landscapes, noting their beauty. For example,

> (161) INTER I'm going to show you some photos to see what you think. Let's start with this one. Can you tell me what you see in this?
> RESP It's very beautiful. There's a little ridge where there is forest, it's a tropical forest, and we can see a great diversity of trees there. . . . We can see nature in it; that's what really attracts attention. Sometimes I go to observe the forest, and these photographs bring back memories. When I came here, there was lots of forest; but now many of them have deteriorated. The great biodiversity that is found in it there. (CR18)

(162) RESP   Well, what I see in this picture is a humid place for plants, very pretty, that's what I find very pretty, because here there hasn't been any fires, nothing has been destroyed.

INTER   And why do you like this one?

RESP1 Because it looks very . . . it has a lot of nature. . . . It has a lot of forest. It reminds me of places I have been; these things and this hill, and all this looks very pretty to me. (CR3)

Yet, even though they pointed out and admired forests in the pictures, it was very common for them note that while the forest was pretty or a nice landscape for a park, they could not live in a completely forested landscape.

(163) This looks like it is all forest. It looks like a park, you can't see any future there because you can see that nobody is working. There's only conservation, and nothing else. (CR15)

(164) Well, for me a photo like this is one of the most beautiful things, because I appreciate nature, right? . . . Yes, very pretty, but let me tell you again that if my farm was all forest, well, I couldn't . . . I couldn't even live there because I wouldn't have these. . . . I wouldn't have coffee, I wouldn't have cattle. These are what we need to live, right? But it's beautiful, right? Because it's part of nature and there is nothing as beautiful as nature. It would be even better if there were a river there in the middle. (CR22)

(165) This is practically a forested area, it is good. I ask myself a question. What would I do if I fell into . . . or if at the time when I got my land it was all forest, and it was all I had? I ask myself this question. With the experience of these years, five years of working as an organic producer. I ask myself this question, what would I do if at this moment I, with the experience I have had, but if the only parcel that I had was forest? I can't live in the middle of the forest. In this case I would look for the tallest trees to make my hut, dead trees, fallen trees. I would look for the crops that are associated with the forest, palm, plantains that produce in the middle of the forest, and I would look for the most appropriate land to clear, do soil conservation, maintain their fertility and produce the rest of the crops that I need. (CR21)

(166) INTER   Which of these photos, of these six, would you like the most if you could pick one of these places for your own land?

RESP   I want to say this one [all forest], but it would be a lie, because you can't do anything. You would have to conserve everything. . . . [I'll pick] this one, with good management. (CR6)

One person separated the park and the lived-in landscape by highlighting how each had different objectives.

Figure 3.13. Series of landscape photos shown during qualitative interviews to initiate discussion

Figure 3.14. Series of landscape photos shown during qualitative interviews to initiate discussion

Figure 3.15. Series of landscape photos shown during qualitative interviews to initiate discussion

Figure 3.16. Series of landscape photos shown during qualitative interviews to initiate discussion

Figure 3.17.   Series of landscape photos shown during qualitative interviews to initiate discussion

Figure 3.18.   Series of landscape photos shown during qualitative interviews to initiate discussion

(167) It looks good to me, that it is worked—that the park can work above and here you can work with the pasture. (CR16)

When people talked about landscapes they would like to live in, they generally chose a mix of agricultural and forest uses. When looking at photos of such landscapes, they offered detailed evaluations of different components that covered both productive and conservation aspects. These discussions showed a great deal of sophistication and complexity in the way that people linked productive and conservation objectives in complex land use patterns.

(168) I would like this one, with one change. Prune all this forest and make it just one place, divide the other part into pasture and for basic grains and vegetables. Three parts, in among the basic grains and vegetables there would be a house. . . . Forest all in one place, a place to plant a diversity of things to consume, and an area of pasture. (CR21)

(169) This photo, it looks pretty because you can still see a lot of trees, there's a pair of good pieces of forest. What has happened, you can see that they are using the land, but they have left something.
[*next photo*] This is pretty because they are using some but not too much. They left forest up above and used part of the land. They are using, but they aren't destroying too much. If everyone would do it like this, it would be nice, because you see that there is a lot of forests and that there

are some places where are a few cows. One cow, right there. They left forest here below, and also there is forest up above.

[*next photo*] This one is really bad, this is really bad. This has all been cleared, too much. . . . Are those crops? Really steep, right? It's too steep. You'd have to go with a rope tied to you.

[*next photo*] This one is very pretty. It's pretty because here where it is steep, they have left it in forest, and they are using this part.

[Which one do I like the best?] Let me be sincere, very sincere. The one I like is this one because it has cattle, and I want to have cattle, and it has forests, too. If we could all live like this, use a little and leave another little bit . . . this one is very pretty, too, but it is pure forest. Man can't live in pure forest. (CR11)

(170) RESP   In this one you see a very pretty area, you see an area that is worked, but not everything . . . you can see it has trees, like in front, so it doesn't get too parched. It looks good because you can see trees. You can see that this area is worked very well, very well.

[*next photo*] This one is pretty, too, but the part below has been worked too hard. They didn't leave anything and you can see that it is beginning to dry up. They didn't leave anything. That's why I say that it is important to leave trees, because you can see that if everything was like this it would all be like the parched area. . . . [But this part is] pretty, with forest. You can see that here what they are working is the low part.

[*next photo*] This one looks more or less like this. Here there was a thinning, and they left the biggest trees. And it looks like it has been worked for quite a long time. The trees look mistreated. At the least the area was burned. Here on the side they cut all the timber that wasn't useful. There is still timber but it has been mistreated.

[*next photo*] I like [this one] because it looks green, because it has been worked, you can see that they have conserved a little bit of timber along the streams, you can see they have used the land, that the farm has been worked a lot. It's a farm that has been worked but it's not all parched, it looks green. Because if you talk about this one that is forest, you don't see anything other than forest and it's not useful even though it looks [nice]. (CR15)

While most people preferred mixed land uses, several people saw examples of, and talked about, agroforestry-type systems in the photos and talked about them as a way to balance productive needs with conservation.

(171) This is half forest [*medio madera*], this is very pretty. Here we have both things, we can use the pasture and there is wood, too. I am in agreement with this. (CR16)

(172) RESP   This one reminds me of this zone here, Coto Brus, where some-times for fear of what we call the forester, who controls the cutting of trees. Sometimes we make our pastures half forest [medio madera] so that the forester doesn't notice. So they make their pastures half forest and they cut it a little at a time; people are very clever. And this reminds me of those times when we were using pastures that were half forest. We had the experience to see that we were using the land twice, for example here, there are trees and they are also using the pasture. If you are go-ing to raise cattle I think that it is important to do it in this way. It is a good way to use the land, to have your cattle where the big trees have been left and people are using the pasture under them. It's a very nice form of management. . . . I have a brother and he made a system where he cleared the small trees, planted pasture, and left the big trees. So he is using it double. At the same time he is using the pasture he is protecting the trees. I think this is a good system that can be used in some places.

INTER   And which of these would you like for your own land?

RESP   Well, the system, on my little lot right now we can't have tropi-cal forest because it is impossible, it's very small. But if we could use what I was telling you about, to achieve a double objective of having trees and getting some other crop, right? But here we can utilize the trees as well as the forest, like on my parcel we can use trees and coffee. It's just that we have to use the right kind of tree so it doesn't cause problems. So I think that this is the photo that I would like, to obtain a double system. (CR18)

Tree- and Forest-Related Behaviors and Their Rationales

The tree- and forest-related behaviors people engage in are ultimately determined by complex interactions between environmental and other values (including liveli-hood values). We asked people to talk about their tree- and forest-related behaviors to learn more about how values are translated into actions.

A number of people had left patches of forest uncleared or, in some cases, reported intentionally leaving trees on their farm. This was done for a variety of reasons, including for the aesthetic values of trees and forests or for more utilitar-ian purposes. Some people discussed the desirability of having a patch of forest or trees on their farm, even when they had to convert part of it to agriculture or pasture.

(173) INTER   Have you cut trees on your . . . ?

RESP   Yes, I'll be honest, of course, I had to do it. Years ago I cut trees to plant pasture and coffee. But not now, no way. . . . [I] always have conserved a large area. Yes, sir, [I have cattle], but I also conserve about fifteen or twenty hectares of forest. (CR22)

(174) INTER   You told me that you have areas of forest on your farm that have never been cut. Why did you leave these trees?
RESP   Yes, we left a part, untouched, virgin forest.
INTER   And do you think it was a good thing, leaving this forest?
RESP   Now it's hard to cut it down.
INTER   Is that why you still have it, because it's hard to cut it down or do you think that . . .?
RESP   No, we left it there, let's say to look at. We left it because we didn't want to cut it.
INTER   And what do you think is good about it? Do you get any benefits from these trees?
RESP   No, nothing for us, just having them there and not wanting to cut them.
INTER   And you never think about selling them?
RESP   No, the idea is leave them there. Look how beautiful all the trees we planted are; beautiful. (CR12)

The idea that forests may contribute to future economic opportunities from tourism was also important, as the following statement indicates:

(175) We have a forest here that we have taken care of. You can't cut it, you can't cut forest at all. . . . The reason we left it was, well here. . . . There will be tourists and they have said that this part is beautiful to bring tourists here to hike, to see the rivers and everything. So we have left it for the future. (CR17)

But other people expressed deep feelings of attachment to their forested land. For example,

(176) Look, I have been interested in selling this farm several times, including right now. There were some men here, from the United States, and they have a farm that they are making into a coffee plantation next to mine, and they had the idea that perhaps . . . truly it would make me sad to sell this farm, because I know if I sold it another person wouldn't protect it like I am protecting it, the forest and everything. The earth is here so we can live from here, but we need to take care of it, too. Love it, not destroy it. . . . To grow crops I have a hectare of land. On this land I grow all of my food, and for several more people. I do it myself. This is proof of what I said, if we think a little bit, if we work the land sensibly, we can get all our food from a small area of land and the rest can be protected in whatever way. (CR3)

Even people with small parcels of land often tried to have patches of trees or forests on that land, as one smallholder explains:

(177) Right now I just have a small parcel of no more than a hectare and a half, where I have a little coffee and the rest is in trees, which logically I'm going to protect to the extent that I can. There are only a few trees, there are ten trees on this parcel. Logically these trees have to be protected—if you start to analyze the situation—because they purify the air, make the environment fresher. (CR18)

Discussions like this also revealed that people could receive government incentives for conserving standing forest, although these incentives seemed to be seen more as additional benefits from forest conservation than as the primary motivation for it.

(178) INTER   And how is it that you were left with thirty-five hectares of forest? . . . Why did you never clear this forest?
RESP   Really I think that it was just left and everyone got used to it being there. I'll say this about my father. He was the only one that conserved forest. He didn't permit anyone to go in there; not to hunt, not for anything else.
INTER   And from your experience of conserving forests, the thirty-five hectares that you have, what have you gotten from this?
RESP   Well, right now we have gotten a little money that came our way, that is helpful for buying a few things we need. (CR2)

(179) There's a family here, neighbors of mine that in the beginning, when I came here, people talked very badly about them. The man, mostly, because he had a lot of forest and wouldn't let anyone hunt or go into the forest. Perhaps you've seen this forest there in the center of town, it gives me pleasure to go and see this, to feel and see this. How can it be that people don't enjoy seeing nature? I congratulate these people every time I can for being able to conserve this. Sure, they are being paid, and I know that it has turned out good for them because a little something is coming in each year. Perhaps, if there were a law that could help, perhaps it would be easier to conserve. (CR3)

We also asked people about tree-planting behaviors. Some people had not planted any trees—even if they thought tree planting was good—because they needed to grow crops, as revealed by this interchange:

(180) No, I haven't really planted trees. The trees that I have planted have been in my coffee plantation. I have a parcel that I have been going to reforest. But I have concluded that it would be better for me to plant coffee, and

at the same time I plant coffee to plant trees, so I would be reforesting and also planting a crop I could live from, right? For example . . . look, if everyone went around planting trees we'd have nothing to live on. (CR7)

Often a few trees were left or planted along fences, property boundaries, and stream banks without any incentives or assistance from the government. Many of these efforts reflected the positive values that people had for trees and, perhaps even more, the way that these positive values become intermingled with livelihood values to produce creative mixes of trees and agricultural land uses. For example,

(181) Yes, and in [my coffee plantation] I have some timber species, that have sprouted there. I didn't plant them, but they sprouted and they are still there. Below there is *cedro* . . . including a tree there by the stream that is dropping seed and propagating new trees. I would like to reforest the bank of this stream, but I don't have a lot of time to spend on it. (CR21)

(182) Of course, I've planted trees. . . . Generally we plant along the stream bank, along the boundaries, and in front of our house. They serve a dual purpose. They mark our boundaries and you also get to look at the trees, and also someday they might provide something for us. They're pretty, because we planted eucalyptus and pine. (CR13)

(183) I planted *cedros*. . . . We leave the trees with the best wood standing on our farm. We also plant some. We put them at the most appropriate place. And here we have planted *amarillón*, and *cedro*, because *cedro* is a tree that provides almost everything. At least in this property there are *cedros*. Do you see that tall tree there? That man there has coffee, but he also has trees there. So if there's an emergency or a need for wood, he can go and ask for a permit. So he has the two things. But the truth is that coffee really doesn't need these shade trees, coffee at this high elevation. You need it, but some *guavas* [*Inga* spp.] are enough; but well pruned. (CR9)

(184) We've planted a few, besides the ones we protect. We've always wanted to do an area of reforestation, but have never been able to. . . . We've planted a few trees along some fences, but only a few. (CR2)

(185) Yes, I have planted [trees], for example, living fences, so I don't have to cut more trees, for example. I have a lot of living fence posts, one that is called *poró*. (CR10)

(186) I have put a lot of living fence posts on my farm. Thinking about this, that one day trees would become scarce and there won't be anywhere to get a fence post. . . . I brought them all the way from San Vito. I brought live fence posts from there for my farm. . . . I did it to have some for later. If a fence is made from living fence posts, you don't have to cut more posts. And this was a good thing because now they don't let you cut any new ones. (CR7)

Other times, people planted fruit trees. Many people lumped fruit trees with forest trees, seeing them as dual purpose (environmental and livelihood benefits) compared to timber trees. One person feared planting timber trees because of government controls.

(187) Well, my farm is small, only about one and a half hectares, plus this lot where I live. I have part of it in coffee, and the other part is abandoned. What we'd like to do is expand the coffee a little. But I am thinking about the fences, planting trees to protect the environment, either timber or fruit trees. We'd have to see which would be better, but yes, I have been thinking about planting trees. I think we have several objectives, not just purifying the air. With the same tree, we can protect the soil so it doesn't get eroded too much, because on open ground the top layer washes away when it rains and it washes away the fertility of the soil. (CR18)

(188) INTER   And of the trees that you have planted here on your farm, how have they turned out.
RESP   There are good trees. At least I have planted a few fig trees. . . . There's a fig over there, out on the farm there are two, and over there I am planting them for shade. Fig trees make a good environment, so I planted some of them and some fruit trees. . . . To have something to eat, and to have a good environment, too. For both. (CR10)

(189) Mostly what we plant is things to eat, like oranges, *guanábanas*, things like this. Trees, well there are some little trees that my husband planted, that he got from my cousin. And we planted them, we planted them, to have them, right over there. Because these are things that you can't touch, right. Once you plant a tree it's not yours, I don't know what sense this makes. . . . These trees that my husband planted, they look pretty, right? They'll make some good shade, the timber trees are still small. I hope they'll get big and we'll get some wood. (CR17)

Other people planted under the reforestation incentive program. Many people did not seem to have embraced planting trees for the long-term production of timber. Of the people we talked to, a number had made creative adjustments to the standard planting arrangements, such as mixing the trees with coffee or pasture. Some people seemed to have planted mostly for the incentives, while some had taken the incentives but their plantations had not been successful.

(190) INTER   And the four hectares are the only ones you have planted in trees?
RESP   Yes, they are the only ones. . . . It's just that I have always enjoyed planting trees, whatever kind, timber or fruit. I have always liked to plant trees. They offered me an incentive and I decided to buy some trees and

plant them with the goal of correcting a little of the damage that has been done, and, at the same time, I should also say, that maybe in the future they will be useful. Perhaps for lumber or at least to protect. I planted them along the bank of this stream, so at least they will protect this water. (CR22)

(191) [I planted] *Amarillones*, yes. I had a big area of *amarillón*, but there also was a lot of damage from leaf-cutter ants. And there were five hectares that were burned . . . the first five I planted. I have received two payments, and for the second I received one. (CR14)

Even when people receive incentives, they often adapt the planting strategies to fit their needs. For example, this landowner rejected the ideal of later felling all the trees for timber and planted a diverse mix of trees, but then planted coffee underneath them:

(192) INTER   Do you think that it is a good thing to plant trees?
RESP   Yes, I think so. Look, they gave us some help for planting trees, the institution [of reforesters] helped us. . . . They explained to me very clearly that after twenty years, the trees would be cut and you would get the money from the trees. They explained this to me very clearly, and I was in agreement with their plans. Later we thought, no, it would be better to leave all the trees, to plant all different types of trees that are here and recreate a forest, because that is what they were looking for. I said to myself, what they are really looking for is to keep the remaining forests and to make new ones. Not that in twenty years you would clear again and get some money, right? . . . Because I have a lot of children, and as a result what I could do was about twenty hectares; maybe forty let's say. With forty hectares and so many children, I couldn't give a piece of land to a child who needed it and still reforest. The land is really good for coffee and agriculture, but I also like the way a forest looks, understand? So, on this land where, starting in 1990, I could have been planting coffee if the forest wasn't there and my children said, "Papi, what are you getting out of this? With making this forest? Why are you planting these saplings, these trees. Coffee would be better. Coffee produces something, but trees, for twenty years you just look at them."
INTER   So it's just something you wanted to do. Interesting.
RESP   Of course, they helped us [financially] with it.
INTER   So you have a total of fourteen hectares reforested, right? That's a lot, it's a lot. And it's all a mix of different types of trees.
RESP   There's *amarillón*, and there's . . . we talked about *cedro amargo*, but it didn't take very well. There was a little moth that damaged it. . . . I have fourteen hectares, and at a few places I have put some coffee in with the trees. The institution tried to get me to clear the coffee, but, for me, watching the trees develop over the years, coffee has never damaged the trees. Now I

have a part that is trees and a part that is coffee, so between the two I have the look of a forest and can earn a little money from the coffee. (CR8)

Another landowner planted trees with wide spacing in pastures in order to have both pasture and trees.

(193) INTER   Have you planted trees on your land?
RESP   Yes, sir.... [But] I haven't had any results. They're there.... *Cedro*. ...They're planted sparsely, so they don't hurt the pasture grass, so it is still there. It's sparse, but quite a bit. It's not dense because if you plant them dense you won't have any grass, just trees.
INTER   So it's what they call "half wood" [*medio madera*]?
RESP   That's it, that's it. So it doesn't mess up the pasture, and you can keep a few trees there in case you need them someday.... The benefits will be seen over the long term. It's not something quick. I can't talk about benefits, because I haven't seen any. But there they are. (CR16)

The rationales for planting trees varied and included many of the benefits of forests that people had discussed with us. A number of people saw tree planting as a way of balancing out forest clearing, something that should go hand in hand with it. Others had less tangible or more spiritual reasons.

(194) I can't really explain the reason [why it is good to plant trees], but thinking about the future. Perhaps I won't benefit from the trees I planted, but future generations will have a place to get things like firewood, the wood that they need. I think if we destroy we should plant, and if we plant trees we have the right to harvest it. But sometimes we want to enjoy things we haven't created. That we haven't created, that which is used mostly by the animals. So if we plant some trees, in twenty years if we're still alive and we need to cut a tree we have the right to do so, because we planted some. Plant a hectare, and then we will have the trees we need. We should destroy less and plant so there's always an abundance. (CR13)

(195) No, no. [It's never bad to plant trees.] I think it is good because some people are deforesting and others are reforesting, so it evens out. (CR15)

(196) Whenever I have been able to, when I find a seed or a shoot that I can plant, I plant it. Wherever I go I find things and plant them. In Guanacaste, I planted some timber trees. Since I have come here, we came here four years ago, and this here was abandoned, there were animals here and it was abandoned. And now, thanks to God, here we have a little bit of everything, but we have everything. Here there is food for, well ... for a lot of people. There are trees. I work the land with a shovel. If I see an area washing away, I make a little ditch and try to fix it. I ... I think of nature as being something very much mine, very familiar to me. So it hurts me. I think the

earth suffers when it is not taken care of, it seems like this to me. It's that all my life ... perhaps I'm wrong ... I think everything is alive. (CR3)

Most people surveyed had not planted hardwood or timber trees; 26 and 28 percent, respectively, reported planting such trees. But three-fourths of those surveyed had planted fruit trees on their own property (see figure 3.19).

Figure 3.20 shows the proportion of the people surveyed planting trees in various locations on their property.

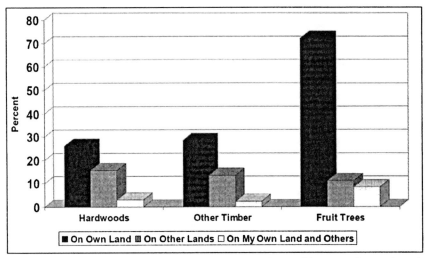

Figure 3.19. Proportion planting trees on their own or other land by types of trees planted, La Amistad, Costa Rica

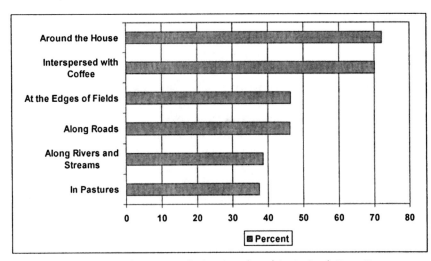

Figure 3.20. Proportion planting trees by location planted, La Amistad, Costa Rica

Conclusion

Costa Rica is an international poster child often applauded for its progress in meeting internationally inspired conservation goals. Certainly the Costa Rican government has played an important role in this success story. The data presented in this chapter show the importance of governmental regulations in shaping people's behavior. The creation of the Amistad International Park and related natural resource use regulations on private lands surrounding the park had a marked impact on reducing deforestation. In fact, the impact of the park's creation could be seen in the clear differentiation between the heavily forested park in the map of land cover (figure 2.2) and the substantially deforested private lands surrounding it.

Our interviews clearly showed that people living around the parks had been exposed to internationally diffused conservation messages, and they were well aware of the laws that defined natural resource use in Costa Rica. Often they parroted these messages in wording that seemed almost scripted. We encountered references to the forest as the world's lungs from respondents independently in a variety of settings. The similarity of the responses was often striking. The responses to our questions strongly suggested the presence of cultural models heavily embedded in local life. These cultural models clearly informed our interactions with local people about forest conservation. The evidence was consistent whether we gathered it with in-depth interviews or more structured survey interviews. Our in-depth interviews uncovered clear articulations of values associated with international conservation thinking, and our survey interviews showed that these values were widely held.

But our interviews also showed that people living around the parks did not simply passively comply with developing forest conservation expectations. While voicing common conservation values, people were also keenly aware of contradictions between demands for conservation and their ability to sustain a livelihood. These tensions surfaced in a number ways, but especially with respect to food production and the construction of houses.

In the case of food production, the most significant tension was created by the limited amount available for cultivation. Both the park and conservation laws had clearly limited people's access to additional land for cultivation. In the context of a limited supply of arable land, the intensification of production became an important consideration. The most important option for such intensification was coffee production, and people attempted to reconcile conservation with the demand for land by mixing coffee and tree planting. They also attempted to maximize the amount of land they had access to, by quietly expanding pastures and carefully controlling regrowth so that it would not become secondary forest that would be off-limits to future cultivation.

The use of timber for local home construction was an important source of tension and highlighted perceived inequities in conservation laws. People living around the park felt they were saddled with responsibility for protecting the natural resource base for the nation, and even the world, without having reasonable access to the very resources they were stewards of. This tension emerged when local residents talked about the difficulties of using timber for home construction. The common sentiment was that requirements for permits for timber use were reasonable but that it was far too difficult to get those permits. At the same time, people perceived that wealthy forest users, like logging companies, had privileged access to forest resources.

The tensions between conservation, human needs, and fairness were apparent throughout our interviews. The cognitive and practical challenge of our subjects was to make sense of their reality with its contradictory demands. Interviews with our subjects revealed six cultural models that mediated between these tensions, helped people make sense of their reality, and provided a guide for thinking about and using natural resources. These models were neither mutually exclusive nor exhaustive of the possible ways of managing the encounter between competing interests, whether local or global, or conservation or livelihood. The most important lesson from our observations is that the encounter between these varied interests is neither uniform nor predetermined. The interests are structured by social organization and practical considerations, but these structures are refashioned in various ways as people attempt to manage the tensions between them.

Notes

1. For more information, see chapter 2 and appendix.

2. For more information about persons reaching working age before or after creation of the park, see chapter 2.

Forest Conservation, Park Management, and Value Change in Honduras

4

BUFFER ZONE RESIDENTS in Honduran parks have a direct relationship with governmental and nongovernmental agencies managing forest conservation and play an active role in environmental protection. They are in a close relationship with agencies that are carriers of the global environmental discourse, and they offer an interesting case study in the processes by which the symbols and practices associated with the global discourse are both incorporated into local life and refashioned to meet the interests and needs of those who most intimately interact with the forest resource.

In chapter 2 we described the relatively recent and only occasionally successful history of forest conservation in Honduras. It was not until the 1950s that the Honduran government established forest management agencies. Although there have been various policy developments since that time, the most significant development for forestry management came in the 1970s with the creation of the Honduran Forestry Development Corporation (*Corporación Hondureño de Desarollo Forestal*, or *COHDEFOR*). This parastatal agency played an important role in deforestation since it generated funds by selling timber harvested from the nation's forests (Barton 2001).

In the context of strong pressures to harvest forests, protected areas represented important sites of potential forest conservation. As indicated in chapter 2, the Honduran government began to create protected areas in 1954, and in 1961 it created the first national park. Since the early 1980s, the Honduran government has created a large number of protected areas. In 1987, Law 87-87 declared all lands over eighteen hundred meters in altitude protected areas, and this law led to the rapid expansion of the protected area system. Cerro Azul Meambar National Park (CAMNP), or in Spanish *Parque Nacional Cerro Azul Meambar (PANACAM)*, was one of the parks created in 1987.

Prior to 1987 *COHDEFOR* had jurisdiction over the forests in the area of CAMNP, and as indicated in chapter 2, it also had initial responsibility for management of the park. But in 1992, *Aldea Global*, a nongovernmental organization (NGO), entered into a park management agreement with *COHDEFOR*. This contract assigned responsibility for management of CAMNP to *Aldea Global*, which has now managed the park for more than fifteen years. After accepting responsibility for the park, *Aldea Global* established a plan that created three management zones. This zoned park, like other similar models around the world, is based on a philosophy of local participation and stewardship. CAMNP has a core zone where use is restricted to scientific, educational, and tourism activities; a special-use zone, which also has restricted use; and a buffer zone where regulated resource use and habitation is allowed. This model is intended to provide for biodiversity, as well as human needs, and a key feature is community participation in conservation projects. This chapter provides a glimpse at the opinions, values, and practices of CAMNP's buffer zone residents who have a direct role in forest conservation.

As in the previous chapter, our qualitative interviewing elicited responses related to forest and park values, social contexts and relationships, conflicts between forest conservation and livelihoods, and forest-related behaviors in a park context. We begin by looking at forest values and their strength at both individual and community levels. Following the previous chapter, we look at a number of issues and themes including conservation policies, laws, and regulations; forest conservation awareness and actions; responses related to the national park and hunting; conflicts between livelihood needs and forest conservation, and mediating models by which people come to terms with this conflict; local notions of desirable landscapes; and forest-related behaviors. As in the previous chapter, we give priority to quotes from our interviews in order to give voice to local people and in an effort to show the full complexity in the way people discuss forests and conservation.

General Cultural Models of Forests

In Honduras, as in Costa Rica, we began our interviews asking a very general question about the first thing that came to mind when trees or forests were mentioned, and then probed deeper around themes of trees, forest conservation, and the national park. This approach allowed us to uncover schemas and cultural models (i.e., networks of strongly connected cognitive elements that are largely built up through human experience). As we indicated in an earlier chapter, schemas are fundamental to people's understanding of their experiences and the meanings they attach to them. As was true in our Costa Rican case study, many of these first responses expressed common themes in a very automatic way. These themes were also referenced repeatedly throughout the interviews, often with great consistency in terminology.

Common Values

Forests are life. One common initial thought about forests was very general: the idea that forests are life, for people as well as for plants and animals, and often with reference to water.

(1)   If there's no forest, there's no life. (H7)

(2)   Trees are life for humans. Almost the most important thing. Often I have told people that the tree is the great symbol of life. Without trees, there's no water, so there has to be trees. (H14)

(3)   Well, that forests, plants and forest directly are the source of life. For each human being, and living beings like animals, too . . . we should protect them to have a better future . . . and we know that we can have a green Honduras in the years to come. (H25)

Part of this cultural model may have come from what one respondent cited as the *COHDEFOR* slogan, that "the forest is life, without forest we will not have life" (H20). The quotes from people often appear to be repeating portions of slogans that they have heard, such as "no forest, no life" and "we can have a green Honduras."

Water. Water was without doubt the most common benefit of forests expressed throughout the interviews. Trees and forests have a strong association with water, often expressed by saying without forests, this would be a desert.

(4)   RESP   It is due to the forests that we have water . . . because if it were a desert here; well, we would be completely ruined. For me it is necessary to care for the forest. (H18)

(5)   There were communities that were ending up like a desert. In the summer they had to live with very little water. The water was disappearing. And here in this community, rainy season or dry season, there is abundant water and excellent water to drink, nice and cool. (H15)

The association between forests and water is twofold. On the one hand, forests in general are seen as being related to weather patterns and rainfall. The year before the interviews took place was very dry, and forest clearing was often associated with drought.

(6)   There's less [water than before], for example this year, with the dry season we had, there were a lot of water sources that dried up. So I think that by protecting the forest, these waters that dried up might come back. (H8)

(7)   It was more agreeable [when I first came here], and the water, too. Here it has at times rained continually for four years. It's no longer the same. . . . It doesn't rain much. The clouds aren't here anymore. They aren't born over there. The clouds are formed in the forest near the

village, but not anymore. . . . It is because of the lack of forest. In the mornings, this forest up above, you see that it settles, that the clouds are born over it and then it begins to rain; the downpours. That's where the rain is formed, that's why it is so important. (H7)

On the other hand, and different from general links between forest and rainfall, retention of forests around specific sources of water is seen as keeping the flow of water in place and the springs flowing.

(8)   Some streams here used to always have water, but now, due to the clearing that has been done, there is only water when it rains, in the rainy season. In the dry season there's no water, the sources of water dry up. You can see that this is not good. . . . This started when people started to strip, to burn, and leave bare the land; without trees. The water started to dry up. Sources of water have been lost. It is because of this. (H19)

(9)   It's important to leave a strip of forest along the stream, *guamil* [short forest regrowth], so that it doesn't dry up. So that all the water doesn't dry up. (H7)

Almost all (98%) of the six hundred persons in our survey agreed with the statement "Without forests, our community would not have sufficient water." Likewise, when asked, 96 percent agreed about the broader national significance of forests in their community: "The forests in our community are the source of water for those who live in other parts of the country." But people did not just associate forest clearing with drought and streams drying up in a general sense. They also cited specific examples.

(10)   INTER   So you have seen other places where people have cleared the forest and the water has dried up?
RESP   Yes. . . . For example, I have seen it in Agua Fría which is just past Meambar. There they cleared the forest and the water disappeared. For example right here in Cienegal, in Cienegal the water has diminished. It is not abundant. It hasn't been abundant because they've cleared the forest and there have been fires. . . . Monte de Dios, Monte de Dios, a little while ago I was over there. There's no water. (H16)

Pure air/coolness/health. Another very common specific reference to forests was their role in producing "pure air" or in purifying the air.

(11)   The forest . . . is good to purify the air. (H18)

(12)   Forests are important so that we can breathe pure air. . . . It's the air one breathes . . . the bad air, that hurts us. The leaves absorb this and breathe out air, pure air, no longer polluted, but clean air. (H7)

Often responses were more specific than pure air or air in general. A number of people made reference to the importance of forests in providing oxygen.

(13) Yes, we are careful not to destroy the forest, but to conserve it . . . so there's more oxygen. (H3)

(14) I think that without plants we could not continue to exist, because they give us oxygen. (H25)

In addition to air quality, when people talk about the air they often begin to talk about the role of forest in keeping the air cool. For example,

(15) INTER   Would you like to have more trees and forests here around the community?
RESP   Yes, I would like to, because when you're close to trees you feel cooler. . . . For the climate, it's important. (H9)

People told very specific stories about the coolness. They were grounded in their experiences, as revealed in the following exchanges:

(16) INTER   But your father taught you to leave trees, *guamiles,* around the springs. How did he know this?
RESP   Well, it's like he had noticed that it is very important to leave the shade there. If you plant a tree, perhaps somewhere where there isn't any shade . . . if you plant a tree and on a sunny day and you go and sit underneath that tree, you won't feel the sun. The sun will hit the tree and not you. (H7)

(17) INTER   About . . . the changes that you have seen since you have been here, what have been the results of this here in the community?
RESP   Look . . . what I have noticed is . . . the first year I lived here it was a very cool place, totally cool. And I have been a little weak, I have to bundle up. Lately, I have seen that the climate isn't the same. I feel like the climate is warmer, it's hotter. Now I hardly ever feel cold, when before I felt it. . . . It seems to me that the climate is changing, it feels warmer than it used to be. If we talk to people who lived here twenty years ago, they will tell you that this was a forest full of mist all the time, and that in the rainy season it rained day and night. So it looks like there has been a big change. Clearly we have to think that this is because of what happened to our forest. Because before this became a coffee-growing area everyone cleared the forest and planted beans and corn. Perhaps this has brought the climate change. I have seen this that it is not the same cool climate that we had my first year here. The climate is hotter. (H21)

The extent of these sentiments is striking and only fully appreciated in the survey results. There was near unanimity about the relationship between forests and the climate among the persons we surveyed. Nearly everyone (99%) agreed that "Without forests, we would not have sufficient oxygen to breathe." The effect of forests on the local climate was also widely acknowledged. Ninety-nine percent agreed that "The forests around here help keep the climate cool."

There were many associations between forests and health. The specific mechanisms that people suggest associate better health with both cleaner air and coolness, which are both seen as benefits from forests.

> (18)   Having the forest, well, what little forest we have left, we will have pure air, and having pure air, we will have better health. (H14)
>
> (19)   We have considered it to be a source of a lot of pure air. You notice a lot of coolness, it is a place where not much disease reaches. Because the climate is good and the disease doesn't come. (H13)

The coolness of the forest and its association to health is also used to contrast it to the earlier landscape, where burning was prevalent, with either an association between burning and a warmer climate or contrasting the air near the forest with the polluted air of urban areas.

> (20)   RESP   There was a time, a long time ago, when we first started here. Here it was cold . . . fearsome . . . not now. . . . It's hotter because there have been fires and deforestation, when we started living here, you needed to warm yourself by the fire, because it was so cold, too cold. People came in here, they cleared forest, and the forest only remained up above. The sun shines and shines more. . . . The healthy thing about forest is the air; it's pure. And the heat is from fire and smoke. That's why it's better to have trees, so one can breathe. It's healthy. (H16)
>
> (21)   In the first place [trees are important], because trees are a source of life. Where there aren't trees you can breath all kinds of air, polluted and everything. For example, here in this place it is very agreeable. But if this place didn't have that little strip of trees that you see around us, you would be breathing more polluted air. Thus, trees are life. They protect and perform a function. (H21)
>
> (22)   Yes, [we need to] maintain [the forest's] riches, maintain these even though these riches are not money. Rather, we obtain them in health; a good, a good—breathing. Now we don't breath carbon but pure air, pure. (H20)

These three categories of responses (forests as life; forests for water; and forests for pure air, coolness, and health) represent the most frequently recurring schemas for the value of forests. All of these came easily to respondents as their first responses and reactions to being asked to talk about forests, and all three themes were referenced frequently throughout the interviews. People often fell back on the key phrases when they were having difficulty articulating forest values in their own words. Each of these three themes has concise terminology associated with it. This language is a "verbal molecule," or a formulaic expression of a common opinion. Forest as life is expressed simply and often in terms reflecting the reported *COHDEFOR* slogan, "forests are life" or "without forests there is no life." Forest for water is expressed with the phrases "without forests this would be a desert" and the need to protect forests around the "sources of water." Forests for air, coolness, and health is expressed through the recurrence of terms like "pure air," "oxygen," and "coolness."

Other Values

Beyond the general expressions of the value or usefulness of forests found in verbal molecules, residents of the park mentioned several ways that forests were particularly important: forest utility, wildlife habitat, ecosystem service provision, nature appreciation, and forest protection. Some examples from our interviews illustrate these specific and widely held forest values.

Forest utility. There were many other values of forest mentioned. Various utilitarian values of forests were mentioned frequently, including lumber for houses and furniture, firewood, fruits, and medicinal plants.

(23) [Forests] give us a lot of useful things . . . there are many things; firewood, lumber, to make houses, things like this. (H2)

(24) If the places where there is forest are restored a little . . . in the future we will have some place to get wood, and so will the future generation. (H13)

Park rangers were most likely to go beyond talking about the value of timber in the forest to also talk about using the forest to obtain food and medicinal plants. For example,

(25) And the forests have some things that people eat, fruits that we call *car-mucas* and ones that we call *pacayas*, others that are called *jilotes*. People go to the forests and bring back these fruits, and eat them. So for a lot of reasons, for all these and other reasons . . . we shouldn't cut down the forests. (H11)

(26) Also we get a lot of help from the forest, because it provides us with firewood, and there are some medicinal trees in the forest. (H8)

The individuals we surveyed gave priority to their subsistence needs over forest conservation, but relatively few agreed that forests should serve a narrowly commercial purpose. For example, almost 60 percent agreed with the statement "It's better to use the land to produce food than to leave it in forest." In contrast, less than 30 percent agreed that "The most important thing concerning trees is to make money from them." These responses are consistent across the communities in the park. The pattern shown in figure 4.1 does not change when we take into account the age or gender of the individual answering the question. Likewise there is no difference between persons who settled in the area before or after the park was created.

Wildlife. The presence of wildlife was also mentioned frequently as a benefit of forests, nearly always in association with a phrase related to the importance of future generations' being able to see them.

(27)   The forest should be the place where the animals live, and so I would like things to really be taken care of. Because there are people who kill the animals and I don't agree with this. . . . Now some of our children and grandchildren won't be able to see deer, they won't know a lot of animals that are in the forest. I would like them to be able to do this. (H18)

(28)   INTER   Are there other reasons why you like forest close by?
RESP   Well, there are a number of reasons. When I was a child . . . because I was born here, I have made my whole life here. During the rainy season I would see a flock of birds, of all colors, and beautiful animals. Now you don't see them, there aren't any, they were eliminated, possibly because of the destruction of the forest and what came with it, they left.
INTER   Do you think that they went to other places and don't come here any more, or that they died?
RESP   I think they died, some of them died, because of what has happened here. The forest was burned, twenty years ago, the forest here was burned. . . . There were monkeys here. It was really beautiful before.

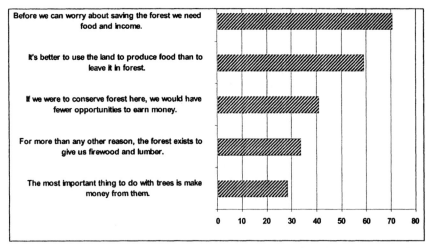

Figure 4.1.   Proportion who agreed with selected statements about forests, Cerro Azul Meambar, Honduras.

There were monkeys, all kinds of animals. Now these children won't know monkeys. Only when we take them to a park. Only in a park can you see monkeys, but here in our forest they can't be seen. (H9)

(29)   Because then you can see the wild animals. They say that there are people from the city, some only know the animals from photographs. And we have seen them, seen the animals. We don't look at them in photographs but see them live. . . . Our children, so that they don't only see them in photographs but also live. (H7)

Ecosystem services. Environmental services provided by forests were mentioned frequently. Air and water, which were discussed above, were mentioned most frequently, but there were others, including forests as windbreaks, forests creating better climatic conditions for agriculture, soil conservation, and the relationship of forests to the production of electricity.

(30)   Look, let's say a hurricane comes, let's say a hurricane comes. If there aren't trees it will pick up our house and take it who knows where, because there aren't any trees to stop the wind. Instead of getting rid of trees, we need to plant them. (H24)

(31)   INTER   You cut down trees when you were starting out here. What happened?
RESP   Sometimes it produced landslides, these lands are very steep and there was erosion, of the soil. . . . And it's worse when the land is steep. . . . Besides, when the rain washed over the land, the soil was carried away. When the erosion came here the soil was washed away and left very poor. (H13)

(32)   Because if we clear forest, the waters may dry up, and it would be a disaster for those who live here. And we are a part of the basin of the reservoir. This is also maintained by the forest; it would hurt it. At the national level, this is providing electricity for the whole country. And it is up to us to take care of this. (H3)

(33)   For example, here we are in a place that has a lot of water. This water is what feeds what is called the *Proyecto de Cañaveral Cortéz*, where all the electricity is. It's what makes all the electricity, the water is harvested here and put into the lake, and from there it goes over there to make energy. (H13)

Nature appreciation. Recreational benefits were often mentioned; even when people did not engage in them themselves, they often mentioned that they had seen others engaging in recreation (generally outsiders, not local residents). Nature appreciation was also associated with tourism and its potential as an economic activity in the region.

(34)   INTER   And people come here? What kind of people come here?
RESP   All kinds come . . . those from the universities; sometimes they
come here year after year; people from the schools. . . . They come and
go up above to see a waterfall; there's one up above. I haven't seen the
waterfall but people are always going up there to see it; lots of people. . . .
They can just walk there, sightseeing. They say it is very pretty. I've never
been there, but someday I will go there and walk around. (H7)

(35)   I haven't been able to go. I haven't gone to the forest. But some of the
people who [have stayed with me] have gone there, and come back talking about beautiful things. That there were birds, many things. Can you
imagine that a person lives in this place and doesn't know the animals;
that they perhaps haven't been able to see them? I see people from the
city, educated people, well-trained people. They grab their backpacks and
walk. They come back tired, but they are always happy. (H5)

(36)   People are living from the forest without damaging it. I think, too, that
when people come from other places, people in the communities will
feel the benefits of having forest. Many people may benefit by, for example, selling food, providing lodging, and such. And in this way I think
that ecotourism will begin. I think that if people try this little by little
they are going to gain interest, and with the little incentive that the
tourists leave, they are going to begin to love the forest; I think they will
conserve it a little more. (H11)

Almost everyone surveyed (96%) agreed that "We need to take good care of our
forest if we want tourism to grow and bring us money."

Beyond recreation, people talked about the beauty of the forest, often in relation to religious values. One person spoke of this beauty in spiritual terms.

(37)   Sometimes I stop and look at the forest and I see the beauty of this forest,
the beauty that it is to see. God created nature and left the environment
for life, there are a lot of people who don't understand this. Here, I have
talked to a lot of people, and they have been deprived, we no longer have
access to this patrimony of ours. . . . It is important, we need to take care of
this. It is a great patrimony and there is only a little left in our country. You
have to be honest. There are forests that have been completely cleared in
our country, lots of crops have been planted, and thank God we still have
a few parks that preserve a little of the beauty of the country. (H21)

Eighty-eight percent of the individuals surveyed agreed that "Because God created
the forests it is bad to abuse them."

Forest conservation was also connected to social concerns and profound experiences in life outside of religion. For example, one woman compared the fate of
forests and nature to that of women.

(38)   RESP   Well, when I think about forests—not only forest, I am referring to nature and covering everything—it can only be compared to the situation of the woman—not only here in Honduras but worldwide—because through the history of the world I think that the beings of nature, or nature, has been violated, has been mistreated, exploited, forgotten, marginalized, just like has happened to women. And because of this I am a good friend of nature. I feel sad thinking about this, but it is because I feel bad, for example, thinking about a tree that has been burned, and I play the role of a mother, and I say, "This big tree that is being burned. All around it there are a lot of little children and they are children of that tree, and have to be loved. And when fire comes the first ones to die are little trees, and sometimes the big tree is saved and the little ones die." So I think, What would happen if my children were burned and I was left living? This is what I think. For me nature is a symbol of life. Do you know why? Because just like the women, in spite of the mistreatment, being forgotten, the exploitation, in spite of everything, everything that has ruined us, we can say that we're still living. Women continue to have children, nature continues to give life. Without her, we couldn't live.

INTER   And this that you are talking to me about, who taught you this, or where did you learn this?

RESP   No, no one taught me this. Rather, I have been interested in training women, mostly advising *campesina* women. The discoveries that we have made have been made together. Little by little, and I think that some of it comes just from struggling against the situation that I have found myself in since I was little. Because I remember that when I was a child I would like to make little things, poems and things. So I would go down to the river to do these little things, as a little girl. I played with it, I talked to it. And when I was a little older and started to think about love and all this, I once again made friends with the river. I loved the river like my friend. I looked at the river like a little boy; a young friend that understood me. And I still think like that. Sometimes I tell myself that perhaps it is something that is born in someone, that no one has to teach you. It is born in you, you just realize it is there. (H14)

Protection. A few people thought about protection immediately in relation to forest, particularly avoiding forest fires, indicating that forests are often associated with messages about the importance of protecting them. Here are two responses to the question, "When you think about forests, what is the first thing you think about?"

(39)   Well, I think that trees are the life of the forest, which I understand that we need to protect. To help ourselves. (H6)

(40)   The first thing is to protect them, not to destroy trees or forests so that we can live a life with air that is not polluted. (H1)

A park guard, in response to the same question, talked at length about protection, and the following excerpt shows the way that the idea of protection is woven through the conservation discourse in the region:

(41) Well, the first thing I think about is that it is a resource that we need to protect, because it is . . . one of the best things that we find in the park and in the communities. Because we see that forests are one of the most important resources that are needed so that everyone who inhabits the community can live. When we protect, protection helps us to make our life better. When we talk about conflicts, when we have forest fires, we see that the solution is protecting the forests—having people that live together protecting our resources. We value it a lot. I do. In four and a half years [that I have been a park guard] I have developed a lot of love for our forests, and it is the future of our children and of our adults. Because there we have life; we have pure air; we have water; we have firewood; we have pine trees [*ocote*]; we have the resources that we live from. Because what we have here in the community is ours. If we lose it, if we waste it, if we don't take care of it, we will end up in a desert. (H15)

While we have presented the various forest values in separate categories in order to highlight the different ways forests are valued and the language used to talk about them, it is important to note that many of the statements made by people in interviews were comprised of complex statements that integrated many different benefits and values. This can be seen clearly in the following responses:

(42) Well, the first thing I think about is nature, or the earth. Principally about protecting the water, the animals. This is what I think about when I think about trees. (H7)

(43) When I think about forests, I think about me first, and then about others. . . . Because the forests are our lungs, they give us richness [*riqueza*]. And after the richness, they give us firewood . . . and after that comes our happiness, because that's where the water comes from. Everything comes from there. I think that they are the greatest thing that God has given us. . . . They're the best. (H23)

Stories of Forest Change

We asked questions about the history of the region's people and forests, including how forests and values had changed over time. As described in chapter 2, our interviewees had lived in the region for varying lengths of time. Early residents told stories of the original colonization and deforestation of the area, and both older and newer residents told of more recent forest recovery and changes in attitudes.

The explanations that people gave for deforestation, and later forest recovery, highlight the many material, institutional, and value-related factors that influence forest change.

(44) INTER   Let's talk a little about the forests in the community. How have the forests changed in the time you have been living here?
RESP   They have changed a lot. Look, when I was a child, everything around here was a big forest, a big dense forest. But in recent times, the people have, well, to grow crops, they have had to fell a lot of, a lot of trees. And there hasn't been, there hasn't been a way to . . . how do you say . . . a way to better manage the land. People have cleared places where they shouldn't have even tried to grow crops. And this is what has bothered us, because we weren't oriented in such a way that we could manage the situation. (H9)

(45) INTER   When you came here thirty years ago, what was it like?
RESP   It will seem like a lie, what there was. We came here on a dirt trail . . . everything that is now the village already had no trees. . . . What is now village already had no trees, it had already been cleared, but all this was forest. I have the images recorded in my mind even after all this time. Later, when I told this to my children, they thought that what I told them was a lie. It was very beautiful here, all around there was forest. Up on those hills, it was forest, but here in the center the virgin forest had already been cleared. It was cleared, but there were no houses. There weren't any big trees anymore, but the squirrels would come on top of the house; the toucans—but we called them knife-beaks here, the toucan. But how we heard them digging around! Beautiful! Here very close. Now you can only have these on leashes; they don't exist—in the forest, yes; but here, no. The animals that you could see were the *agouti*, that passed right in front of the house. This was unusual, but the thing that had the greatest impact on me was the river, that the river had so much water compared to what it has now.
INTER   And how can you measure, or how do you remember this?
RESP   In the first place, here we don't have any pools for bathing anymore, where we would wash the children. There were great big pools where we could swim as much as we wanted to. Now these pools don't exist. And the noise of the river! This noise was loud. Not now; now you can't even hear it. And the quantity of water, of course you can see that. It wasn't easy to cross the river in just any place. Now you can cross the river jumping from rock to rock. Before, no. You could cross it, yes, but you had to walk a ways to find a place to cross.
INTER   What do you think happened to the river?
RESP   It was the felling of the forest. After we came here we saw how they were felling everything, all the forest around here. I saw how they

were felling the trees, because they felled them, and they felled them . . . in places they didn't even use them. I remember this ridge over there, in front, it was something beautiful, like something you would draw. Here in the park there's a species they call endangered. . . . It is a species that is called *palmiche*. . . . This ridge was full of *palmiche*, and when they felled the forest they felled without stopping, and so they cleared all the forest, all the forest. And in places they felled just to fell trees. They didn't use them. It was too steep.

INTER   How did you feel when you were little, seeing them cut all these trees?

RESP   Well, what I remember, when they were clearing this hill over there in the front, that you could see the trees coming down. At first, when they began felling some, we felt . . . we liked it . . . the way the trees fell down. . . . We lived over there by the church, in my mother's house. We liked to see them fell those trees, but after a while we felt the difference. In the afternoon we no longer could see the *palmiches*; when storms came through with wind it was so pretty to see the *palmiches*, to see the palms shimmering. So we couldn't see them anymore. We no longer enjoyed them. But we didn't feel bad. Sincerely nobody would have said so. We didn't know the consequences it would bring, or things like that. We didn't feel it.

INTER   Of the changes that you have told me about . . . how has this affected the community and the people?

RESP   Well, some of the changes have been positive, for example, the highway, the school, the bridges, the water, the latrines—very positive. But the disappearance of the forest, this has not brought anything positive. For example, this year we were very worried because there was a time when we felt like the river was going to stop running, that it was going stagnant. There was so little water. The rocks were very dirty. This is another change that is due to felling of the forest. There are more farms. There is more income for families. Life has improved, but there has also been pollution of the river. . . . For example there is terrible pollution. There are more farms, more coffee. And having more coffee there is more *aguas mieles* [runoff from coffee pulp] that go into the river. Like I was just telling you, there was a time when the water got really thick and stagnant, the rocks got really dirty, and if you bathed in the pool it would get stirred up and you would come out like a pig, stinking. This is not how it used to be. We are trying to fix this. (H14)

The reasons given for forest clearing are a combination of the need to grow crops and ignorance about the importance of forests to people, as indicated in the following interchange:

(46)   [The forests] have been destroyed. They have been destroyed. . . . Since I came to work here. . . . It seems before there was a very immense forest. But, perhaps because so many inhabitants have come here, it looks like it has been destroyed. . . . They have cut the forest beyond measure. Perhaps because of the ignorance of people, because you can see there are ravines where it was cut. . . . Look how it is . . . these ravines . . . they cut the wood. . . . This isn't good for anything now. And the trees, they thought they were going to use some of this, but everything ended up underneath a lot of dirt. There was a landslide. This was not beneficial.
INTER   Why do you think these changes have happened?
RESP   I would think due to ignorance. . . . Not knowing that this would affect us in the future.
INTER   And who did all these changes?
RESP   Well, those that were here before. Almost all the inhabitants did the same thing. And we did the same. . . . Everyone, everyone did this. Nobody can say otherwise. (H6)

Some people showed a sophisticated understanding of the political ecology of colonization, realizing that they had come to an area of steep terrain and poor land quality because they had been driven out of the flatter parts of the country that were better for agriculture.

(47)   INTER   How have the forests here in the community changed since you began working and planting here?
RESP   The change that there has been here . . . well, we came to this zone. . . . When we came here, this was a forested zone. There was a lot of forest here; all this was forest. But because of the situation that we live in here in this country, the situation of the migration of communities, of people . . . we came to this place and started to clear forest to grow coffee and bananas, which are the products that predominate here on small parcels for family subsistence. So the change that we made to the forest is that we planted coffee, which is appropriate here, and banana, which is what substitutes for shade for growing coffee. . . . This is the change that has happened here.
INTER   Why have these changes happened?
RESP   The changes have been rooted in the fact that we came here. . . . Well, in Honduras in general the communities of poor people, those of us who have few resources, are forced to live however we can. And we will look for land wherever we can. Because we practically don't have access to the areas that are flat. There are a lot of steep areas, and those of us who don't want to be always fighting for land in the flat places, what we do is come to a place like this to be able to possess a little piece of land and to be able to subsist on this. So this is why we have been obligated

to be here. Not so much because the benefits are so big, but because at least we can survive.

INTER   So mostly to look for a way to make a living?

RESP   That's right. Yes, yes. . . . A lot of times people aren't trying to destroy the forest. When you do, it is because you need some land to grow crops, not because you simply do it. To meet your needs, you have to do it. Now when it is a big landowner that wants to cut a lot of forest for his own benefit, to exploit the wood, this is another situation. In that case it is done with the intention to make money. But in our case, no, in our case it's that we live from the parcel that we have and that parcel is stuck in the middle of the park. We have done it because we didn't have any other place to go. In the case where the government would maybe say that they would pay us for our land and resettle us in another place where we could have land. We can't leave because there would be more social problems there than we now have. (H13)

Many of the explanations piece together a process of agricultural change in response to changing material conditions, beginning with shifting agriculture and then, with population growth, the establishment of permanent farms planted in intensive crops like coffee. For example,

(48)   The farmers, or the farmers that started to work here, didn't work in a conservation way, they practiced migratory agriculture. . . . I think that if in the beginning if there had existed . . . if protected areas had been declared, people would have learned how to work. Our parents surely would have learned and all the people would have learned how to work correctly. But when these laws were made, it was too late. . . . But I don't really think it is too late because we still have a quarter of the forest left. (H11)

(49)   INTER   And this was a good area to grow crops?

RESP   It has been good, yes, it has been good. But now. . . . Before it was good. But now, well, almost all the places are getting so it is very hard to grow much; a lot of disease, a lot, yes. And the land doesn't have any force. If you don't throw on some fertilizer you won't harvest anything. You have to be throwing on fertilizer and other things to be able to harvest anything.

INTER   And why do you think that the land has changed, that it doesn't produce like it did before?

RESP   Well, I imagine that, like we were saying, that there were fewer people. And now there are a lot. So before, these forests, or *guamiles* as we say . . . one year you would work here, and the next year, not here but over there, in another place, and the following year not over there. Not now. Now it's right here every year, in the same place, right here. . . . Now you have to stay in the same place, whether it's productive or not. (H2)

Ethics of Tree Felling and Forest Clearing

We asked questions about when it would be acceptable and unacceptable to fell trees and clear forest to understand the moral dimensions of human behavior toward forests. The general parameters of the acceptability of felling trees were that it was unacceptable to waste trees by cutting them without using the wood. But felling trees when you are going to use the wood is acceptable. It is also considered unacceptable to fell trees near springs or streams. For example,

(50) If you just cut them to cut them [it's bad]. But when you use them, yes [it's acceptable]. (H11)

(51) If it is close to a spring, you shouldn't cut it. If nature wants the spring to dry up, it can dry up, but you shouldn't mess with the sources of water. (H14)

(52) For me, I don't think that cutting a tree that you need hurts much, but to fell trees just to fell trees and leave them there, that is doing damage. You should cut them with a permit and talk to the *patronato* here, so that they can make sure that it is necessary. (H2)

There are, of course, a wide range of reasons, circumstances, quantities, and ways to fell trees or clear forest, and these determine whether a particular action will be considered acceptable or unacceptable behavior. Important factors in determining acceptability include the number of trees felled, whether large trees or small trees are being felled, whether the trees are live or dead, and whether the person felling the trees has a permit or a management plan. It is helpful at this point to look at some longer excerpts of interviews from several individuals to illustrate the complexity of the rationales that people used to determine appropriate and inappropriate tree felling.

(53) INTER   Do you think that sometimes it is good to cut trees?
RESP   As long as it is something that you need. . . . But now if someone goes around cutting trees without reason or perhaps near a spring, I think that this can affect and hurt us, and I am not in agreement.
INTER   Do you think it is necessary to fell trees to plant coffee?
RESP   Close to a spring, I'm not in agreement [with this]. But if it is far from water, I think it is perfectly fine as long as you have a permit.
INTER   And talking about clearing forest, not just cutting a tree here and there, do you think that sometimes it is good to clear forest?
RESP   Let's say, true forest [*montaña montaña*], no. Because you can imagine what problems we would have in terms of trees and their felling. But not everyone thinks the same. At least for those who have a true need, perhaps they don't have any land to work. So I think it can be understandable.
INTER   How can they live if they don't have any land?

RESP   For example, there are people who live from beans, from making *milpas* and they don't have any place to do it. No one will rent them land. If there is forest, it is reasonable that they should be able to take it. (H5)

(54)   INTER   Do you think that sometimes it is good to cut trees?

RESP   Sometimes it is good to harvest a tree, to use it; if you need it, for example to make doors for the house, or beds, or something like this. If you are going to use it, it is good, because sometimes people need lumber. But only for use in your own community. To cut them just to cut them, you can't. (H11)

(55)   INTER   Do you think it is good or necessary to cut trees sometimes?

RESP   I think that it depends. Because, sometimes, someone here in this community, or wherever, doesn't ever burn, and they have a lot of trees on their private property. For example there are people that have *cedros, caoba, laurel*, trees of this nature . . . so the people who are in charge of this . . . to get a permit, you have to pay money to get permission . . . and if you need a tree for something in the house, when you're fixing up your house, you need it for the roof, for the doors, for chairs, things like that, they should be given permission. But they should use it, not just fell a tree. That's not permitted. It is prohibited and you should never be able to do it.

INTER   So what do you think about it being sometimes prohibited?

RESP   Well, I think that it is good because if we are going to use a tree we should at least ask for a permit, and if they give it to you, then get your wood. I think that if it wasn't like that things would be worse here, because people would be selling wood and all the forest would be cleared. If they didn't have to pay a fine or anything like this. Now it's not like this because people are scared that someone will see what they are doing. They have to get a permit. They can't just go and do it.

INTER   So sometimes you think it is bad to cut trees?

RESP   Yes, I think it is bad if it is done like that. Like I told you, for a personal use to meet a need is one thing, but to cut it to sell, I don't think that is good.

INTER   And if we talk about clearing forest, do you think that sometimes it is good to do it?

RESP   I think that it depends, because if a person has land that they live off of, for example, someone who lives from this, from agriculture, they have to do it because there's no other way to crop their land. (H17)

(56)   INTER   Do you think that it is sometimes good to cut trees?

RESP   No, no, it's not good. . . . Never.

INTER   And if you need some lumber for construction?

RESP   Yes, well, if you are going to need a tree, then you should plant another tree. Not just one, but some five trees. If you fell a tree, you should plant some. Not just leave it lying there where no one uses it, and it continues to mess up the forest. (H7)

On the other hand, clearing forest, as opposed to felling trees, is often talked about as being generally unacceptable, as indicated by the following response:

(57)   INTER   Do you think that sometimes it can be good to clear forest?
       RESP   I don't think so; I don't think so. . . . Because you shouldn't take away what God created. I say that it is not advisable because all of us have a right to life. Just like we need to live, the trees also need to live. I don't think there are any benefits from cutting trees. I think that the soil will be washed away. You are throwing away the organic layer of the soil. I don't think it is good to fell trees. . . . The problem is that when you clear land, water destroys the organic layer. There are landslides, and the land is ruined. If you want to ruin land, clear the forest. It will be ruined. You have to leave trees there. (H20)

Our survey results show that these types of sentiments about the cutting of trees and forests were widely held in the park communities (see table 4.2). For example, almost everyone (93%) agreed that it is alright to cut a tree as long as you plant a new one. Four-fifths of the persons also agreed that cutting old or dead trees was acceptable. But relatively few felt that indiscriminate felling of trees was acceptable. Only one in five persons agreed that "It's alright to cut forests because they easily grow back." This pattern of sentiments was widespread in the park, and there was no difference based on age, place of birth, or when residence in the park was established.

A park ranger talked about the problems with forest clearing, using common terminology about preventing the area from becoming a desert and emphasizing

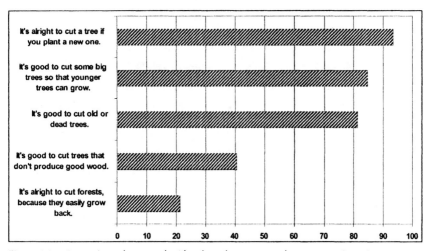

Figure 4.2.   Proportion who agreed with selected statements about appropriate circumstances for cutting trees, Cerro Azul Meambar, Honduras.

links between trees and food crops. The park ranger saw his job as making people see these links and benefits.

> (58)   For me [forest clearing] is never good. The forest will lose its equilibrium and be left a desert, because if a tree is cut it doesn't recuperate. Recuperation is when another tree is born. This is what we have tried to do while working with *PANACAM*, to make the people aware that they can't cut. . . . [There are] many abandoned lands that have recuperated, and people don't lack land. They agree with [not clearing land] because they have seen the benefits that the community has received. The abundance of water, as well as the harvest of corn, beans, and coffee—in their yards as well as their crops. We have this parcel that is looking really good. It's a work of art, which before you couldn't have because it was so dry. There is a lot of communities that don't have this environment, to be able to have something, like fruit trees. Like here we have oranges in abundance; mangos; all kinds of trees are abundant here; bananas; all kinds of fruit here. This is why people here don't like to clear forest. (H15)

Park rangers have been effective in informing people living in the park about regulations protecting trees and forests. For example, the persons surveyed were practically unanimous (93%) that clearing forest in the park was not permitted. Four-fifths were also supportive of park restrictions on the commercial harvesting of trees, agreeing that "The government should be able to prohibit people from cutting trees to sell lumber."

Changing Values, Changing Forests

Forest values have changed. Earlier, people focused on the agriculture as their source of subsistence, but in recent years people have begun to link trees and forests to having an environment favorable to their own well-being, and there is a growing concern about forest loss. Changing values were generally attributed to outside groups, such as *COHDEFOR* or CAMNP, that made people aware of the importance of forests and began programs to promote forest conservation. Yet, observation of noticeable changes in climate, water, and soil also appear to have been an important factor in people's receptivity toward environmental conservation messages.

People recognized their role in forest destruction, as indicated in the following responses:

> (59)   Years ago, we didn't take care [of forests]. At this time, the forest was destroyed because people went in and felled trees. They took pieces of land and burned them. But later, the government formed an institution which was called *COHDEFOR*, that is still around. And from then the

forest began to be taken care of; from then to now things have been changing; from 1970 until now. . . . Before 1970, no. They felled everything. . . . There were big forests here, they say. There were forests—enormous, virgin—they say; and it was all felled. But then these government organizations, came, from then on . . . [*COHDEFOR*] came here to give talks and to make it clear to people that they should be respecting the law and taking into account the damages that were going to result from this. Because, if in that time there hadn't been all this, this place would be a desert now, all this forest. But after that, people stopped. The forest was maintained; today we are taking care of it. (H3)

(60) RESP We have all more than once participated in the destruction of the forest, the majority of us. . . . Almost everyone. . . . Before *Aldea Global* came in. That's when everything stopped. Since there have been one or two problems, but it has always . . . it has always gotten everyone's attention that they shouldn't keep doing things the same way. . . . Many of us, before—perhaps I have never cleared forest where there is a spring, but many of us have done this. The result is that when the dry season comes, the water dries up on us—water that we used to have during the wet season—because of the clearing of the forest. (H9)

(61) Well, sometimes . . . the people here don't understand that forests are important. It's because of the national park. We would have continued to fell all the forest. . . . Now people have changed a lot, because people have noticed that forests have to be taken care of to keep the waters from drying up. . . . I think that about one-third have become aware that we definitely have to take care of the forest and the animals. . . . There are a few people that don't understand, but there is always an organization, in the *patronato*, that is always calling meetings and teaching people that they need to take care of [the forest]. (H7)

One of the notable ideas found in these quotes is that, although people saw outside conservation actions by the government and NGOs as the instigator of the change, they also talked about a key role for the local community governing body, or *patronato*, in this process, showing an alignment between external and internal institutions in addressing deforestation.

(62) INTER And when did [forest clearing] stop?
RESP Look, here this stopped about six years ago. Six years, yes. It stopped six years ago because they [the *patronato*] organized a committee here. (H6)

People generally believe that the changing values have led to a change in people's behaviors toward the forest and, ultimately, to changing forest conditions. For example,

(63)   INTER   How have forests and trees changed here in this community and around it?
RESP   Here, a lot of forest was destroyed, a lot. Now they are taking care of a lot of forest here in Cerro Azul. They have put into place a lot of groups that care for the trees. There hasn't been much burning. Because where we are, everything has been burned before—all these hills. This year there hasn't been any burning, but we have seen around us how people have destroyed the forest, thousands of forests, the little forests that are sprouting are killed by fire; animals that are there are destroyed by the fire. (H22)

(64)   INTER   When you think about all the years you have been working here in your parcels and all this, how have the trees and forest changed?
RESP   Now I think the environment will get better, with respect to forest. Because we have received a lot of talks and many people have come here to explain to us that it is necessary to conserve the forest, not destroy it. Now people are taking care of things.
INTER   And why do you think things have been conserved?
RESP   Oh, because one knows that it is necessary to take care of it, if you use something from the forest, like a tree or two to make a house, something like that, then you do it carefully. . . . One has to take care of the forest; it is necessary. (H18)

Social Relationships

To probe this subject more deeply, we asked people where they had learned about the forest in order to gain insight into social environments where forest-related knowledge might be transmitted. Reponses clearly reflect earlier indications that forest knowledge and values were seen as originating from outside the community, from government agencies and NGOs. Some of this dates back to earlier programs of *COHDEFOR*, the government forestry agency, while most of it was associated with CAMNP and the management of the park and its inhabited zones. At the same time, people noted that their own observations and experiences in the landscape supported the forest conservation-related messages disseminated by these outside sources. People often said that it was through the outsiders that they began to notice what was happening. A park ranger who has been active in conservation for many years says,

(65)   One place I have learned is from *COHDEFOR*. About fifteen years ago *COHDEFOR* was working here with cooperatives. Around 1985 we planted some nurseries of pine trees. We always worked with *COHDEFOR* on this, and I was working there so I have had a lot of instructions from *COHDEFOR*. . . . And from *PANACAM* . . . I learned that it is

important to take care of the forest, that was where we began to notice that the forest was giving us what we needed to live. They pointed out the pure air and also protected the water for us, and the forest is where animals are produced. . . . They took us to see the forest, what the forest produced, and why it should be taken care of—for example, the animals, too. It's that now the animals—before we didn't see them because the forest had been burned earlier. It had been cleared. Also there was hunting. People hunted animals. Now there isn't. This is prohibited so that the animals can reproduce rather than disappear. So they have given us a lot of ideas and given us a lot of talks about this. (H8)

The arrival of the national park was commonly credited with calling people's attention to the importance of conservation, sometimes highlighting ideas of unequal knowledge and power.

(66)   The National Park has come to teach us to stop [cutting trees]; it is not prohibited, it's just bad for us. The mother [knows] but her son does not; the child does not know. So the mother says, "Shhhh, do not do that because it is bad." She says it causes damage. She knows how it damages. The child does not know. (H26)

Other NGOs, as well as religious groups, also had an impact, including those working on changing agricultural practices and forest conservation in relation to watershed management and those working on social issues.

(67)   Well, a lot of people have come here and have explained to us, have given us classes. Engineers have come from the institution of *El Cajón* and from *Aldea Global*, and others have come. They have taught us how to technify our parcels so that we don't need so much land and don't have to go from one place to another. (H18)

(68)   [I learned about forests from] the small program for women's development that I participate in. We have a number of women. It is composed of three parts: The part about the development of a personal identity as a woman. The part of health is focused on problems that women see and feel. And the third is the part that deals with women and nature. So, of course, we have reflected a lot. We have read, and through the Bible we have analyzed a lot and found that all the catechism of the church is very closely related to nature. And clearly because the reserve was placed here and we are inside it, through this we have learned, too. (H14)

(69)   The people, many people are changing. Because there are organized groups that bring people here, for example through the Catholic Church. They are training lot of people, who are learning a lot about the environment and what they say has a lot to do with the environment.

And when they came here people began sharing these things. They are doing them, and they think the same as what they have heard. (H11)

Park guards recruited in the local community play an important intermediary role in transferring information to local people in their communities, and local people noted the role that they have played in transmitting information.

(70)   We have the park guards. They go to training sessions and learn things like how to use wood. They are here, and we learn from them. They have helped, because [the park guard] lives here. (H16)

COHDEFOR and CAMNP presented videos and gave talks in communities, and these clearly had a significant impact on people.

(71)   [I learned about forests], in part from COHDEFOR and the other part from *Aldea Global*, who also came in and gave us ideas. What we could do to survive in this place. Teaching us to no longer burn, not to cut. Showing us a program of agriculture where you work the same land so you don't continue to clear . . . we had a video . . . brought by COHDEFOR, and also by *Aldea Global*. (H3)

(72)   I have been learning [about forests], I came from the school in the main valley. . . . They brought a film [about the Cerro Azul Park]. . . . [It was] very nice, there were forests. . . . It was pretty, one would be very cool there. (H12)

The radio was also an important source of environmental knowledge and information, again although people often talk about it in relation to, or supporting, other sources of environmental information, as indicated by the following responses:

(73)   Me? . . . [I learned] mostly from the radio, they are advising people and that is when I think about this. . . . In the dry season there is a program that advises people not to burn the forests, but now this program is over. . . . Yes, I like it when I hear a program. I like it. I wish everyone would think like this. About taking care [of the forests]. (H22)

(74)   Most of what I know [about forests] I have learned on the radio, from news, and in meetings with people who know about this subject. (H21)

(75)   In school they taught me about the benefits of the forest and all this, and also [I learned] from programs I have listened to on the radio, and talks that they have come to give here, talks at the school. So, through this one begins to see the benefits that one has, what hurts and doesn't hurt the forest, or how to maintain the forest. I learned like this because I like to learn a little of everything and I have always enjoyed learning something everyday. . . . I have listened to a [radio] program. There are several on

international broadcasts. There are programs from the government, for example I have listened to a program that is called *Eco Radio* that talks about the benefits; why the forest should be taken care of; about the ecology—including the flora, the fauna, all this. So I listen to it all and I think that it is true, what they say about needing to take care of the sources of water. There is one program, for example about how the water comes from the forest. (H17)

(76)   [I learned from] programs on the radio . . . because right now the radio station always has a program, *Green Horizons*. It seems like *Aldea Global* is giving them this program during the weekdays. . . . It talks about important things. It is a very good program, and I think it is resolving a few of the problems that exist in many communities. (H1)

In many ways, taking care of the forest was seen as something new that came from outside and something very different from what was learned from one's parents, who mostly felled trees and converted forest to agricultural lands. But people changed over time, and parents often changed their environmental views along with the younger generation. Parents and other mentors were often seen as important influences. In fact, parents were most often cited when we asked, "Of all the sources of information about forests, which was the most important." One in five persons surveyed indicated that their parents were their most important source of information about forests.

(77)   RESP   If I learned about forests from [my father]? No, I have learned from other people. [My father] didn't talk about this. These people were from the older generation. My father died when he was one hundred ten years old. . . . And the way things were in those times . . . to fell a tree, you just grabbed an axe and did it. But the times have changed. (H2)

(78)   My father only felled trees. When he came here this was a great big forest. But he came here when people were planting crops. Later he worked to restore the forest. . . . At the end, he saw the damage, so he dedicated himself to protecting forests. Because if you do this, it protects the springs. He always did his part for growing crops and his part for protection. (H9)

(79)   I used to work with a German "gringo" over there in Mazcala. I worked in the coffee. He was the foreman for the owner of the farm, in charge of the workers in the processing plant. We would talk on occasion. He had a pine plantation there. And I told him that it would be good to cut those pines to make farms. "No, no," he told me. "No, no, no." "No," he told me. "Don't fell trees, it is better to have some young *guamiles* in another place for agriculture, but these pine trees, no. I'm not going to fell them; I'm going to conserve them." He told me about erosion and about conserving the forest. "You have to take care," he told me. This was many years ago. You have to take care of things. (H10)

(80) I learned this from my father, because he would take us out with him to help him. He told us a lot about taking care of things. . . . He didn't know anything about knocking over a great big tree in the forest. When he came here, he bought the farm already made, he didn't fell the forest, the people who felled it were the natives from here. And since we came from another place, we came to fix up the farm; we didn't know what it was like to knock over the forest.

INTER   And later he taught this to you, telling you these things about leaving trees, for example?

RESP   No, it's that for them, there wasn't any of this yet. There wasn't any of this about having to take care. . . . There wasn't any of this, they hadn't come here planning to take care of the trees. . . . [But] Papi has received a lot of training. . . . I never went to any of these trainings, but he has. . . . It's that he is now a part of this. It took a long time for him to learn about having to take care of trees, but now, now that he has received this training, now he knows more, now he has more experience with protecting the forest. (H7)

It is clear in many of the above quotes that personal experiences validated outside messages about the need for forest conservation, and a number of people indicated that an important way that they had learned about forests was on their own, through personal experiences. For example,

(81) It is mostly nature that teaches a person. . . . Because, look, I have this forest, that I told you about, on my property. And there I learned that the parts near this forest stayed more humid, and you notice the coolness. . . . That's where it seems I learned the most, from nature. . . . Nature teaches you a lot. (H6)

(82) I have learned [about forests] from working the land. And I know that where there aren't trees you can't grow crops. Because I know the wind will blow, and when the wind blows the trees will stop it and the crops won't fall over. Because I have tried it. And besides this, where there is wood, there are springs. . . . I know it because I have grown crops, because I felt the grace of God, and . . . that is why I am . . . why I can give testimony for the forest. (H23)

(83) I learned it in, or I have had courses from *COHDEFOR*. But more than anything I have learned here, in this place. Because I have learned that the forest is useful when it is there, and about the changes that have occurred when the forest was destroyed. There are changes that you see; not because someone tells you something, but because you have seen it in real flesh. You know about the changes . . . so you already know that forest is the best, it is better to regenerate the forest than to destroy it. . . . Yes, from living here. I have seen the change in the community due to lack of forest. (H20)

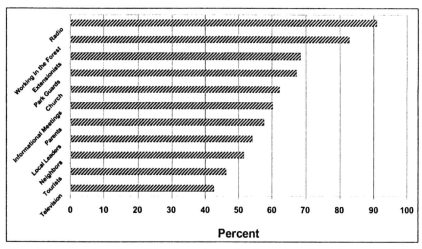

Figure 4.3.   Proportion who said they learned what they know about forests by source of information, Cerro Azul Meambar, Honduras.

The results of our survey show the relative importance of the different sources of information about forests. In terms of media, radio programs were most important in this region. Radios were widely available, while access to a television in the region was relatively rare. Lack of electricity in most of the villages in the park

Figure 4.4.   Group of landowners in Cerro Azul Meambar National Park, Honduras.

limited the use of televisions. As indicated above, radio programs about the forest were widely received and an important vehicle for information dissemination by both *Aldea Global* and *COHDEFOR*.

We asked people whether they talked about trees with other people, and then with whom they talked, to gauge the salience of topics related to trees and forests in everyday life. It was common for people to indicate that they talked about trees mostly with friends and family members. In some cases, there was a feeling that talking about trees and forests more generally in the community was not a socially acceptable topic or could provoke confrontation. Yet there were some indications that it is growing in importance as a general topic as effects attributed to forest loss are observed.

(84) I talk with my children. . . . Things have changed. My father didn't, because of the way he was raised. . . . I talk with my children, about how things are. (H2)

(85) RESP [I talk to my children] about the forest. . . . That we have decided to never burn; to never smoke the earth; to not deforest. And about trying to plant trees around springs so that they never stop existing.
INTER So you talk about this within your family?
RESP Yes, but just with the family in the house. (H1)

(86) INTER Do you talk to other people about trees and forests?
RESP In the first place with the children . . . [and] I talk to friends. Close friends. (H6)

(87) RESP Not everyone thinks the same. There are people who, the more they are told to take care, the more they burn and fell trees. There are all kinds of people. So they don't like it when you give them advice. They get mad.
INTER Do you talk to other people about forests or trees?
RESP Very little. (H22)

(88) INTER Do you talk to people about forests and trees?
RESP Only like this, commentaries that one makes sometimes with family, friends, but not with other people. (H17)

(89) RESP [I talk about trees] with a group of women, with children from the catechism, with my children, with all my friends that I can talk to, with anybody I can talk to about the natural environment, I do.
INTER And what do they think?
RESP Some of them share my ideas. Others no, but I don't talk to them much.
INTER If they don't have the same opinions you do, what do they think?
RESP To give an example, one day I was talking to a friend who isn't from the community. He's a very good friend, and we were talking—there were about four of us talking—and we came to this theme of the pol-

lution of the environment. We were talking about this, and one of them said to us—talking in the words he spoke, "In the end this is what I know, everything you people are saying is garbage," he said, "because how many years have we been living here in Cerro Azul?" He said, " and in Cerro Azul . . . the river has always been there." He said, " and the coffee has always produced, and now why do you say that the river is polluted, if all this time it has been the same? Let's stop talking about this," he said, "and understand that the things we are seeing are signs of the end of the earth, like the Bible says. The punishment of God is what is going to come here to us, it's not the pollution of the environment or of nature and all this," he said. So someone told him, another person with whom we were sharing opinions, told him, "Look, you are wrong," he told him, "because, look," he told him, "the way things actually are—we don't have water, the river is dirty, and all this; these are consequences of what we have been doing all these years," he said. "And the other thing that you haven't noticed about these things you say," the other person said, " we were three children growing up along this river, and it was big, I had more water. I don't think it is a punishment from God, I think they are consequences of our sins," he told the other. So the first man said, "I believe this, you are three donkeys that don't even believe in God anymore," he said. So these are the opinions that we have here. (H14)

The community-based park guards believed talking with people about trees and forests to be an important part of their job and talked about how they did it.

(90) Sometimes [I talk about trees and forests] when I am with the others, from other communities, for example the park guards from other places. Sometimes the park guards get together to take care of the forest, because, they are park guards. . . . I like to tell others that they should plant trees, that we need to take care of the springs, all this. (H7)

(91) [The park rangers have] worked with a lot of communities; we have visited a lot of communities. . . . We tell people that each [park ranger] is responsible for their zone, for their community, and that we will take care of things together. That we don't let people start fires; that if a tree is felled just to fell it, that the tree is wasted, even the firewood is wasted, it is burned up. . . . And when someone starts to commit an infraction, I go and say, with good manners, "Look at this here, if you need a tree you need to ask for a permit, so you won't be punished by the law." I get things started, and they do it. (H15)

(92) I have the opportunity to talk to people; people ask me things. I have the responsibility to make them aware and make them know a lot of things. . . . For example, when someone wants to cut some lumber, or something like that, they ask me how to do it, why a permit is needed,

and how to get one. And I tell them why they need a permit, and that if you cut a tree you are supposed to plant two more. I explain all this to them. . . . When they cut trees, they are asked to plant two for each one they cut. . . . They ask me why they need to plant trees, and I tell them that the trees that they plant are replacements for the one they cut. That with time these trees will grow and be the same, and will provide benefits. Someday they can cut these trees too, I tell them. . . . They have a lot of questions, they send me to see if a tree is okay to cut or if it is not okay and they have to look for another one. They say that I have good knowledge of which tree to cut, because before they cut trees that were not good. They were too soft and were only good for firewood. And they don't want to cut trees and waste them. People don't know how to do it. If the tree is soft, or when the wood won't last, they say that the tree isn't any good, when the real reason is that the tree wasn't ready to cut. Trees have a time when they should be cut. (H11)

Regulations

People attributed a great deal of the change in behavior to the laws and regulations for forest clearing. In some cases, the effect was getting people's attention and making them aware that forest clearing is no longer permitted. There are several different ways that people think about laws. Some people think that most people realize that felling trees and clearing forest hurts their own interests and think of the laws as something extra that provides additional support. But there was also an acknowledgement that there would always be some people who would tend to cut trees and not follow guidelines and that the laws provided the authority that was necessary to stop these people.

(93) INTER   And how are the forests and park protected now?
RESP   Because people are a little afraid, because it is visited more often by people from *PANACAM*, from *COHDEFOR*, and people now are afraid, to destroy much; to go into the forest. (H20)

(94) No, [forest clearing around water], no. Because today there is a rule that if someone is clearing, this person attracts attention and has to pay a fine. So now we all know that we have to protect the springs, not clear around them. (H8)

(95) INTER   So, is it because people here don't want to destroy the forest any more, or is it because of the law against this?
RESP   It's partly because of the law of the government that prohibits entry [to the reserve] to clear forests, and also because we, the people who live here see that it is bad for us. Because if we clear forest, the waters can dry up, and it would be a disaster for those who live here. (H3)

(96)   Like I told you, I think that a lot of us aren't in agreement with burning, nor with cutting trees improperly. But, like I told you, without authority there's nothing one can do. A long time ago, I had a field up above and some men came by and felled some great big *cedro* trees, the slash is still up there. They took out just a little wood and left the tree, the slash is still up there. (H10)

These sentiments about the importance of government regulations in protecting forests were widely shared as indicated by our survey results. Most people agreed with the following statements:

- "If we did not have laws to protect forests, we would have far fewer trees" (96% agree).
- "If people were permitted to cut all the trees they wanted, they wouldn't know when to stop" (95% agree).
- "People don't burn on the land they cultivate because they are afraid of the government" (80% agree).

The general sense of what people say is not that they are completely opposed to tree cutting and even forest clearing, but rather that they are opposed to indiscriminate cutting. Although getting a permit can be an onerous process, there is a sense that it is reasonable to require people to get a permit, that the permit system works fairly well in that people who really need wood for household use can get a permit, and that without permits some people would find it too easy to fell trees and clear forests and that this would have detrimental effects on the community as a whole. The following responses express these sentiments:

(97)   I think that it is good [that cutting trees is prohibited] because if you are going to use a tree, you ask for permission and they give it to you; then you can use your wood. I think if it wasn't like this things would be worse because people would make deals and clear all the forest if they didn't have to pay a fine or anything like this. . . . It's not like this now, the people are afraid that someone will see what they are doing. (H4)

(98)   INTER   And do you think that there are people who need a guard to maintain the forests?
RESP   Always, because there are people that always say, "Now we are happy, we can do whatever we want." So it is always necessary to have a guard; it is always necessary. (H3)

(99)   INTER   And if you need a tree here in the community, for example to build a house, let's say, what do you have to do to cut one, can you just go out an cut one?
RESP   No, you can't. . . . You have to get a permit in Meambar, go to *COHDEFOR*, to the municipality, and they will give you a form. This

has to be signed by the *auxiliar* from here, the president of the . . . *patronato*, and after the president . . . it has to go to another person, a man here in Cerito, too. And from there it goes over there, to the town of Meambar. . . . He signs it, and when this permit gets there with all the signatures and everything, you go and find a tree, a pine tree. And you ask the owner of the land, too, and he has to sign it, too, the owner of the land. . . . That's the way it is today. It's very well regulated. . . . For one of these permits you have to do a lot of things for them to give it to you. . . . Before you just went out. . . . You cut something. You cut yourself a little piece and the rest was wasted. Not anymore.

INTER And which do you like better, the earlier system of just going out and cutting, telling the owner to give you a tree, or the system now where there's a lot of hassle to do this?

RESP I . . . well . . . the way things are now, it's better to have to ask for it. Like it is now. . . . I like it better. Do you know why? Because I may not cut any wood, but there are others who cut a lot. . . . I like it better like this because they always give you the permit, where before, you couldn't cut because all the wood had been destroyed. (H2)

Responsibility

When we asked who had the responsibility for taking care of the forest, a number of people mentioned park guards, undoubtedly because they are present in the community and have official responsibilities for forest protection. In a community where a park guard had resigned, people said that no one was responsible anymore. Other people noted that the *patronato* and other local political authorities had responsibility. But an equally large group felt that everyone had the responsibility because everyone received some benefits from the forest. The following responses show the range of parties considered responsible for forest care:

(100) In the community, they name a park guard. . . . The park guard spends all his time going around where there is forest so that they are not cutting *guamiles* and forest, and takes care of not only the forest but also the animals. (H1)

(101) Look, here, right now, I don't know [who is responsible for taking care of the forest]. Because there was a man, he was in charge of taking care, for example, of these permits when you have to fell a tree and things like that. He was in charge of giving them out and everything. But a little while ago he died, and so now I think that there isn't anyone. I don't know if they have named anyone, but I don't think they have, yet. (H17)

(102) RESP Well, I think that it is the *patronato* [that is responsible]. . . . The *patronato* has to be on top of everything, they have to look and see if anyone is damaging the forest, they have to go and be sure that the forest isn't cut.

INTER   And can you give me an example or tell me a story about when the *patronato* has taken care of the forest?

RESP   Some guy had gotten permission to saw a tree, and went out with his chainsaw, and he didn't just saw one but he felled several trees, and they had to call the municipality. . . . They stopped it. If they had let it continue, they would have sawed all the wood, all the trees. People always saw some, but this person was going to sell outside the community, wood that was to be used there in the community by someone who needed it. But [you have to use the wood] in the same community; you can't sell it outside. If they see someone taking a piece of lumber out, they demand it back. (H7)

(103) Well . . . I think that the responsibility in the village for taking care [of the forest] belongs to the communal authorities. Like the *patronato*, the assistant mayors. . . . If the assistant mayor or a communal authority sees someone that is destroying the forest, that has cut down a tree, he sets them straight. (H25)

(104) I think everyone [has responsibility for taking care of trees and forest]. . . . The community, and each person has personal responsibility, every person has to take care of forests. Everyone in the community can take care of something or other. (H22)

(105) [The responsibility for taking care of the forest in this community] is with us, the inhabitants of the community, because we are the beneficiaries. Not the institutions, because we are the ones who take care of this. Perhaps the organizations that have this responsibility can guide us. But it's the community. (H21)

(106) RESP   I understand that we have [responsibility for taking care of forests and trees]. . . . I think that one part is the community's, and also the organizations'. Because if a community is left alone perhaps they won't be able to carry out all the work that is required, they always need help from the organizations.

INTER   And why can't the communities do it alone?

RESP   I think that maybe is because of the economic aspects; because we can't take care of the forest ourselves and protect it with only the little fund of money we have. Because, to protect, to plant—you have to make nurseries and plant trees. So perhaps the community can't develop this, only because some people are needed to do the work. . . . The park guards are paid for by *Aldea Global*. (H8)

What Happens When Someone Cuts a Tree or Clears Forest?

To assess the strength of social norms against forest clearing, we asked what would happen if someone felled a tree or cleared forest. A few people said that they would report that person to the authorities or the *patronato*. The question of reporting people seemed to depend to some extent on an assessment of whether real damage was being caused, as opposed to felling a tree for a need. Similarly, there were indications that the local officials from the *patronato* make judgments similar to those of our interviewees about the balance between damage and needs in deciding whether to report people to higher authorities in the municipality or *COHDEFOR* or whether to deal with an infraction locally.

(107) INTER   What do you think would happen if someone started to cut down trees here in the community?
RESP   They would be cutting . . . cutting . . . ruining nature.
INTER   Would someone scold them, or what would happen if they were there doing something, damaging the environment by cutting trees? What would happen here in the community? How would they react?
RESP   They would react by reporting them. . . . People would report them, they would make a lot of noise and the *patronato* would notice and send the people to the municipality.
INTER   And has this happened here in this community, that someone reported another person?
RESP   Yes, it has happened. . . . If they are deforesting and are damaging the same community, you have to take action. Because if not, there isn't respect. And it's for the good of everyone, the person who is reporting as well as the person who is felling. (H1)

(108) INTER   What do you think would happen if someone from this community started to cut trees?
RESP   I think they would have to be reported.
INTER   Would you?
RESP   Perhaps, perhaps. I might tell someone, perhaps.
INTER   Is that what you should do?
RESP   It is, if someone is really destroying. (H6)

A park guard talked about how he would work with the *patronato* to enforce the laws against tree felling, at the same time indicating flexibility in cases of true need.

(109) INTER   What do you think would happen if someone cut trees here in the community?
RESP   The force of the community would be thrown upon them, because we are organized to take care and if someone wants to use resources they should look for a legal way. But to keep people from making a mistake, people are made aware why they shouldn't do it. People have responded in that, if they need a tree, it's worth coming to me and I will talk to the *patronato*. Then we will do an analysis and give the right tree. When the person is poor and doesn't have any money to

go to the municipality to ask for this tree, and from there they will be sent to Siguatepeque, we don't let it leave here. We try to resolve it here, that they can pay a little more, some three lempiras, to the *patronato* so that this *campesino* doesn't have to waste time and money—rather than sending him to Siguatepeque where they will tell him "no" because he is poor. For people with connections, they might get this resolved. They solve their problems. When it deals with five pine trees, they will resolve it. But if it is just one, they get lazy and can't do the work. So, to avoid creating these conflicts, we solve the problem for him. The person gets to saw his wood because we can tell it is for the roof of his house. (H15)

When respondents indicated that people would be reported or have trouble with the authorities if they felled trees or cleared forest, we sought examples of when this has happened in order to gauge the likelihood of, and circumstances under which, this would happen. It was often the case that people could not come up with any examples from their own community but may have heard of examples from other communities or from the radio. Many respondents suggested that the reason that their community was doing everything right was that people had been made aware and were taking care of forests. But we did get a number of firsthand accounts of what had happened to people when forests had been cleared illegally. But instances of tree felling in the community were often left unreported if people felt the clearing was justified by need.

(110) INTER   In his community, if someone cut trees how would the community react?
RESP   Look, in general I think that the community is completely on the side of the trees. As you know this is very regulated by the highest authorities of our country. I think at least this person would be condemned. Perhaps not by the community, because the community is very humble, in this respect, but the authorities are strict. Because I heard in the news on the radio, bad news about someone being reported some place or another, they had been seen starting a fire, because they had been cutting trees. So I don't think the community would react, but the authorities would react. . . . They would punish the guilty person. Because many people have already been punished. I heard on the radio that some people had had to pay up to five hundred thousand lempiras [US$42,016] in a fine, for felling trees or clearing forest.
INTER   So you have heard of cases on the radio, but do you know of anyone here in this community?
RESP   No, look, not here in the community because up until now this hasn't happened in the community; nothing like this. You hear rumors

that they are going to be looking for people, that they are going to see whoever is setting fires and take them to jail. They are going to fine them, all this. But up until now they haven't punished anyone yet, that I know of. (H21)

(111)   RESP   Here, where I live, no, but in other communities, yes. There have been some reports; perhaps when someone makes a *milpa* near a spring, fells a *guamil*. It ends up cleared and they have to be reported, perhaps because of the spring.

INTER   And if someone in the community cuts one, two, or three trees, what would happen? What would the community do?

RESP   If it is to use, well, we wouldn't say anything. If someone is going to build a house, for example, and they are going to fell a couple of trees to get some wood, they wouldn't be reported because it is for use. (H19)

(112)   RESP   We respect the land and we respect the trees. We conserve the trees like we conserve our children, that's how we conserve the trees. We no longer go around felling trees, rather we take care of them and if we see a person ruining trees, felling them, we report him to the authorities. . . . If it is a serious crime we call the police, and they will come here and see where they are sawing or where they are taking out wood, and they will give them the ticket and call them to court.

INTER   Perhaps you could tell us about a time you had to call the police.

RESP   The problem was when they were taking out some wood over there. Well, it was here, near Buena Vista that someone was milling wood. They took them away. They were reported to a village here on the other side. Not here, no. Here if people are going to cut a tree it is to use. We sawed a tree that had been there for a long time; had been felled maybe fifteen or twenty years before. We took out some wood, but we justified [doing] it for the house, for the stove. (H24)

(113)   INTER   Have you yourself reported people?

RESP   One time a man came here from another community, one very far from Cerro Azul. I saw him mill some *cedro* trees and a mahogany. He had a permit from *COHDEFOR* and permission from the municipality, because he was going to mill a tree to sell the wood in Zimatepec. But those people over there gave him a permit, and he knew that mahogany and cedar were here near the river. It said that they had given permission to the man to take out the wood. The man asked the *patronato* to put their seal on the permit. But we didn't put our seal on it, and this man went and reported us, said that we weren't following the law because we wouldn't give him the wood. And we went and fought for our rights with *COHDEFOR*, with the municipality, but we wouldn't let him take out the wood. They tried to put us in jail for what we were doing, but we didn't let the wood be taken. We weren't afraid. (H14)

(114) INTER   What do you think would happen here if someone went out and cut trees?

RESP   There was an example. A man from down here below started to cut some trees, and it was to make a house here in the community. But he hadn't communicated with the people in the *patronato*. He hadn't gotten authorization from the *patronato*. They called a meeting and they looked at a lot of things and afterwards they fined him one hundred fifty lempiras [US$12.60]. . . . [He was fined] by the *patronato*, and he paid them. And from this date forward they authorized a permit so he would be guaranteed to be legal. . . . The fine that they assessed was one hundred fifty lempiras for having cut those trees without knowledge of the *patronato*. This was just a little while ago, it was about a month ago.

INTER   And what did this man do?

RESP   He was mad when this happened, but after a while he understood the reason and he paid the one hundred fifty lempiras and after that they met with people from the municipality and people from *PANACAM* to give him the permit.

INTER   And do you think that the community here in general supports the *patronato* in this? When they fined this man, was the community in agreement with the fine?

RESP   They aren't in agreement with the fines, but . . . it was a part of the agreement that they had with the municipality that when someone does things illegal they are going to call a meeting here. And if they agree with the opinion of the *patronato* then they will settle the problem. And if not they will pass it over to the municipality.

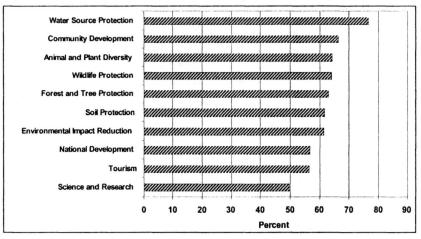

Figure 4.5.   Proportion who thought the park was very important for selected reasons, Cerro Azul Meambar, Honduras.

INTER   But why aren't the people in agreement with the *patronato*?
RESP   They say that the *patronato* doesn't have legal authority and it is
true that there's not really a law to enforce. But with this man they did
a whole lot of things that day, and they said if he was in agreement he
could contribute something to the community. And if not, they were
going to confiscate the wood. So he agreed. He said, "I will pay you. I
will pay what you ask . . . give me the authorization." Because it was a
failure to communicate that he had with the people here. He had cut
three green trees. (H11)

Forest Conservation and the National Park

The communities that we studied in Honduras were located inside the park, in an
area zoned for human use and sustainable development that surrounds a strictly
protected core zone. We sought to specifically engage respondents in discussions
about the park since, for local residents, the park had different implications than
forest conservation alone.

Why the Park Exists

We asked them why they thought the park was created, what benefit the park
provided, what damages or problems it caused, what they thought would happen
if the park were eliminated, and who they thought benefited from the park.

In general people understood that the park had been created for environmental
purposes like maintaining water supplies, protecting wildlife, and keeping forests
intact for all the benefits that they associated with them. Water and its link to forests
were widely seen as important reasons for the park, both for local use and for the
reservoir and associated water and electric projects. For example,

(115) I think that the park exists, because . . . I think that this side of this park
is where all the springs are. I think that this park that was made here is
for the protection of the water that is here. So I think that this is why
the park was made here. (H8)

(116) It seems to me that the national park is good for many people. It is not
just good here for us—it's good for people who live here because of
the water. These waters are going to end up near [Lake] Yajoa and these
waters are going to be used in the hydroelectric projects. That's why its
important to take care of forests, so the waters don't diminish; aren't lost.
And also for us . . . before there was abundant water here . . . but today
we have to collect water even here. It's starting to rain and the waters are
coming back a little. But the water is diminishing. Now we're beginning
to often lack water here. I think that taking care of the forest is important
for many people. (H10)

Wildlife was also frequently mentioned as a reason for the park, both as the main benefit and also as one of a set of reasons that often included the most frequently mentioned benefits of forests: air, water, and wildlife.

(117) I think that this park is there, because there was so much destruction. There are [parks] in different places . . . for the animals . . . so that the birds, trees, forests, and water aren't destroyed. All this, I think this is why they made it. (H22)

(118) INTER   And why does the park exist?
RESP   Well, for one thing to breed animals. So, for example, there are more, more animals, and . . . because they have been persecuted. You can see that before, a long time ago, before 1970, there were all kinds of animals. There were monkeys, all kinds of animals. Now you don't see anything. Why? Because people destroyed them. . . . By hunting . . . so it was being lost, all the fauna, the animals. That's why it is important, and now there are starting to be animals again. . . . I think besides the animals there is the maintenance of the water. Always, because of this, we have a great abundance of water. . . . And the oxygen. . . . Pure air, I think that this doesn't only benefit those of us who live around it, but that it is giving oxygen even to, I think, other nations. . . . Because the air travels. (H3)

(119) The benefit that I find from having the park is that we have abundant water, the timber is developing there, and also the animals are reproducing; and clearly we are receiving pure air, it's a different climate, because it is cool. (H8)

(120) The benefits that [the park] brings involve a better way of living, because we no longer drink contaminated water. Because if you drink water that is from the forest, you will drink good water. Good water, not like water from the town; the water that you drink there is very polluted. If you drink water there in the forest it is good water and very cold, too. (H7)

The idea that that park existed to meet global interests, or the interests of unknown outside interests, was pervasive. The following interchanges were typical:

(121) RESP   Why does the park exist?
RESP   I think it came about because of the international need for more production of oxygen. (H14)

(122) INTER   Why do you think that the park exists, what's it for?
RESP   Well, I think that because these are natural reserves, that . . . I think that I have heard in various programs that there are . . . because here in Honduras there are a lot of national parks. So I have heard that the government. . . . I don't know if they have sold them. . . . How do I explain it? . . . So that these zones will be maintained virgin, like they

are. So I think that people have the responsibility to take care of this park, the owners. .... I think that it is for this reason ... they see the forest deteriorating more every year, and these zones are important. And because of this they want to take care of and make people understand that they should take care of them for their own benefit. This is what I think. (H17)

We asked the individuals surveyed how important the park was in fulfilling a number of functions. Water source protection was considered very important by the largest proportion of individuals, but other environmental protection functions were also considered very important: maintenance of animal and plant diversity, wildlife protection, forest protection, and soil protection and environmental impact reduction. However, community development was also considered to be one of the most important functions of the park. This function is especially significant since the communities are located within the park's buffer zone. Not only are residents expected to contribute to the protection of the park, but they expect to benefit materially from a well-conserved park.

Consistent with the idea that the park was affiliated with outside interests, there were a few people who said that they knew very little about why the park was created, even though they resided in the park buffer zone. For example,

(123) INTER   And do you know what the purpose of the park is?
RESP   I'm not involved in the park right now, no.
INTER   Nobody has come here to talk about this?
RESP   No, or perhaps they came. I have been sick, or if not, I was out in the field weeding beans. (H23)

Figure 4.6.   Buffer zone sign in a village center, Cerro Azul Meambar National Park, Honduras.

(124) INTER   In your opinion, why does the park exist or what is it good for?

RESP   Look, I will tell you again, I have a bad memory. I have been told. I know that the park helps the village. But after that, I know there are other reasons for it, or benefits that it has. . . . I have been told, but I forgot. (H5)

Many of the benefits that people talked about in relation to the park had more to do with potential benefits. There seemed to be significant hope that the park would lead to some improvements in their life by bringing tourists and fostering development.

(125) RESP   Well, I think that . . . I think because I have seen, for example, over time I have seen that things have changed here, that foreign people come. That more people come and there are opportunities so that one can sometimes, if the community needs something and there are organizations, that one can obtain some aid. . . . I have also said that with the opening of the highway tourists will come, there will be more tourists coming to see the park, and all this is progress for the community, because it can open up opportunities for people. (H17)

(126) For us, [the park] is good, because, for example, tourists are already coming to [our] village and more will come. For us, no, but for those that are living modestly, well they will see something good. . . . Look how people come, even those we don't know. To have contact with the people, to be social with the people. To have contact with people from other places, because they are coming, have already bought things. . . . Little things; for example, they eat fruit. . . . I don't know if you noticed that we put little things out in front—bananas, oranges, mangos—we sell these. And sometimes a person comes who wants to buy to resell, and I would like the foreign tourists to come here. Later, God willing, if it is fixed up right, the people will keep coming. Because this park is at the level—it seems to me, although people won't believe me—this park is at the national level. What I mean is that it has been advertised, it has already been advertised. Do you think it has been advertised in other countries? (H25)

A number of people seemed to think that the creation of the park by outsiders indicated that the area was important and that, to be managed well, the park would have to have development associated with it. In many ways, the park was seen as something that could be a positive agent for development.

(127) I hope and I think that one day [the park] will make us better off in some way, because they are going to fix things, like the roads. . . . Because in other places the national parks are different from this. They have good

roads. They are well cared for, and there are a lot of animals and many things. Wildlife is conserved. And here we need a little of this. Up above there . . . is a landing strip, a landing strip up there and now it is covered with many trees and all this. This is a good example, you will no longer want to came here in this Toyota, but in an airplane. (H18)

(128) [The park] is mostly to conserve the water, because, look, without forest there is no water. This is certain. What the national park needs is a little bit of care, as is starting to happen. But it needs good means of communication, it needs other care. . . . Here, here many things are needed. Electricity is needed, access to other places is needed. . . . We use a splinter of pine to provide light for us at night. . . . Here, if you want to go to the park, you can only walk there. . . . There should be roads. . . . Here we need a lot of things, we need so many things and we don't have anything. Because these roads are so bad, we don't have light, we don't have communications, we don't have anything. . . . It seems to me that a park should have a telephone in each town to communicate from one place to the other for whatever. You can't do anything now. (H18)

(129) INTER   Do you think that there are any problems associated with having the park? Does the park hurt certain people?
RESP   Look, we don't all understand things the same way. Sometimes there are people who make it out to be bad. These people say things like, Why do you think that this kind of people have come here to say that this is a national park? . . . Honduras has been sold to the United States, they say. That's why they are walking around these mountains. I repeat, at times one tends to look at all these people who are coming and get a little scared. . . . But one knows that the people from these institutions are here for the good of the village, and clearly, who wouldn't want the village to improve? Because we want electricity, we want everything, and without this help I don't think anyone will offer us anything. (H5)

When asked, people generally said that they had no problems with the park, sometimes suggesting that those who objected to it had ulterior motives, like wanting to fell trees, or simply had not yet been educated or gotten the conservation message.

(130) INTER   Any problems that exist because the park is here?
RESP   No, I don't think so. I don't think there are problems. (H6)

(131) INTER   Here in these communities, do you think that there is any problem or damages caused by the park?
RESP   The park? No, for me there is no problem.
INTER   And the park doesn't hurt anybody?
RESP   Some people think so. Some people who perhaps aren't well educated. They say that they are hurt. Because some people, I'm not going

to say everyone, but the majority are educated. . . . There are a few people who can say that they are harmed because they would like to go and fell trees at their pleasure, go and fell and fell. But not all. Perhaps a few. The majority of us are educated now. (H3)

More commonly, people recognized the general benefits of the park and forest conservation, such as the often mentioned air and water benefits, but did not think that they received any specific or more tangible benefits.

(132) INTER   What do you think are the benefits of having a park?
RESP   Here, for us, our only benefit is that it would be good if this helps us not to lose all the forests. I repeat. I have seen things that my children haven't seen, so at least we won't be clearing all the forest. But direct benefits to the community? No, we don't get any. Except for the oxygen, water, things that of course come to us, but direct benefits to the community? No, nothing. (H14)

(133) INTER   So what do you think about the park? Is it important?
RESP   It is important, of course, in the sense that the little bit that is there will be there for the future generations. But the government should see with more clarity the population that exists in it. They should give them some help so they can survive there. So that they don't destroy everything and so that the people can live with what they already have and with that make a balance.
INTER   What are the benefits of having the park here?
RESP   The benefits? No, for us, the community, the only thing is what I told you at the beginning. To have pure air, water. This is the only thing. Because from the government there aren't any benefits. (H13)

Although park residents were less likely to expect benefits of the park to accrue to them directly than to others in their community, more than four out of five surveyed thought that they benefited from the park, however intangible those benefits might be. Almost everyone surveyed (94%) thought that park guards benefited from the park, and almost the same proportion (93%) thought that their own community benefited from the park. On the whole, residents believed that the park was widely beneficial, not only for themselves and their communities but for others in the nation and the world as well.

There were a number of specific complaints about the way that the government had treated people and made allowances for their livelihoods. On the other hand, a number of people indicated that things had not turned out as badly as they had feared when they first heard about the park and that in fact the government had allowed them to continue to meet their livelihood needs. The following responses are examples of such sentiments:

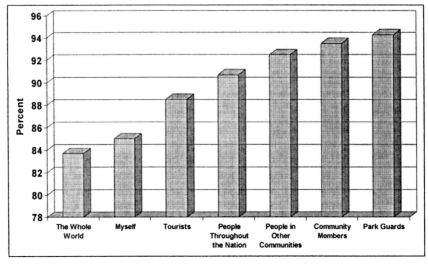

Figure 4.7. Proportion who believed selected groups benefit from the park, Cerro Azul Meambar, Honduras.

(134) INTER   And you said [the park was established] in 1986, but you didn't know about it until 1990. What was the reaction of the community on knowing that the government had decreed this national park?
RESP   Look, there was a lot of anticipation, because when they announced all this to us some people said that they were going to remove us from here. Others said that we were going to have to give up our farms and they were going to fill them up with trees; that they were going to "knock us off," as they say. Others said that they were going to make laws so we wouldn't be able to live here. So many things were said. But I would say that the community became partners two or three years ago. It wasn't easy for the community to become a partner, for the situation to become more balanced. From our perspective, they were above us and they were going to squash us. . . . But [to be better], I think the first thing would be to prepare the people so the impact wouldn't be so hard. It would be another thing to start with the communities. They made decrees, made laws, and all this, perhaps from the point of view of the people who gave the money for these projects. But the communities are the last. I repeat, in 1986 this was decreed a national reserve, and we began to notice this around 1990. There's no reason. They should think about the communities. (H14)

(135) INTER   And does the park hurt anyone in any way?
RESP   No. In the beginning it seemed like it did, that it prohibited us from cutting from the forest. It seemed like this would bring us problems. We said that we wouldn't be able to work anymore. But as it has taken

shape, this project, we have seen that it also benefits us, because of the fact that it has kept us from continuing to fell the forest. . . . In the beginning [we were against the park], because we didn't know what form it was going to take, we said, "We aren't going to be able to grow crops." . . . The majority now are well aware that this brings us benefits. It was at the beginning that everyone thought that if it came we were not going to be able to work, but that's not how it turned out. . . . Now we have many benefits, good results. (H9)

(136) INTER   And do you think that there are any damages or problems from having the park?

RESP   No, I don't think that there is any problem, because in the beginning they said that this was a zone. That there was a zone where it would be prohibited to fell a tree even in your own yard; that everything would be prohibited. So everyone was thinking. We were all worried that we were going to have to do things that we did not want to do, things like that. This is what we understood. But so far, I don't think so, because we haven't felt any change. We don't feel like they have pressured us in any form. (H17)

(137) INTER   Do you think that the park hurts anyone? The fact that the park exists, does this hurt anyone?

RESP   I think it doesn't hurt . . . not anybody. Do you know why? Because in the area of protection, we, how should I say it? We live with our horses, cows, pigs. We live mixed up in the protected area, and this circles us up above, and the water never dries up. (H16)

If the Park Were Eliminated

Another way of getting at people's sense of the importance (or lack of) of the park was to ask them what they thought would happen if the park were eliminated. In answering this question, people returned to many of the common cultural models of forests. Some cited that water would dry up, and the area would turn into a desert. Others thought that there would no longer be pure air, that crops would suffer, that ultimately people would no longer be able to live there, or that the desirable and healthy aspects of the countryside would be replaced with urban ills.

(138) INTER   What would happen to the trees and forest if the park were eliminated?

RESP   Well, it would become a desert, like I said, and we would have a lot of conflict because we would run out of pure air, water. All the resources would run out and we would starve. (H15)

(139) INTER   What do you think would happen to the forests and trees if the park were eliminated?

RESP   Well, we would have a grave problem, because of the problem that there might be a prolonged drought. There wouldn't be any life if the water dried up. We would be eliminated with everything else. And the future generation would have a desert. If there's not some good management of this thing by somebody, it will be the death of us. Especially, those of us who live in this zone. (H13)

(140) INTER   And what do you think would happen to the trees if the park were eliminated?

RESP   [It would be] left like a desert, it would be ugly to look at. It would look ugly. There is nothing like looking at forest, the trees, the birds that are seen going around there, the squirrels, the monkeys and all this. They need it, and like they need it, we need it, too. For coolness, like I said before, all the fresh air that one breathes, all these clean things that one breathes here. Go to [the city of] San Pedro, what you wake up to are the bad odors, dead animals, and rotten things. Because it is polluted there; ferment and pollution. I saw it when I was there recently—two barrels of rotten trash and more. (H24)

Many people felt that the rules and authority of the park were what kept people from clearing forest, that if the park were eliminated people would clear forests and claim land.

(141) INTER   What would happen to these forests if one day there wasn't a national park?

RESP   We would fell it. I would grab my *manzana* [a measure of land, approximately 0.7 hectares], and I would clear it. (H12)

(142) INTER   And what do you think would happen if the park were eliminated?

RESP   I think the forest would be destroyed. . . . Because if the park were eliminated, if there wasn't any one taking care of the park, for example if this park were to be eliminated, the guards that are here would not exist. So anyone who wanted to could go and start a fire in the forest; start a fire and destroy the forest. Clearly, the sources of water would dry up. (H8)

(143) INTER   And what do you think would happen if one day they decided to not have or to change the status of the park?

RESP   Well, I don't know. What I think could happen is that the people would not be afraid. Because the way it is now, at least the people that want to go into the national park are afraid. Because if they wanted to do something, if they were going to kill an animal or start a fire, I think they would feel more free and then we would be left a total desert in a few years. . . . I think that it is probable that they would burn all the forest and the animals would go extinct, because talking about the way it was before, before they weren't afraid of there being park guards; that someone was taking care of the forest. People went out and hunted.

Because I remember when, here, close, there were deer, pacas, *agoutis*. All of these are gone. I remember before, around the community, there were abundant deer, and now, no. And I think these are gone. If no one takes care of the forest, we will end up with nothing. I think, at least I had the opportunity to see deer, and I think that what follows, these children that are growing, are not going to have the opportunity, perhaps only in books. They are not going to have the opportunity to see the wild animals and things like this, so I say that because of this it would be good to always maintain the forest. (H17)

The survey results show that most people agreed that government regulations had an important impact on conservation. There was almost unanimous (96%) agreement with the statement "If we did not have laws that protect the forests, we would have far fewer trees." In addition, almost three-fourths (73%) agreed that the government was responsible for protecting trees. Interestingly, a majority (66%) also agreed that "people in the community could protect the trees without government assistance."

As the response above indicates, some people felt that attitudes and values had changed enough that people would not immediately go back to their old ways. Some also saw that enough community experience had been built up that people would work to try to establish new institutions for forest conservation. For example:

(144) RESP   Look, I think that [the park] exists to maintain the life of the human beings, because . . . if this wasn't here, if this zone hadn't been declared a reserve, I think we would have cleared all this forest.
INTER   Now that the park has existed for five or ten years, if the park disappeared what would happen?
RESP   Well, I can't say, because some of the people are very aware, and others, no. . . . Perhaps [they would] not [go back to clearing forest], because we now are aware that it is very damaging to fell the forest. . . . But without help, from those who are helping, perhaps the people . . . who knows? . . . It would be very difficult. The help that these people from parks give is very important. They help a lot with their training and everything. (H9)

(145) INTER   What would happen here if the park disappeared? Suppose tomorrow came and they said, the park no longer exists, we have erased the law and it doesn't exist? What would happen here?
RESP   To give you an opinion, about the national park, we would have to see what could be done to continue the protection by the authorities. Because the people, without order, will do what they feel like. Let's take an example like when a person has a fence and they take down the fence. It is left open and everyone comes and messes it up. . . . A lot of people

now would like the park to be here always, and if it disappeared, we would
have to do the same thing; protect it. Because we depend on it for life,
because food is life, too. But we won't last even two days without drinking
water. I can withstand hunger, but if I don't drink water I'll dry up.

INTER   So you think that the community could do it? Could they do
it, without funds and everything?

RESP   This place is almost all poor people. All they can do is feed their
bodies. But I think that there would be someone who would send some
things so it could be done, to protect here. There are people, yes, here we
have about fifty men. . . . Here we are ready to [protect the park]; do what
is needed. Because, look, the protection is not only felt here locally, but
it is felt even in other countries. Because I have talked with some people
there in Tegucigalpa, and they told me that these could be jokes, but they
say that the same watershed of *El Cajón* was going to sell electricity to
Nicaragua. (H16)

At least one park ranger believed that the community had gotten to the point
where it would organize itself to protect the park.

(146) If, for example, the organizations in charge of its management no longer
existed? I think that some community leader would take charge. For
example, the people here, the people that I know, that understand everything, I think they would take charge of managing something like local
reserves. Now, what would happen in other communities, I can't say anything. But one responds based on the community where one lives. . . . I
think it would depend on the consent and awareness of each community.
If the laws and the institutions in charge of managing the park would
disappear, I think it would depend on the awareness and consent of each
community. . . . If there weren't any more organizations and there weren't
any more laws, I think the communities would have to wake themselves
up about this to continue to conserve to protect our benefits. (H11)

Who Benefits from the Park

As the responses indicated above, many people feel that they receive some benefits
from the park. Only a few people thought they received no benefits. However,
the benefits that people do recognize are often general and not directly economic.
Many were expressed in the terms of the widely shared "verbal molecules" that
were also used to describe the benefits of forests in general ("forests are life," "pure
air," etc.). Yet people also have a hope that the park will be an agent of development
in the area, both for infrastructure and for a level of tourism that could provide
economic benefits to the communities. There were also indications that some
people felt that many of the benefits of the park accrued to people in other regions

or countries. We asked people who they thought benefited from the park to learn their perspective on the distributions of costs and benefits. Many of the benefits were seen as being universal, as these interchanges demonstrate:

(147) INTER   And who is benefiting from the park?
RESP   Well, I think that who benefits, from all this nature, we all benefit. All, because we say that forest is life for us, and so I think we are all benefiting. (H17)

(148) INTER   And who benefits from the park?
RESP   We all receive them, those of us who live on the edge. Because we are receiving the pure air that is being produced. (H3)

A park ranger described extensive benefits from the park, clearly indicating his enthusiasm for forest conservation.

(149) [Who benefits] from the park? Well, there is a collective benefit as much for us as for the same plants and animals that live in the forest, and I think the birds live from the fruit trees in the same park, and also the animals that live there in the forest, pacas, *agoutis*, these depend on fruits from the forest and also they come to the cultivated zone to eat what man plants in fields there. . . . [The benefit of the park] is collective, for us as well as the animals. . . . I think that here we are very much benefited by this forest, because of the river. Right now the community needs it and this river is useful. We see it as a very large benefit that comes from the forest and is a gift. We don't pay for its health, nor to bathe in this river, nor to wash clothes in the river. Everything is a gift, and I think it is a very large benefit that the forest is giving to us. And there is the firewood that we bring from the forest, which is also given. We don't buy it. And I think that we can say that we find ourselves in a corner of glory where everything is given. And there are great benefits that come to us for free from the forest. And, because of this we should struggle for conservation. (H11)

A number of people felt that the primary beneficiaries of the park were the NGOs and government organizations and their employees who received money for managing the park. Resentment toward this is often tied to the lack of direct economic benefits from the park for residents of local communities.

(150) INTER   And who benefits from the park?
RESP   There are people in charge of watching it. And there are others who are working with it. . . . With *Aldea Global* and *PANACAM*. (H25)

(151) INTER   And who do you think benefits from the park?
RESP   I don't think anyone benefits, because the park belongs to the government. (H24)

(152) INTER   But are there benefits for people here?
RESP   Well, for here, I couldn't tell you. There could be. It would only
be the work that they have given; some work to help these people. But
there's no aid. (H23)

(153) From what I know we don't have big benefits, because from what I have
seen in the park here, no. Nothing like concrete projects. I haven't seen
them. There has been some motivation. There has been a lot. Where
people are getting aware; this is the only thing that you can clearly see
that they have done. But projects, the only thing they have done is increase the awareness of the people. . . . The community is not clear [what
the benefits are]. Because last year we strongly pressured them to help us,
that they would give us a project. In the end they showed us some plans
for a highway, but it was under pressure. A concrete project . . . we need
something . . . I don't know . . . there is the awareness that people have
gotten, but nothing more than this. (H13)

A few people discussed the fact that, due to drinking water and hydroelectric
projects, people in other places were actually receiving more benefits from the
park than local people. Interestingly, even when invited to complain about this,
the tendency was, rather than to begrudge other people their benefits, to use this
as a justification for why communities near the park should be the recipients of
infrastructure improvements to match those people in other places had. In essence,
people used the unequal distribution of benefits not to complain about unfairness
or what others had attained but to make the case that some benefits should be
provided to local people in return for their taking care of the forest. This might
be a reflection of benefits observed to accrue to some park communities. A higher
proportion of those living in more inaccessible communities distant from main
highways or roads agree that local forests benefit people elsewhere more than
those living in local communities. As indicated in figure 4.8, people in the community with best highway access and some success in attracting tourists (Cerro
Azul) are least likely (37%) to think that outsiders benefit more from local forests.
In contrast, people living in the most remote community (Palmital) are more
likely than their counterparts in Cerro Azul to think that outsiders benefit most
from local forests.[1]

(154) INTER   Are there some groups or some people who benefit more
from the park than others? Or are the benefits general?
RESP   The benefits are general.
INTER   There aren't any groups that might receive more benefits?
RESP   No, here, no, because . . . from here there are benefits for other
villages. For example, water, because over there in [another community]
they receive water from here. From the waterfall to there, they get water,

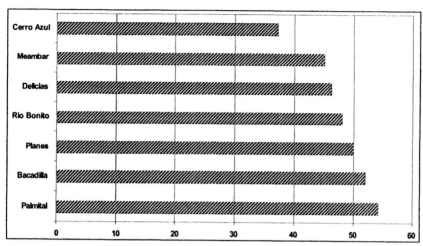

Figure 4.8.   Proportion who agreed that local forest benefited persons elsewhere more than those living in local communities, Cerro Azul Meambar, Honduras.

good water. . . . The water that we drink in the village is bad water. They drink better water in [the other community] than we drink here.

INTER   Do you think this is fair or unfair?

RESP   I think it is unfair, because it is us here that should have good drinking water. . . . Because [the benefits should go to] the ones that take care of the forest. That waterfall up there, we have planted trees. . . . We have gone to this waterfall to plant trees, because the waterfall there, when they declared it, when they said that they were going to see the waterfall, there didn't used to be any trees and now they are there. (H7)

(155) INTER   Are there some groups of people in the community who benefit from the park more than others?

RESP   I think that it benefits all of us. The benefit is for everyone.

INTER   But are there other communities that receive more benefits than this community?

RESP   Perhaps in some ways, yes, because [our community], for example has always been, well . . . it is that [our community] has always been left for last . . . because we have been trying to get *Aldea Global* to bring the boss here, the general boss. . . . Whereas in other places he has come more frequently, the general boss of the park. But for us it has been really hard to get him to come here. We were thinking he had forgotten us.

INTER   And do you think this is fair?

RESP   No, because the truth is that we are very, very interested in conserving this park. We had always thought that *Aldea Global* would treat us in another manner; that we at least get what we deserve, because we really want to take care of what we have. (H9)

(156) INTER   Who benefits from the national park?

RESP   From the national park, I think that those that are in this sector are benefiting. And the companies are benefiting, and [the national electric company]. Business, that is to say businesses that are factories, because that is where the electricity is going from this watershed of *El Cajón*. Also, we are benefiting from the television.

INTER   Because you have electricity to watch television, or because . . . ?

RESP   Let's say, some people already have their electricity. Where does this come from? The watershed of *El Cajón*, there is a benefit because there is something with which to freeze things. It's not here yet, but we are thinking about it. . . . The electricity isn't here, but we are thinking about it. To have electricity is to have some advancement here because we can have new things. For example there isn't a repair shop here, because there isn't electricity. There are cars, but you have to take them out.

INTER   And do you think it is fair that some groups of people benefit more from the park than others? For example, do you think it is just that some companies are benefiting while this community doesn't have electricity?

RESP   Of course.

INTER   It's fair? . . . Why?

RESP   Because here we depend on what we take care of. We benefit here, and others are benefiting. . . . For me, it is unfair for us but fair for others. But we're going to catch up.

INTER   So the situation, as it is now, is unfair, but when the electricity arrives here it will be . . .

RESP   Fair, because now we have it within our reach. (H16)

Hunting

Although wildlife was often mentioned as one of the values associated with the park and forest, we had very few productive conversations with local people about hunting. It appears as if hunting was still going on in the area to some extent. There were some indications of the emergence of an antihunting norm, although it was not clear if this was as developed as it appeared to be in Costa Rica because people seemed more reluctant to discuss hunting with outsiders.

(157) INTER   Are there hunters that are killing animals?

RESP   It is possible that, very quietly, there could be. (H18)

(158) INTER   Do people here hunt; hunting of animals?

RESP   Yes, there are some people that, yes, that have been caught various times hunting animals, but they are people who don't pay attention. I always see them going around catching [animals].

INTER   People from the community or from outside?

RESP   Yes, from the community, yes.

INTER   And do you do this?

RESP   No, not me. . . . No, I never have liked this, going around getting animals, it is better to take care of them. Sometimes they come over there, sometimes. They come there to my farm, and I never harm them. . . . Because I don't like to harm animals. (H7)

(159) There are still people in these streams, picking up rocks looking for crabs, there looking. I don't say anything, but I don't like this. . . . I hunted some animals once before, but to protect the *milpas*. I make *milpas* here. I killed a few animals like *agoutis* and *coatis*, but I don't go looking for animals in the forest anymore because I never get excited about hunting. I hunt only to prevent damage to the *milpa*. . . . There are people who hunt a lot of birds. . . . They put ladders with nails. Like this. Look. There in the forest there are trees like this, for example, nailed like a ladder and they climb. This I have seen and I don't like it, but because one isn't an authority, doesn't have authority, one can't do anything . . . without authority; but with authority, yes. But this doesn't happen often. Before there was a lot of hunting of animals, there were [professional] hunters of animals, too. But now they've all retired because it was announced that the hunting of animals is prohibited. But when I first came here people lived from hunting . . . there were people who devoted themselves to this. (H10)

Our survey confirms that there is an antihunting norm emerging throughout the park communities, as well as an apparent awareness of the diminished wildlife populations in the park. More than 80 percent of the individuals surveyed *disagreed* with the statement "It's always alright to hunt or kill wild animals." An almost identical proportion *disagreed* with a more narrowly commercial objective for hunting expressed in the statement "To hunt or kill animals is alright if you need money." A smaller proportion objected to hunting in different circumstances where larger populations or animals were present. About 53 percent *disagreed* with the statement "The hunting of animals is alright when there are lots of them in the area."

Livelihood Conflicts and Resistance to Forest Conservation and the National Park

Forest conservation in both the core, strictly protected area and the sustainable-use area of the park has potential to conflict with the agricultural-based livelihoods of rural people.[2] Livelihood conflicts exist, as we have seen, even when people place great importance on forest for fundamentals of life such as water. This is because people need to fell trees for timber to build houses and firewood for cooking, to clear forests to grow subsistence crops like corn and beans, and to manage the density of tree cover to grow cash crops like coffee. Strictly protected forests, even when appreciated for water, wildlife, and aesthetics, reduce the amount of land that is available for rural extractive forest uses and growing crops. Even when rural people are not directly opposed to forest conservation, this conflict between environmental values and livelihood values is present, and they are forced to come to terms with it in some way. Our interviews revealed a number of mediating models that people used to establish beliefs and values that enable them to support conservation and meet their livelihood needs. Four of these models deal with the forest as a utilitarian resource that can be managed to meet human needs. One opposes wasting trees but finds that cutting for personal use is acceptable, especially when done for true need or mitigated by planting new trees. A second finds that temporarily clearing forests to grow subsistence crops or integrating cash crops into forests is acceptable. A third develops local definitions of trees; in one case, this broadens the definition by finding the same environmental benefits of forest trees for fruit trees and coffee, and in another case, it narrows the definition to exclude some tree-based land covers from the forest category by classifying young forest as *guamil*. A fourth finds that the real source of environmental damage is not local forest use, but rather logging by outsiders. Two more mediating models explicitly deal with the conflict between forest protection and livelihoods. One is based on a belief and expectation that the government has to allow them to grow their crops. The second suggests that if local people are going to be restricted in their use of forest and growing of crops, the government is obligated to provide them with an alternative. Unlike in Costa Rica, however, we did not find people to be willing or interested in talking about direct opposition to conservation.

Mediating Model 1: Trees Should Not Be Wasted, but the Forest Can Be Used and Managed to Meet Our Needs

Almost universally, people said that it was bad to cut down trees if they would not be used. This seems to reference earlier frontier clearing of forest for agriculture, when trees were often wasted. People agreed at equal levels that it was acceptable to fell a tree if you needed it to build house, make furniture, or for firewood. They tended to see forest as a resource that could and should be managed for human benefits. Trees that were not valuable to people could be felled to favor more valuable trees. If tree cutting was done under a management plan, it was acceptable. If you felled a tree to meet a need, you should plant some number of trees (for example, two, five, or ten) to replace it in order to have wood available in the future.

> (160) INTER   Do you think that sometimes it is good to cut trees?
> RESP   The way I think, if you need a tree to make a fence, I think you can make one. But to cut one just for mischief, I am not in agreement. But if you need a tree to make a fence, or perhaps we need a little corn crib, and we cut a tree and it's not wasted. But just to cut and leave it . . . no, not me. (H22)

(161) INTER   Do you think that sometimes it is good to cut trees?

RESP   Yes, I think so, depending on the need. What is needed; because sometimes it is necessary, like to cut some lumber for a house, something like that. . . . For something useful, for a house or something, I say then it is good. . . . If you are going to use it, it's good, it really is. (H2)

(162) INTER   And do you feel that sometimes it is bad to cut trees?

RESP   When you cut without need, for me it is bad. Because, for me, if you are going to cut a tree you should do it because you need it. Because God created plants, he created them so that man could use them, so that man could make use of them, as well as to be the clothing of the earth, according to the Bible. Man has to have products from them, because these plants, many are unique, many bring a good environment—pure air and everything. So for me, to cut a plant mercilessly is bad, because I am not going to cut a plant just to watch it fall. If I am going to go cut, I should go and cut because I need something and it should be a plant like a pine tree. And I'm not going to just go and cut. First, I have to go to the authorities who will give me permission and then I can go get this tree legally. . . . But there are plants that dry out the soil. Here we have a plant that we call *mozote,* a plant with broad leaves. This plant seems to stop the decomposition of the soil and dry out the area below it. It is not a plant that is very beneficial. It seems like this plant, well, if you have a plant near one of these . . . there is no life around it. . . . Your plant will get yellow and shriveled. And there are plants, very low plants that don't provide much protection. This kind of plant it is perfectly fine to fell. (H21)

(163) INTER   Do you think that sometimes it is good to cut trees?

RESP   Sometimes, yes, trees that are in decline. Sometimes it is good to use them; but trees that are alive, it is bad to cut them. (H20)

(164) INTER   Do you think it is good or bad to cut trees?

RESP   It's bad. . . . It's not good because we have seen that it brings us problems to cut trees, most of us have lived with problems caused by having cut trees. . . . Sometimes you need a little wood to build, but now it has to be done under the law. Here there is [a park guard]. We are always looking for him because he has a lot of experience in this. . . . So he looks at the tree to see if it is of the age for cutting or if it is not its time yet. So if the community needs a tree, for wood, they want his permission to mill one, but with an obligation that if you cut a tree you are going to plant two new ones where this tree was cut. (H9)

(165) INTER   Do you think is it good to cut trees?

RESP   Yes, but always regulated. Under a management plan or for an urgent need, such as someone needing to make a house for his own use. But a business to cut wood in exploitation, I no longer think this is necessary. Because this will use everything up. . . . It's not bad [if you cut under a management plan] because the truth is that the whole time that you are cutting trees, you are planting others. That is to say you are looking for this kind of relationship. So, I tell you, go ahead and cut what you need, for example, in the community, for example. Here the only person who cuts a tree is someone who needs to build a house. But for someone that wants to take out wood to exploit, that is not permitted. (H13)

(166) If you are going to need a tree, then you should plant another tree. Not just one, but some five trees. If you fell a tree, you should plant some. (H7)

Mediating Model 2: Clearing for Crops, or Integrating Crops into Forest, Is Acceptable

When faced with a genuine need to plant subsistence crops like corn and beans and no other land, it is generally considered acceptable to clear forest (see quote 53). That is, a true, immediate livelihood is more important than forest conservation (even though it is considered to be regrettable to have to make this choice). In the case of coffee, the mediating model is more nuanced, finding it acceptable to clear small trees and undergrowth to plant shade coffee, including a general feeling that this has few negative environmental consequences.

(167) INTER   Do you think that it sometimes is good to clear forest?
RESP   Look, it depends on the kind of clearing that you do, because I think that planting crops is not prohibited. I think we should cultivate the earth, and each place has a way of being cultivated. (H21)

(168) You know about the *milpa*. We need to do it to get our food, even though it's really not good. We have to have our *milpas*, and some trees die. (H6)

(169) INTER   Do you think that sometimes it is good to clear forest? Do you think it is good, or necessary?
RESP   Look, here in Honduras, let's talk about Honduras. We live from agriculture because nobody from the government or any other institution is going to come and give us some food. We have to produce it. That's the detail, no one from any government. They say if you don't work you don't eat. We have a parcel to grow food. Because if you go to the market you will see cassava, sweet potatoes. We produce all this, plantain, banana, sweet potato, cassava, vegetables; we grow them. What we don't have is money to buy crops. We have a little piece of land, where we can plant anything. But things need to be made better. If there's no money, there's nothing. I'm going to tell you again—is it good to clear forest? No, it's not. Because we need water, the coolness of the trees, we have to feed them so they feed us. (H24)

(170) To grow coffee you don't have to go and cut the forests, fell the whole plantation. To plant coffee all you need to do is perhaps clear the area under the plantation. So there are trees. . . . I think that to grow coffee you don't have to clear everything and expose the earth to the weather

and the sun. So for me, I think that if it is to plant crops like corn, like beans, you have to clear, but you should already have your land dedicated for this. . . . For me, to clear without using is bad, and to grow crops you also have to leave some trees, clean the area underneath. From what I understand this is not prohibited in the forest. They have said that planting coffee is not prohibited; that growing coffee on the land that is good for coffee, being careful not to clear—this is what a lot of people have told me. (H21)

(171) INTER   I want to talk a little about clearing forest. Do you think that sometimes it is good to clear areas with trees or forest?

RESP   I don't think so. There is what is called *socolar*; *socolar* is, where there is a big tree, and you clear underneath it to plant coffee. I don't think this is bad. . . . *Socolar* is good, but clearing is not, because clearing is felling all the trees. (H22)

Mediating Model 3: Fluidity in the Definition of a Tree: What Counts as a Tree and When a Tree Is Not a Tree

There are several ways that the local definition of what is an environmentally beneficial tree has been adjusted to be different from the way that outside conservationists may think about this. First, fruit trees, coffee, and other cultivated plants are considered to be trees that provide the same benefits as forest trees, or planting them is considered to be reforestation. In this way, the definition of a tree is broadened to include woody plants that have direct livelihood benefits. Almost 85 percent of the persons we surveyed considered coffee to be a type of tree, and the same proportion agreed that "Fruit trees are just as much trees as pines are." Planting these trees, then, is seen as having both environmental and livelihood benefits. Second, the definition of a tree is narrowed to exclude the young second-growth trees (*guamil*) that people frequently clear as a part of a shifting agricultural system for growing corn and beans, known as *milpa*. In this way, by excluding *guamiles*, which are regularly cleared for agriculture, from the category of "tree" or "forest," clearing them is not seen as contradictory with forest conservation.

(172) INTER   When you think about forests, what's the first thing that comes to your mind?

RESP   Think about trees?

INTER   Yes, about trees.

RESP   Like fruit trees, right? Because fruit trees are a plant, right? They need to be cared for; not destroyed but cared for. (H22)

(173) INTER   And why is coffee expanding?

RESP   Well, now we want a plant that is permanent. It is a plant that is more permanent than the other crops. . . . Coffee is a permanent plant.

So I saw that it was necessary to cultivate it. Furthermore, to cultivate coffee is reforestation. So, also, for the forest.

INTER   Does coffee produce air or water like forest?

RESP   I don't think so. Because it is a small plant. But it is a part of the protection, because where there is a farm no one is going to burn. And also, you plant a few trees in the coffee for shade. You can plant citrus, you can plant mango, avocado. So you will be planting plants that always are going to help you and protect the forest. (H8)

(174) INTER   Do you think that it is good to leave land in forest? You told me you had a piece of forest, do you think it is good to leave it like that?

RESP   Yes, it's good. For me it is good not to touch the land. But sometimes we need to plant some basic grains, but just a little. The important thing is not to burn. And to reforest, plant trees like we were talking about. I'm a fan of planting trees. . . . But often we need to cut a little forest to plant corn, because we need that, too. But forest shouldn't be felled, man, nor big trees. No. None of this.

INTER   Just *guamiles*?

RESP   *Corralitos*, yes, low growth. Like that over there. Above the streams is a clearing that I would like to convert to grass to see if I can buy a calf. If there's a place, if it would be possible. I am thinking about making a little pasture because we have very little land here and we're going to need it, with the children that are coming. (H10)

There is a logic in the local definition of forest and fallow land, and it has to do with the protection of access to land for agricultural production. According to the national laws and the park management plan, forest clearing inside the park is not allowed. The individuals surveyed were by and large aware of this fact. Eighty-six percent were aware that clearing forest inside the park is not permissible. Almost everyone (94%) was aware that forest growth on fallow land is considered forest when it grows very large. Finally, 80 percent were aware that when fallow land becomes forest, it is illegal to return to that land for crop cultivation. Although there was some confusion about whether it was permissible to clear fallow land, about one-half correctly indicated that it was allowed. The important point is that most residents of the park communities were aware of their interest in managing fallow lands so as not to lose access to them for crop cultivation.[3]

Mediating Model 4: Real Forest Damage Is Caused by Outside Loggers or by Selling Trees for Personal Gain

Another mediating model builds on the previous ones, finding little damage from local use but blaming the real problems with forests on logging or sale of trees to outsiders. In some cases, these models cast the local community as the defender of the local sustainably managed forest against outside loggers, people from the cities, and even the government forestry agency.

(175) INTER   So when is it bad to cut trees?

RESP   It is bad when someone wants to do an illegal harvest. . . . You should do the legal things that are necessary to cut wood, and it should be a harvest for the community; for a roof of a house and not for sale. Because the resources of this zone are not sufficient so people in Siguatepeque [a nearby provincial city] can use them. What is here is for the benefit of the community, and others can't come and take away our resources; because they belong here, to this community. (H15)

(176) INTER   Do you think that sometimes it is good to cut trees?

RESP   It depends on the need. I think that if we need to build a home, well, I think our country has a law that says that we have the right to five trees; five trees, of pine.

INTER   Each year?

RESP   No five trees, if you need them. Because if we're building a house, then we can ask for a permit and they'll give it to us. But perhaps there are some who go and do it without getting a permit; go and fell whatever trees, sell the wood. Nobody might see you. But the truth is that we should be able to do this. Because following the laws of our country, such and such person, inhabitant of the community, has the right to five trees, five trees for construction. But you know that, regarding the law, well, there are always important people who have their shops; they have their wood. These people always have permission. What can a community do against these people, these people who are there with their machines, their offices, and things, who generally are respected? But to me, someone shouldn't be deprived. The inhabitants should have use of perhaps a tree or two, always with a permit. Done right, but not abusing these permissions like a lot of people do. Perhaps not here, but I have seen people go and take their axes without mercy, as we say, to the forests and fell and everything, and the water dries up. (H21)

(177) RESP   Here we have that hill over there. We call it the lumberyard, this hill. There you can't touch a tree just to touch it. . . . There are no permits to go and take out any wood. But it depends what it is for, and if there are sufficient reasons to take one of these trees. If not, you don't touch it, because it is a wood lot . . . for the community. . . . Those of us who live in the community, we can [request permission to take out wood or a tree].

INTER   And you said that there are certain people that don't know, or that continue to cut trees. Do you have any idea why they continue to do this?

RESP   Oh, it was some old guys, some rich men who came from other places. They came to fell trees to plant coffee. It didn't matter to them because they weren't from there. They were looking for a business or perhaps a harvest. . . . I don't know how it happened, but they were stopped. They didn't continue felling trees. . . . They were from this side of San Pedro. They paid a fine and didn't go to jail, because they were caught by people who were able to . . . what is it called? . . . They helped them, it is better to say, get away with just this, with just the fine. But it is something delicate. (H5)

(178) RESP   COHDEFOR has come here, but COHDEFOR has done a lot of damage. You can see that they have messed up the country.
INTER   Why?
RESP   Because the poor people are denied a tree, but a rich person, a company, gets a permit. (H23)

Survey findings show that concerns are widespread in the park communities about privileged access to forest resources by elites. Nine out of ten persons surveyed agreed with the statement "It is easier for large landholders to obtain permits to cut tress than for common or poor people." There was near unanimity (97%) in the view that lumber companies destroy more forest than people who live in the local communities.

Mediating Model 5: They Have to Let Us Do It

The fifth mediating model expands on the four discussed above. Because local use of wood and local agriculture are seen as more important than strict forest conservation, enforcement, at least by CAMNP, generally seems to reflect this. People seem to have drawn the conclusion that the government cannot implement forest restrictions that do not provide for these uses. They believe that the government and CAMNP have no choice but to allow these uses to continue.

(179) They can't keep us from planting beans or corn. How are we going to live? (H21)

(180) RESP   The way I understand it, if we're going to build something, they won't keep us from getting a tree. If we're going to build our houses, they won't prevent it.
INTER   And [if you needed] to cut trees to build something? Do you think they would give a permit? Do you have any doubt if they would give a permit for construction?
RESP   No, they have to give it, right? I don't think they would not give it to us. (H6)

Survey results support the notion that local people's subsistence needs must be addressed before they can reasonably be expected to protect forests. Seventy percent of the individuals surveyed agreed with the statement "Before we can worry about forest protection, we need food and money." But the insistence on reasonable access to forest resources did not include unconditional access to resources. Those surveyed were generally not opposed to government restrictions on forest use. The low level of agreement with the following statements is indicative of this orientation:

- "They should permit people to sell trees that are on their own land without any government restrictions" (27% agreed).
- "They should allow people to clear forest to cultivate or plant coffee without any government restrictions" (26% agreed).
- "They should permit people to do what they want with trees found on their land" (17% agreed).

However, there is an important exception to the support for government restrictions on land use. More than 70 percent of those surveyed agreed that people should be allowed to cut trees to build a house without any government restrictions. This finding indicates that access to trees for home construction, just as access to land to raise food crops, is seen as a basic subsistence need.

Mediating Model 6: They Need to Provide Us with an Alternative

Although people are generally accepting of the park and forest conservation efforts, it was very common for people to say that the government needed to provide some sort of alternative option to people so that they could meet their livelihood needs without damaging the forest. To some extent, this may be because they sometimes think of the park and forest conservation as being something to be done by outsiders to benefit outsiders and that if these are going to be imposed on local people, there should also be an increase in development activities so people can meet their livelihood needs.

(181) INTER   Do you think that it is sometimes good to clear forest?
RESP   Forested areas, you said? Well, in the area where we live, I think that you practically can't do this anymore. You can't do it. . . . In the first place because there really is very little forest. There really is not much forest, and we are also seeing a situation where the climate is changing. There is little water and pure air. I think that you can't do it anymore. Really what we need to be doing is trying to find someone to help us . . . find a way to work in another way . . . Create sources of work so that people can work in another environment and restrict ourselves to staying on the parcels that we have. Because if we fell more forest and people stay here, the future will be worse. So we should think about how we

can find some way that this doesn't happen. Create sources of work for people in the future. It's a solution to the problems that we have. . . . I think that we have to look for sources of work for our children so they don't have to clear forests.

INTER   Do you want them to have opportunities here, or for them to go to [the city of] San Pedro, or . . . ?

RESP   No, No, No. It has to be right here, because if we send them over there they will be ruined by the social problems that are there. (H13)

(182) RESP   Do you know what we really need? People that have the big picture. Because I think . . . that if there were a little business here where people could earn a little money to sustain themselves, then there would be a means to protect more forest. Because if there were, let's say, a factory, something like that, then there would be a place to work and you could live. . . . This is needed because there are times when someone has to clear a little spot, because they don't have any place to grow crops or to work. There are a lot of things you have to think about in this. . . . If there were a source of work perhaps it wouldn't be so necessary to work in agriculture. This is a zone that has prohibitions, so it should be taken care of. But more is needed here, because if we all go to the United States they'll throw us out and send us back. (H18)

(183) In this case I think that the areas here in [this community], the areas where you can grow crops have run out, as we say. What is still in forest is land that can't be cropped. Sure, there are a few places that could be cropped, but it wouldn't be right to cut them. It would be better, and I hope they do, if the organizations in charge of protecting the areas of forest, like in this community, would look for other alternatives, other solutions so that the people can survive. Because we have this need to survive, there are a lot of children. Many people are forming new families and don't have any place to go. So the option that is left sometimes is to go to the mountain and make a little farm there. . . . There are pressing needs, but I understand that the organizations, the NGOs in charge of protection have to look for alternatives; come up with solutions for the people so they can survive. It's like they say, we find ourselves "between the sword and the wall." Sometimes we don't know what road to take because we see the needs, the need that people have to work. (H14)

(184) We have already been taught how to take care of the forest. They should put a little business here that would give us work, so we don't need to go around in [the park]. It seems to me that they might be able to help us with some things, and that way we wouldn't have to continue to make the parcels that we do. . . . We are already [conserving trees], and the only thing that we don't have is a source of work. This is the problem, and you know that without having one you can't live. I think that if we take care of the forest, they need to take care of us. (H18)

(185) Well, the park exists because supposedly there was a decree on the part of the government. I don't know in what year it was. I don't have the decree here at hand, but in 1987. . . . But the government complicated things in the decree, because, following the law that it created, it says that the park is where there are communities. . . . There is going to have to be something additional, there are going to be plans with activities for these people, which we haven't had. They decreed the parks to purify the air that they themselves breathe without noticing the damage that they were doing to the communities, who are giving up a lot, who need to look for a place to live because they didn't give them access. . . . Now they have to leave the park. If they don't throw some jobs this way, they are going to create a more serious social problem in the country, this is clear. If the government believes what they say, in clear conscience, in creating parks they also have to supply something for the communities. . . . Sometimes they talk about parcels of soil conservation and all these activities; doing all kinds of things. But the people don't have any clear financing from the government to do these activities. They create laws, but up to now they haven't actually done anything. On paper is one thing, and doing it is another. (H13)

(186) INTER   What do you think that the government could do, or the people from the park, so that this won't hurt people?
RESP   That they create an environment of work, an environment of work of another kind so we don't have to work the land and so that there is a way that we can work without bothering the land. Even though it is a national park, like they say, they need to do their part by putting in a factory where everyone can work. Because if they put in a factory, everyone can work. Because, look, things are bad. Put in a factory and everything . . . . Shoes, cloth, all the things that people consume, everything. We have a peaceful environment here, because we have the park, but it's not worth anything if they don't let us work. In my case, they included some land that I already had cultivated in the park. Now it's prohibited for no other reason than that it is in the park. And there's no way to work, because they have prohibited it, people are afraid to work. (H24)

Desirable Landscapes

As in Costa Rica, at the end of each interview we showed people a series of photos of landscapes with a range of different amounts of forests, croplands, and pastures. We asked them to talk about the pictures, and to tell us which one they liked most and which one they would like to have for their own land. Discussions of these pictures invoked many of the mental and cultural models from earlier in the interviews. People often made negative comments about deforested areas like this one:

(187) Here it looks very deforested. You see pastures, farms . . . almost only farms. And you can also see some landslides; it's very steep. . . . Here, you don't see anything, you see a land without trees, and the trees that are there don't want to be because they are all alone and very deforested. You can't see anything useful that has been planted. All they have done is to fell the trees. (H1)

At the same time, many people pointed out forested areas, noting their beauty, association with water, and the habitat for wildlife that they provided.

(188) INTER   What do you think of this landscape?
RESP   I like it. I like it . . . because it looks very green, there are a lot of trees, pretty. . . . Pines. I see a forest up above. High forest. . . . I imagine that there are rivers or streams that pass through there. . . . There are streams in the forests. . . . There always are.
INTER   And which one do you like the best?
RESP   This one, because it is full of trees, and there are a lot of animals. (H2)
(189) This is really beautiful, it looks like a landscape, a very beautiful type of forest. Very dense, and you don't see any degradation. There aren't any dead trees. All the trees you see are really green, deep in the clouds. (H15)

Yet people did not necessarily see a place for themselves in forest landscapes. They explained that they had no choice but to clear some forest to grow crops in order to survive. For example,

(190) RESP   Here you just see trees, national parks. (H22)
(191) RESP   This is what I see in the photo: it tells a part of the reality of the deforestation of Honduras. We see these forests, but here they all have been felled; we see cattle. The reality of what has happened in Honduras is that the flat parts—where crops can be grown, where *campesinos* could grow something—are full of rich ranchers' cattle. So us *campesinos* had to come to the forest, and we had no other option but to fell the forest to live. . . . [Sometimes we have to] continue to kill forest to grow crops. This is necessary, let me tell you again, if we are going to live. To eat, we have to grow crops. But it has to be done the right way, with rules. . . . I repeat, we need to grow corn and beans to feed ourselves. . . . *Campesinos* shouldn't be criticized for making their little *milpa*. What we need to do is coexist, bring together the reality of nature with the reality of our poverty. (H14)

People were attracted to landscapes that had mixed land uses, including crops and trees.

(192) INTER   Which one do you like the best?

RESP   They're all pretty, but I like this one because of the crops that it has. Because it has gardens. It has coffee, and there are also trees for protection. And in the middle there is a vegetable garden. This is a garden. (H8)

(193) INTER   Which one of these photos would you like your land to look like in the future?

RESP   This is better, because it is more oriented. . . . It is called sustainable agriculture. . . . It has both things. The forest protects. It is making soil. There is no erosion. (H13)

(194) INTER   Which one of these would you like for your own land?

RESP   I would like to have this one. Because it has a place where you could grow crops. And there is another place that is full of trees, protected. And over here is another plantation. That is, in this piece of land there are places with different things planted. . . . Different things all in one place. It's much better. It economizes the land, the water. Because if you take care of the soil and water, you are also taking care of yourself. Right now we are doing pretty well. We understand that by arranging things right on the land we can conserve the water. (H18)

Tree- and Forest-Related Behaviors and Their Rationales

The final questions that we addressed in our open-ended interviewing were: How have changing environmental values and attitudes toward trees and forests influenced rural people's desire for forests on their land and in their community? How, ultimately, have they affected decision making and behaviors in relation to trees and forests?

Desirable Amount of Forest

The majority of the responses favored more forests, often citing many of the benefits associated with forests that we have already discussed—changing rainfall, water availability in streams, pure air, coolness, wildlife, firewood, and religious associations. Several people drew relationships between reforestation and improving these benefits. Several people thought that there were enough forests now, often recognizing the conflicts and complex relationships that can exist between agricultural sources of livelihood and forest. No one suggested that they would like less.

Many people wanted more forest, as indicated in the following responses:

(195) INTER   Would you like to have more forest or trees in your community, or in the areas around it, or are there now enough areas with trees?

RESP   I think that right now, almost everywhere in the community, there is a need for a lot of forest. Because now, in a lot of communities, they don't have forest. We have forest here, but we need to have more forest than we have so that there is a good fortification of the sources of water. Not only for the sources of water, but also for their purification. INTER   Would you like to have more trees and forest in the community? RESP   I think that for me it is very important that there are more forests. Because with a forest close by, for example, firewood is closer to prepare food for the rest of the people, the children, to do a lot of things. In the forest there are fruits, wild fruits like *palmiche* that today is very far away in the forest. If it were closer, right here, one could go. Now, it is very far. (H11)

(196) INTER   And would you like to have more or less [trees] than there are now?
RESP   Well, I think that more, because the more the better because I always think that nature is what God made and that it has to be maintained. But I think that even if there isn't more than what we have now, at least what there is now should be maintained, because I don't want to see a desert. That would be the worst that there could be, because if there are no trees everything ends. (H17)

Some people felt that there was adequate forest now.

(197) INTER   Would you like to have more trees here in the community, or less, or do you like it the way it is now? What do you prefer?
RESP   I would like it if it stayed the same as it is now. (H16)

(198) INTER   And would you like to have more forest or trees in your community, or perhaps less, or do you like it the way it is now?
RESP   For me it is fine, because, the little that we have, if they are taken care of, I don't think any type of problem will happen. (H5)

Tree-felling behaviors. From a conservation point of view, the effects of forest-related values on a variety of tree-related behaviors are important. To address this, we asked people about tree-felling and forest-clearing behaviors, conservation of forest patches, and tree planting and reforestation. When asked about tree felling, only a few people denied having felled trees at all. Since trees and forests can conflict with people's livelihoods, it is not surprising that many people's answers were structured in relation to land use practices. Several people indicated that they hadn't felled trees because they purchased their farm already "made." Others, while admitting to having felled trees, generally gave a series of explanations that follow our previous analysis: this was something that they did only when they first came here; they manipulated forests to grow crops and coffee; they had only cleared *guamiles.*

(199) INTER   Have you cut trees on the land that you work?
RESP   No, I have never cut a pine tree. I have never felled a tree, never. (H15)

(200) INTER   Have you cut trees on the land that you work?
RESP   This, not me . . . not me. . . . I have worked lands that have already been cleared. I haven't cut trees, no. (H20)

(201) INTER   I want to talk about the lands that you work. Have you cut trees on the lands that you work?
RESP   Like I told you before, when I came here we felled some forest. Because we came here to occupy land, we didn't come to protect trees. . . . When we started, yes, but lately, no. (H13)

(202) INTER   Have you cut trees on your own land?
RESP   Only a few. . . . Because, look, over there we have a little forest of coffee, but there are trees that aren't good for shade and so we cut them. There are still a lot left, but there are some still that need to be cut. On the farm we regulate the shade. Because the forest is very rich with trees, so we cut the little ones and plant others that give products like coffee. But the big ones stay; the forest always stays. (H18)

(203) RESP   You have to control the shade for coffee, so you don't have problems. . . . When coffee has too much shade, it won't produce much. So it has to be regulated. . . . [But] big trees, no; just clearing underneath, low underbrush. . . . We practically shouldn't call them trees, what I have cut. They're shrubs, not trees. (H11)

(204) INTER   And on your land, have you had to . . . or what was your land like when you bought it recently?
RESP   When I bought it was in *guamiles*, but small *guamiles*, because here other people had felled the forests. (H19)

(205) INTER   And on the land that you work, have you cut trees on your parcels?
RESP   Well, I have worked on these lands, and when my father left them to me it was a low *guamil*. But I haven't cut big trees . . . just low *guamiles*. (H8)

People generally supported the idea of leaving a patch of forest on their land, and many people did it, either along streams or in a woodlot type of situation.

(206) INTER   And can you think of a case when it would be harmful to have a tree on your land?
RESP   It would not be harmful. . . . You have to have your parcels of land to grow crops. But you also need to have trees, to take care of them. Don't fell them, because if you fell them you're not making something. You are ruining the earth, drying it out. Without trees, land without trees won't have the coolness—the leaves, the wind, the breeze—that the trees give. (H24)

(207) INTER   And have you left forests standing on your land?
RESP   Where I grow crops, I always leave forests along the edges of the streams. . . . Because I see the necessity to leave a reserve to protect the

water, so it won't go away. Because if we cleared everything the springs and the streams would clearly dry up. So, because of this, I have seen that it is good to leave trees. . . . I grow corn and beans, and the tree that I leave there, the shade from this bothers the other plants. But it is also important to me that the water doesn't dry up where I work, so I have to leave them. (H8)

(208) INTER   Do you think it is good to leave forests standing?
RESP   Yes. . . . You can leave some forest so you can take out a tree when you need it. . . . Where I have my land, I have my pieces of forest. . . . [Where] there may be some springs of water. . . . The springs don't dry up, and if you need a tree you get one. (H19)

Of the people surveyed, 58 percent reported having cut trees or cleared forest on their land, and persons who arrived or reached working age after the creation of the park were no less likely to have done so. About 30 percent of those surveyed were adults who had moved to the area after creation of the park or were born locally but reached working age after creation of the park. The creation of the park does not appear to have reduced tree cutting to meet basic needs. Figure 4.9 shows the reasons for cutting trees and indicates that people were most likely to have cut trees to meet basic needs for food and shelter. A very small proportion of those surveyed indicated that they had cut trees for commercial timber sales.

Tree-planting behaviors. When we asked people about tree planting, many people indicated that they had planted trees. The only large-scale reforestation project was the one sponsored by the *El Cajón* project for watershed management purposes

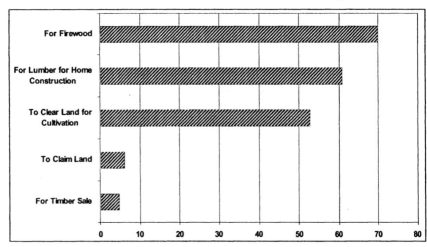

Figure 4.9.   Proportion who cut trees on their own land by purpose, Cerro Azul Meambar, Honduras.

through a cooperative. This was mentioned by several people, although there was some doubt about the possible future benefits for the community or even the motives of people involved in the project.

(209) RESP   Because they are reforesting a zone where there are not many trees, they are planting five hundred thousand plants. Pine trees. So this means that after ten years pass there will be more plantations. . . . I think this is a benefit for the community. . . . I don't have a lot of information, but it is [being done by] a cooperative organized by *COHDEFOR*, the *El Cajón* project, and also the municipality helping this cooperative. They are private people and they are working for this. Now some people wonder if they will have any ownership of the trees after they are planted. That is to say, if we reforest here, will we be able to take out the old trees from here? That there could be some personal profit, but this is imagination. (H21)

(210) RESP   I see that they are planting [trees] where they aren't going to survive. . . . Where they are planting them they are not going to survive, because the animals walk around there and it's very degraded. . . . [It is] in a pasture over there. There are animals and they are planting and the animals will eat them. . . . It's the cooperative that is planting, and where there are pines the same pine trees will shed seeds and sprout. . . . To plant where there are pine trees, this doesn't make sense. . . . [They do it] because they give them some money and . . . they get money for doing it and it puts people to work. (H23)

More common and perhaps less controversial was the planting of a small number of good timber trees on farms. Many people indicated that they had done this in the past, often obtaining the trees from government agencies or NGOs working in reforestation or forest conservation.

(211) INTER   And you have told me that you have planted trees.
RESP   Yes, trees for shade. . . . There are pine trees in general, there is *cedro*, there is mahogany, there is *laurel*. . . . Some are natural, others have been planted. They have had nurseries here, and a lot of plants have been planted. . . . *COHDEFOR* was making nurseries. (H3)

(212) INTER   Do you think it is good to plant trees?
RESP   Well, for me it would be much better, to plant trees of *cedro*, various kinds, of mahogany and pine, because in this zone, in the times when it wasn't protected, the mahogany and *cedro* trees were used up. There are very few of them. They were used up. So the youth, the future generations won't know what a tree of mahogany, or of *cedro*, is. If they do, it will be because there are still a few trees that *Aldea Global* has come here giving to people, and *COHDEFOR* has brought some, too. . . . I have planted my ten trees of *cedro*, my ten trees of mahogany. I have children,

and some day they are going to use these. . . . We are trained and we have talked to people about if you cut three trees of pine you should plant ten pine trees so that they are growing, pay the bill for those that you have cut, the three that you have cut. (H15)

(213) RESP   If you see my father's farm, it has *cedros*, big *cedros*, small ones. My father likes to have trees near the house. . . . He always says, "If I can't use this wood, my grandchildren will." (H9)

In many other instances, tree planting was carefully integrated into farms—around houses, in coffee plantations, and along fencerows.

(214) INTER   Do you think that there is anything bad about planting trees?
RESP   There's no bad in it, because . . . that is to say, it's not bad because on the parcels that we have, we would maybe plant trees in the zones that perhaps have some forest or that have had landslides and can't be used for crops. If you can't grow crops there, you can reforest. But in these places that are practically filling up with trees, we can't plant any more, we could reforest a part, but not all because with trees we can't grow crops. . . . But in a way like I told you, near the sources of water or in some place that you won't be able to grow crops in very well. There are many very good places where it can be done. (H13)

(215) INTER   And do you have a forest . . . or something that has trees?
RESP   We have a little piece, about three *tareas* (0.3 hectares), of a tree that is called *encino*. . . . We have about twenty trees. They are useful when we need them. If a post rots you can fell one of these and you can bring the branches to use for firewood. (H22)

(216) INTER   And have you planted trees on the land that you work?
RESP   I planted the corners and the boundaries of my land, I planted pine trees. . . . The corners and the fences, so the land is delineated. And I am thinking about planting some two hundred trees of *madereado*, which would be good for shade and would improve the soil. It is a tree that is very useful, not only the leaves but the roots. The leaves fall apart and these leaves fertilize the soil, and the land is also fed some nutrients from the roots. And at the same time the tree is good for reforestation because it's big. (H11)

(217) INTER   Would you like more forest or trees in your community and the surrounding area?
RESP   Yes. For the water, the streams of water. I have even asked for more trees to plant in some pastures that I have there. I asked for more trees and planted near the streams. . . . [*PANACAM*] gave me some trees and I planted them and there they are. A part of them survived and others no, but the trees are pretty there. . . . I have [also] planted along the fences, a tree called *madreado* and . . . we have planted a lot along the

fences. We plant along the fences so we don't have to cut more trees later for posts. Because if they are trees they keep growing big and they produce, and you don't have to go back and put in more posts in the fence. You don't have to cut trees again. . . . And on the farm we protect a tree that is called *perpetuo*. For shade, to protect. . . . This tree, there's one over there, look, this is *perpetuo*, the one over there. This is *naranjo*, the one there, there, look, a tree that grows very rapidly. We planted it there because it grows rapidly and gives shade to coffee. . . . We protect [the shade] here, even though farms are being technified.

INTER   So you have planted these. What were the benefits of planting these trees?

RESP   Well, it's like reforesting, in the first place. And in the second for the coffee; to make shade there. And also to reforest the environment. (H6)

Often, when talking about tree planting, the conversation turned to fruit trees, which many people saw as having the same or similar environmental benefits as forest trees, along with the direct benefits from the products they received from them.

(218) INTER   And can [tree planting] be bad, sometimes?

RESP   I don't think so, perhaps. . . . I think it is good to plant trees. Not just any tree, but trees that provide benefits. For example, here in Honduras what is planted most is pine. Because it is what there is a lot of, pine; hardwoods, *caoba, laurel, cedro, cipres*, all these types of trees are useful, and, for example, one plants pretty trees around the house, ornamental plants, things that serve for shade to cool down in the dry season. I think fruit trees are good. (H17)

(219) INTER   Do think that it is good to plant trees?

RESP   Yes. . . . In the first place, for me to plant trees, principally fruit trees, for me it is good because it protects the forest and also it helps us because they are fruit trees. (H8)

(220) INTER   Let's talk a little about planting trees. Do you think that it is a good thing to plant trees?

RESP   Yes, in this case it is good to plant trees in the parts that need to be reforested, for example the parts that have been burned where there are big clearings that don't have anything. So it would be good to reforest them. And with a type of trees that are beneficial to people as well as the environment, and beneficial for the person who plants them. That is fruit trees. . . . It is good to plant fruit trees at the same time as timber trees are planted, so that there will always be one type of benefit or another for people. (H11)

(221) INTER   Have you planted trees on the land that you work?

RESP   Yes, I have planted trees. . . . Oranges, mango, *urracos, zapotes*. (H20)

As indicated in figure 4.10, a large proportion of the individuals surveyed had planted fruit trees on their own land. About one-third had planted hardwoods on their own land. Only a small proportion had planted pines on their own land. A larger proportion of those surveyed reported planting pines on lands in the park as part of the conservation project mentioned above. This conservation project was one of the limited opportunities in the area to earn a wage. The other significant wage employment was the coffee harvest. Interest in tree planting was most closely related to the potential for household use. As shown in figure 4.11, those surveyed were most likely to have planted trees near their house, and these plantings were most often fruit trees.

Conclusion

In Honduras, the influence of governmental and nongovernmental organizations on local forest values and practices is undeniable. Both *COHDEFOR*, the parastatal Honduran Forestry Development Corporation, and CAMNP, the Cerro Azul Meambar National Park managed by *Aldea Global*, a nongovernmental organization, weighed heavily in people's thinking about the management of forests. In fact, we observed this influence most strikingly in the canned responses offered by local residents when asked about forests and trees. These responses were not only uniform but very similar to those we elicited in our Costa Rican case study, suggesting that residents in and around parks in both countries were influenced by the global environmental discourse. In Honduras, *COHDEFOR* and *Aldea Global*

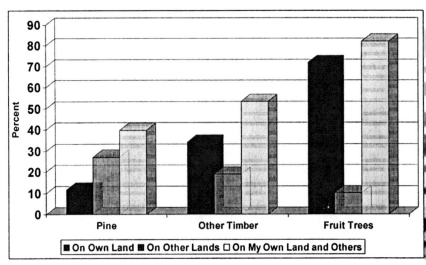

Figure 4.10. Proportion planting trees on own or other land by types of trees planted, Cerro Azul Meambar, Honduras.

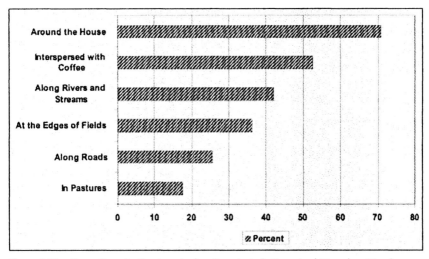

Figure 4.11.   Proportion planting trees by location planted, Cerro Azul Meambar, Honduras.

are strongly implicated as the carriers of this discourse. And it appears that they have been effective carriers of the conservation message. The accounts offered by a number of the persons we interviewed indicated that there had been a marked change in forest values and behaviors since the 1970s. Up to that time, there had been a heavy emphasis on forest clearing. Since that time, attitudes and practices have changed, and there is a strong local sentiment for forest conservation.

The creation of the park in 1987, and more importantly its institutionalization by *Aldea Global* in 1992, is a central feature of forest conservation in the area. Forest conservation efforts have concentrated on education to help local residents balance their livelihood needs with the conservation of forests. This approach was necessitated by the fact that a significant number of people lived in the area designated as the park. We estimated that by the late 1990s there were about 19,600 persons living in forty-two villages within the park's buffer zone (Pfeffer et al. 2001). Given this organization of the park, local residents were directly impacted by the park's forest conservation policies and had a direct role in managing the park's natural resources.

The close interactions between local residents and park authorities and their careful parroting of the forest conservation messages disseminated by conservationists belie more subtle ways that the park residents attempt to manage tensions between their livelihood needs and the demands of forest conservation. Local residents do this in various ways, as we have indicated in the mediating models described above. All the models indicate different ways that people justify their efforts to earn a livelihood in light of the widely accepted need for forest conservation. Our interviews indicate that individuals are actively engaged in constructing these mediating models and that they come up with a wide range of creative solutions.

This chapter shows that local forest conservation is a diverse and dynamic process that is informed by the global environmental discourse but is fashioned according to a wide range of local needs. The diverse livelihood and conservation strategies reflect the local resource endowment, access to resources by individual households, and the location of communities and households relative to economic opportunities created by the park. Clearly, local communities are responsive to the global environmental discourse, but the responses are far from uniform or predictable. This lack of predictability stems from context-specific natural and cultural features of communities and the creativeness of local people in responding to global influences. In other words, these influences might be the same everywhere, but how people respond to them takes myriad forms.

Notes

1. For a more detailed analysis of the expected benefits of the park, see Pfeffer et al. (2006).

2. It should be noted that people in the Honduran site were more dependent on subsistence crops than people in the Costa Rican site.

3. For a more detailed discussion of the fluidity of definitions of trees, forest, and fallow, see Pfeffer et al. (2001).

Situating Environmental Values in a Globalizing World

THERE IS A LOT AT STAKE in the global spread of national parks and protected areas and tropical forest conservation efforts. From a conservation point of view, the stakes include the future of many of the world's species and ecosystems, or biodiversity, and perhaps the nature and extent of future global environmental change. At the local level in tropical countries, rural households and communities often depend on these same resources to meet their livelihood needs and aspirations. Various outcomes have occurred when global conservation meets local people and communities, ranging from extreme conflict to mutually beneficial situations. The most desirable outcomes will be those that conserve biodiversity while also providing for the development needs and aspirations of local people, and finding such outcomes may be the only way that conservation or development gains can endure over the long term. Crafting programs and policies that meet these diverse objectives will require an in-depth understanding of social and cultural processes.

Our goal in carrying out this research and writing this book has been to learn more about forest and environmental beliefs and values, specifically the nature of environmental values, how these values are shaped, and the motivating force that these values carry. In the introduction, we made our case for the idea that rural people in lesser developed countries are at the receiving end of certain forest and environmental discourses and values that emanate from core areas of the world. We hasten to add that this does not mean that rural people do not have their own environmental values or that the values that they do have are somehow inferior to those coming from core areas of the world. Rather, we are suggesting that the concepts and values underlying current national parks and other protected areas and forest conservation policies and laws derive from core region cultural and political structures and that these have considerable power in peripheral regions for both material and symbolic reasons because they may be viewed or disseminated as "global" standards (Grimes 2000).

If the spread of conservation ideas, values, and practices demonstrates certain patterns of global flow and interaction, then globalization and the environment offer a productive connection for understanding local environmental values and practices. In the introduction, we identified three key ideas from social science research on globalization and the environment: (1) the imposition of core conservation values and practices on local people living in remote forested landscapes by more powerful interests, (2) the use of global and universal constructions of the environment in this process, and (3) differences in the content of global (core) and local (peripheral) forest and environmental values that result from complex interactions between, on the one hand, local livelihood and environmental values and, on the other hand, global environmental values and conservation actions under unequal power balances and unique local conditions.

Our approach is based on the idea that unique local environmental values often emerge when the global meets the local. Schema theory, or mental and cultural models, provides the theoretical underpinning and methodology for our research for several reasons. First, it takes a view of environmental beliefs and values in which they are located both in individuals and in culture, as well as in which they are constructed through lived experience. These properties, in turn, allow for concrete processes of value emergence and change that can be studied. A model of this nature enables us to empirically examine the ways in which environmental beliefs and values change in processes of globalization through encounters between dominant global and less powerful local cultures.

We have analyzed transcriptions and field notes from interviews we conducted in rural communities adjacent to or inside of national parks in two countries to identify shared schemas related to forests, national parks, and wildlife; and we have sought to reinforce our findings with quantitative results from surveys administered in these communities. We have based our analysis on, and provided in these pages, ample first-person narratives drawn from the qualitative interviews. We believe that this provides the greatest evidence for our findings, best conveys the nuances and complexities of environmental beliefs and values, gives voice to local people, and allows the reader to form his or her own conclusions somewhat independently from our analysis. The quantitative results are helpful because they gauge how widely held some values or attitudes are and concisely represent some of our findings from the qualitative research, which allows us to look for differences and make comparisons both within and between the two research sites.

Thus far we have presented the results from our two research sites separately. We chose to carry out our research in two contrasting sites because we believed that the different contexts and histories of these sites would help us understand the nature, formation, and motivating force of environmental values in ways that research in a single site would not. We limited ourselves to two sites because we used labor-intensive methods that required us to build on our previous research experiences and contacts in each site, and our time, funding, and social networks did not allow for more. Yet we felt that the two sites we chose for our research offered an interesting series of similarities and contrasts in terms of conservation history, strength of and exposure to environmental messages, levels of development and rural livelihood strategies, and forms of protected area management.

In this chapter we will draw on a broad range of data and analysis from within each research site, as well as comparisons between the two sites, to discuss the nature, shaping, and motivating force of environmental values. We will first look at environmental values themselves in several contexts: forests on private land, wildlife and hunting, and national parks and adjacent communities. Then we will look at how environmental values interact with other value spheres, in particular, livelihood values. Throughout, we will be specifically attuned to using differences in social position and context to illustrate the dynamic and contingent nature of forest values and behaviors and to the processes through which values are formed and change at the local level in an increasingly globalized world. Following this analysis, we will briefly discuss theoretical perspectives on values and then examine the practical value of our research for the promotion of fair and effective forest conservation.

Global Environmentalism and Local Forest Values

Each of the research sites discussed in this book is a place where nonindigenous migrants from other parts of each country arrived over the past few decades in search of land on which to build houses, grow crops, and establish communities. In their initial stages, these colonization processes resulted in widespread forest clearing and conversion of forests to agricultural lands. The evidence from our interviews in both countries suggests that forests had little place in early colonists' thoughts other than as obstacles to this colonization process and impediments to development. Forest knowledge, beliefs, and values were not well developed, particularly in contrast to those of long-term forest occupants such as indigenous or traditional people that have been studied by other researchers (e.g., Alcorn 1996, Pinedo-Vasquez and Padoch 1996). However, while early colonists in our two study sites did not conserve forests, our interviews indicate that their experiences living and working in the forest did make an impact on them and that they frequently developed some level of appreciation for forests and wildlife. In spite of this, forest clearing was widespread as colonists carved farms out of forests, less to obtain timber for sale or household use than to create agricultural lands. Large amounts of timber were reportedly burned or left to rot at both sites, and colonists, using extensive shifting cultivation systems involving slash-and-burn techniques, repeated the process on new forestlands when crop production declined. About 40 percent of the persons we surveyed in Costa Rica and almost 60 percent of those surveyed in Honduras reported that they had at some time cut trees or cleared forest on their own land. Of those who cut trees or cleared forest in Costa Rica, the most important purpose was to clear land for cultivation, while in Honduras, the harvesting of firewood was most important. In both cases, the harvesting of wood for home construction was very important. Little cutting was reportedly done to claim land or for commercial sales of timber, although Costa Ricans were slightly more likely to have cut trees for these purposes.

Today people look back at past deforestation with different eyes. They now associate many important benefits and values with forests, and people in both countries considered past clearing excessive and done in ignorance of the importance of forests. There has been a change in local people's beliefs about, and values related to, forests. In both study sites, the people we surveyed were nearly unanimous in agreeing that "These days people in this community are much more careful with the forest than they used to be." About three-fourths in the respective sites agreed that "Young people should be angry with earlier generations for the damage they did to the forests around here." And again, there was near unanimous agreement in both sites with the statement "We should think about future generations when we make decisions about our forests."

These changes in people's beliefs and values related to forests coincided with the arrival of national and international conservation programs to the sites. If the

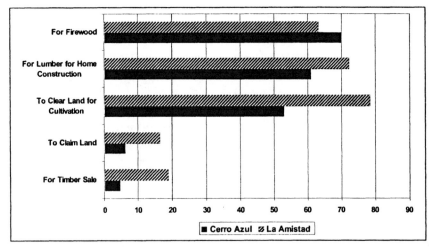

Figure 5.1.   Proportion who cut trees on their own land by purpose, Cerro Azul Meambar, Honduras and La Amistad, Costa Rica

increase in conservation awareness has been due, to a significant extent, to outside forces, the appearance of a team of expatriate researchers who were on a familiar basis with park and forest conservation staff and were asking questions about forests almost certainly led people to put forward the most positive conservation beliefs and values that they had during interviews. However, as discussed earlier, people's underlying mental and cultural models—the subject of our study—were necessarily revealed when they engaged in in-depth conversations with us and answered our follow-up questions.

It's worth mentioning that our results also reflect our choice of research sites and past conservation experiences in these areas. Places where greater tension existed between local people and conservation programs or where people were openly hostile toward conservation would have produced different results and likely would have also required a different research approach. Our results best reflect processes that happen when conservation programs are imposed on local people without provoking a strong reaction. We do not mean to suggest that local people in our research sites were not reacting to, and pushing back against, conservation programs in some ways, only that open conflict had not ensued. Later in this chapter, we will situate our research in a broader range of possible local responses and discuss some of the conditions under which different responses may be provoked. But, for now, we will focus on our findings in the Costa Rican and Honduran research sites.

The Nature of Local Forest and Environmental Beliefs and Values

One of the first things that emerged in our interviews was what we called, in the field, the "party line." These were responses that suggested near complete adoption of conservation rhetoric, often varied little from one person to the next, and seemed very automatic and superficial. After we had heard them a number of times, these statements sometimes frustrated us, especially if they constituted most of what we heard in an interview. We made efforts in our interviewing and analysis to get behind and underneath these responses, and these efforts were generally successful. But eventually we also came to see these nearly automatic and canned responses as highly significant and worthy of detailed analysis and discussion. As we have already discussed, these responses correspond with what Claudia Strauss (1997) has termed "verbal molecules," which she sees as indicators of lip-service motivation (endorsing a value but not acting on it) in response to powerful themes from dominant cultures.

In Costa Rica, the most common themes expressed and the verbal molecules associated with them were (1) forests and the park as important for producing pure air or oxygen, often expressed as the "forest is a lung" or "without forests, there would be no pure air"; (2) the role of forests in maintaining rainfall, stream flows, and water for human use, often expressed as "without the forests, this place would be a desert"; and (3) the importance of continued existence of wildlife so that different species could be seen by people in the future, often expressed as "if we destroy the forests, the future generation won't know the wildlife." In Honduras, the major themes were similar, but slightly different: (1) the association of forests with life in a general way, often by repeating a government slogan, "forests are life"; (2) the role of forests in bringing rainfall and maintaining stream flow, often expressed as "without forest this would be a desert" and the need to protect forests around the "sources of water" (fuentes de agua); and (3) references to the perceived role of forests in producing clean air, a cool and pleasant environment, and good health, using terms like "pure air," "oxygen," and "coolness." These schemas are different in each case because social discourses of global conservation are expressed differently from place to place in the media and in conservation programs.

As an indicator of the extent and power of these ideas, in both Costa Rica and Honduras nine out of ten persons surveyed agreed with the following statements:

- Without forests our community would not have sufficient water.
- Without forests we would not have sufficient oxygen to breath.
- The forests around here help to keep temperatures cooler.
- The forests are a part of our national patrimony.
- [This country] is helping the rest of the world by preserving its forests.

In each research site, these ideas and verbal molecules were nearly universally mentioned early in each qualitative interview, and some interviewees never really got far beyond them. Strauss (2005) notes that verbal molecules can provide people with something prepackaged to say when a topic comes up and also may seem a safe thing to say because you have heard them many times before. It is tempting to see them mostly as attempts by people to tell us what they thought we wanted to hear by repeating phrases they had heard associated with forests when talked about by outsiders in environmental education programs or through the media rather than as genuine representations of local forest beliefs and values. Yet there are several things that suggest they are of greater significance. First, everyone knew them and repeated them to us, indicating that they had been absorbed by most people and were seen as important enough to repeat. Second, they provided the dominant general structure for the way people talked about forests. They were often frequently mentioned and referenced throughout individual interviews, and people often fell back on them when they had trouble expressing an idea or answering a question. In the Costa Rican site, where people expressed more outright opposition to forest conservation and the park than in Honduras, people often expressed their opposition by taking these same verbal molecules, looking at them in a different light and talking about them in a different way, and suggesting that they were factually incorrect and thus provided little justification for conservation (e.g., "We have plenty of oxygen here" [10:CR27][1] or "Costa Rica is not a desert . . . there is more forest than cultivated land" [11:CR26]). In these cases, the verbal molecules provided the terms for, and structured the opposition to, conservation. Thus, we argue that these expressions indicate a widespread model of what people believe outsiders expect them to think and say about forests. But we go further than this and suggest that the power imbalance between outside conservation interests and local people is such that outsiders set the terms of any discussion, and local people adapt to them. In other words, these outside models play a significant role in structuring the way local people actually think about and value forests. This may be especially true in our two cases because people were recent colonists from agricultural zones and did not have a long history of interacting and living in close association with the forest. Thus, many of our interviewees used these ideas as a foundation on which to build more in-depth and complex mental models of forests.

As Strauss (2005) has said for verbal molecules in general, these expressions appeared to sometimes be very superficial and not to have been broadly incorporated into people's thoughts and actions. As mentioned above, Strauss (1997) calls this lip-service motivation, rather than lack of, or weak, motivation, because it indicates that people have internalized a coherent view of what they think is common opinion with reference to how they should (according to outside norms and pressures) be thinking about something—in this case, forests—and these ideas may in fact be accepted by them as appropriate beliefs and values. These ideas thus exert a significant influence over any new, local forest values that are developing, a process that we will discuss in detail later. The other possible outcome would be for new, counterhegemonic discourses to emerge. We encountered little of this, save for some limited expression of opposition to conservation grounded in economic and livelihood values in Costa Rica. We will address some possible reasons for this later.

People living in rural places interact materially with forests and receive some real material benefits from them in the form of products and environmental services. Rainfall and water, a pleasant climate, aesthetic experiences, and the knowledge that these will be available to descendants are all examples. Although verbal molecules and other expressions of environmental values take on social and cultural elements that go beyond the material, material benefits are important, and people discussed a broad range of products and services from forests. Utilitarian views of forests were strong in both countries. Forests were used as sources of lumber to build houses and furniture, for firewood, and to obtain food and medicinal plants. While it was considered inappropriate to waste trees, cutting trees for these purposes was generally considered to be acceptable by local people in both countries, and trees were seen as a renewable resource for human use that could be managed for sustained production. While it was clear in the questionnaire responses that people did not see utilitarian benefits as the only thing important about forests, they were a dominant category of benefits that they considered themselves to be receiving from forests. One interesting difference between the two countries was that in Honduras people could scarcely imagine not being permitted access to these utilitarian benefits of forests, while in Costa Rica people sometimes thought that there were viable substitutes. This may reflect differences in the livelihood contexts of the two countries, with rural Hondurans more dependent on the subsistence foods and products they obtain from the nearby environment and rural Costa Ricans using more purchased foods and products from the country's industrializing economy and well-developed transportation infrastructure. Our surveys in the two countries provide further evidence of this pattern. Figure 5.2 shows the level of agreement with statements expressing various dimensions of a utilitarian attitude toward trees and forests. The overall pattern of agreement with these statements is similar in our two sites, with individuals in both countries in greatest agreement that basic livelihood needs should take precedence. In both countries, individuals expressed less support for commercial uses of forests. As indicated above, concerns about satisfying livelihood needs were slightly more pronounced in Honduras, where local residents were relatively poorer than their counterparts in Costa Rica.

The role of forests in maintaining rainfall patterns and the flow of water in streams was pervasive in our interviews in both countries. People told very specific

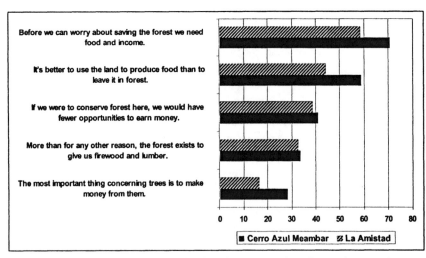

Figure 5.2.   Proportion who agreed with selected statements about forests, Cerro Azul Meambar, Honduras, and La Amistad, Costa Rica

stories about streams drying up and changing rainfall patterns (e.g., 47:CR3, 17: H21). Although the scientific evidence associating forest clearing with changes in climate, rainfall, and stream flow is complex and not conclusive (Bruijneel 2004, Kaimowitz 2005), people clearly believed that changes in water regimes had occurred, and they associated these changes with forest clearing. The association of retention of forests with continued water availability was without doubt the strongest forest-related belief and value that we found in both sites and also provided the strongest justification and impetus for forest conservation for local people (e.g., 6:CR10, 47:CR3, 5:H15, 6:H8).

However, as we mentioned above, people value forest more broadly than for just utilitarian purposes. In both countries, people made statements about the beauty of forests and people appreciating this beauty (e.g., 20:CR6, 37:H21). There was, however, an interesting difference between the two countries. Many of our Costa Rican interviewees made heartfelt and impassioned statements about the beauty of the forests, such as "It is something that is beautiful, it is something that fills one with the spirit of life" (20:CR6) and "I am in love with this forest . . . I have always been a lover of nature" (23:CR3). Our Honduran interviewees, while sometimes talking about experiencing the beauty of forests (e.g., 45:H14), were more likely to talk about others enjoying it, for example "They say it is very pretty. I've never been there but someday I'll go and walk around." (34:H7) or "Some of the people who have stayed with me have gone there and come back talking of beautiful things" (35:H5). This suggests that, in Costa Rica, aesthetic and recreational values of forests may be more widely experienced and perhaps more deeply incorporated into people's mental and cultural models of forest than in Honduras. In both sites, nine out of ten persons surveyed agreed with the statement "We should have a lot of forests here because they are so beautiful."

Religious associations with the forest and the environment were common, as has been found elsewhere (e.g., in the United States by Kempton et al. 1995). Taking care of the forest was often discussed as taking care of God's creation, as a human responsibility. In some cases, this takes on aspects of all species being important or having the right to live (26:CR18, 57:H20). More frequently, people suggested that God created nature for people to use and live from, not just to be appreciated (26:CR8, 28:CR7, 43:H23, 162:H21). While we did not find significant differences in environmental values by religious affiliation (i.e., Catholic or Evangelical), there were reports in the interviews (e.g., 89:H14; see also Jantzi et al. 1999, Pfeffer et al. 2006) of evangelical Christians interpreting environmental degradation as God's punishment rather than the result of human actions. Other important social values also became integrated with forest values. For example, a Honduran interviewee (38:H14) talked about parallels between the plight of forests and the plight of women and parallels in the way they had been treated. In other cases, forests seemed to symbolize the rural environment and its cleanliness, health, and lack of social problems and to be contrasted with the opposite characteristics of urban environments (e.g., 18:CR9, 19:CR3, 22:H20, 140:H24). These examples show the way that forest beliefs and values become intertwined with beliefs and values from what are largely social, and not material, domains and, thus, highlight the social and cultural nature and construction of forest values.

Forests in Social Relationships

One way we sought to learn more about the source of forest values was by asking a series of questions that explored the ways that forest-related beliefs and values were shared among people, including where people had learned about forests. One of our interests was the roles played by the media and representatives of government conservation agencies or nongovernmental conservation organizations, since they potentially play a key role in the transmission of outside conservation beliefs and values into the local community. Park management and forestry organizations— the *Ministerio de Ambiente y Energía* (*MINAE*) in Costa Rica and the Cerro Azul Meambar National Park (CAMNP) and the *Corporación Hondureño de Desarollo Forestal* (*COHDEFOR*) in Honduras—were often cited as important sources of information. They were often talked about as the people who had brought environmental awareness into the communities, calling local people's attention to the problems related to deforestation and forest degradation by organizing meetings, giving talks, and showing movies in the local communities (e.g., 66:CR23, 65:H8, 71:H3, 72:H12). This form of awareness raising seems to have reached more of the local residents in Honduras than in Costa Rica. Figure 5.3 shows that a higher proportion of Hondurans reported having learned about forests from extensionists and informational meetings. In fact, in Honduras, people tended to talk about changes in environmental awareness that clearly showed the influence of outside authority figures, for example "we weren't oriented" before (44:H9), "the majority of us are educated now" (131:H3), "people would have learned how to work" if the park had arrived sooner (48:H11), and "the mother [the park] knows but her child [local people] does not" (66:H26). In Costa Rica, environmental awareness was described more as an organic process of increasing awareness within individuals in response to a broader cultural shift (61:CR3).

The presence of park guards living in the community was often cited as important in Honduras (70:H16), but our survey findings show that about the same proportion of individuals in Costa Rica reported that they had learned about the forests from park guards. In Honduras the park guards worked closely with local community leaders (the *patronato*), and as indicated in figure 5.3, a majority of the individuals surveyed in Honduras mentioned that they had learned about forests from local leaders. This highlights the importance of local community members as intermediaries between globally driven conservation interests and local people. The media, television in Costa Rica and radio in Honduras, represented another very important outside source of environmental information (see figure 5.3). A number of interviewees reported being avid fans of environmental programs on television and radio (61:CR3, 76:H1).

People in both countries reported a variety of other organizational disseminators of environmental messages. Churches were an important source (62:CR8, 69:H11), and when people talked about churches, they generally talked about learning through participation in local church activities rather than learning from religion or theology more broadly. As indicated in figure 5.3, about half of the Costa Ricans and 60 percent of the Hondurans reported that they had learned about forests from the church. Other local groups, generally organized with outside guidance, were also addressing environmental issues, for example a women's group in Honduras (68:H14) and a tourism board and a local environmental organization in Costa Rica (68:CR18, 72:CR20). It is notable that communication generally occurred through local organizations affiliated with, or organized by, larger religious or conservation groups, highlighting the importance of local social connections, as well as how they differ from place to place (28:CR7, 69:H11). People also learned through informal social contacts—parents, family members, and fellow workers—although these, too, were often intermediaries between the local community and outside organizations (68:CR18, 69:CR20, 71:H3).

Notably, though, many people reported that their principal source of information was their own experience living in the region and seeing changes in the forest

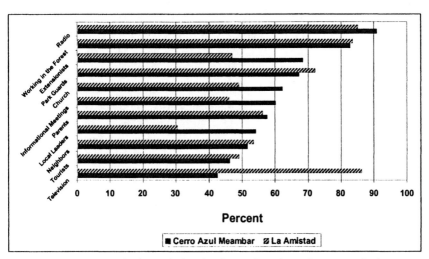

Figure 5.3.   Proportion who learned what they know about forests by source of information, Cerro Azul Meambar, Honduras, and La Amistad, Costa Rica

and the environment. As one Costa Rican said, "It is not necessary for people to tell you things if you have already seen it" (63:CR10). Some of the most eloquent statements about forests and wildlife came when people told about experiences they had when they were young—sitting by a river, looking at trees and forests, or seeing wildlife around their houses (38:H14, 45:H14, 30:CR18, 67:CR13). In fact, our survey findings show that working the land was cited as the most important source of information after radio, in Honduras, and television, in Costa Rica (see figure 5.3). Thus, while outside organizations were credited with getting people to think about forest and wildlife values, people did not necessarily see these as being their sole source of inspiration. Rather, they found clear confirming evidence from their own lives of forest and environmental change and were motivated by emotionally powerful experiences with forests and wildlife. This was particularly true in Costa Rica, where many people in open-ended interviews talked about learning about forests through their own experiences ("This I didn't learn. It was born in me from being raised in the forest" [61:CR3]). This was the most important source of information reported in the Costa Rican survey, but it was also important in Honduras, where it was the second most important source. In summary, people attributed their knowledge about forests primarily to a combination of media sources, learning through park rangers and extensionists, and their personal experiences with forests and forest change. Parents were of moderate importance, and while this was sometimes discussed as a transmission of core values from parents to children, it was often the case that parents themselves had undergone recent value change from their frontier attitudes by being involved in conservation activities.

When we asked people whom they talked to about trees and forests, they reported that much of their discussion was among family and friends. There was a tendency to feel that talking about trees and forests more broadly in the community—which generally was interpreted as talking in favor of forest conservation or against burning and forest clearing—had the potential to stir up social discord since not everyone agreed. Although there were some people who said that they did not hesitate to talk to people about these things, in general our results suggested that the outside conservation values were not necessarily universal norms that were effective in stopping tree felling and forest clearing. Although people tended to report that forest conservation was becoming widely accepted (38:CR24, 39:CR18, 61:H7, 64:H18), they also talked about there being powerful interests associated with tree felling and forest clearing and that ordinary local people felt helpless in the face of this (78:CR10, 90:CR6, 104:CR18, 110:CR21, 152:CR11, 113:H14, 176:H21, 177:H5).

Forestry Laws

Another way of learning about local acceptance of forest conservation was to ask what people thought about forestry laws, which placed restrictions on, and required permits for, tree felling and generally prohibited forest clearing. We also asked people what they thought would happen if someone in the local community began to fell trees or clear forest, because if forest conservation norms were strong and widespread, we expected people to be willing to participate in their enforcement. In both countries, people gave significant credit to forestry laws for having slowed or stopped previously widespread forest clearing. They generally felt that even if forest values were widely recognized and supported, there would always be some people who would fell trees and clear forests if there were no laws prohibiting this. People generally saw the law and associated punishments as creating an effective disincentive for tree felling. In each country, people talked about communities wanting to be able to call on forest authorities to stop forest clearing when it occurred (e.g., 96:H10, 84:CR10), indicating how communities and government can sometimes work together. There was nearly unanimous agreement in both Costa Rica and Honduras with the following statements expressing support for government regulations:

- If we did not have laws that protect the forests, we would have far fewer trees.
- If people were permitted to cut as many tress as they wanted, they would not know when to stop.

In addition, about three-fourths of those surveyed in Costa Rica and Honduras also agreed that there had been a behavioral impact of government regulations in that fewer people were burning forest.

When asked who was responsible for taking care of the forests, a number of people took the question quite literally and responded, "The park guards." Yet in both countries (although perhaps more in Costa Rica), significant numbers of people felt that people in the community were actually the ones who should be taking on this responsibility because of the benefits that they received from forests (e.g., 96:CR5, 97:CR13, 104:H22, 105:H21). Yet responses were mixed about how local people would respond if someone started felling trees and clearing forests. In both countries, some people said that they or someone else would report them (112:CR13, 107:H1, 113:H14), while others said that no one cared enough or was willing to risk the conflict that doing so would engender (108:CR3, 109:CR20, 111:CR6). In Honduras, people seemed willing to overlook felling of trees for necessary personal use (e.g., 108:H6, 111:H19), while in Costa Rica, if this sentiment existed, it was not stated so clearly.

In both countries, people had complaints about complicated and expensive processes for obtaining permits. Park guards often talked about trying to negotiate a middle ground: trying to stop people felling trees for personal profit, while accommodating genuine local needs for timber without subjecting people to complicated bureaucratic permit processes. In Honduras, in particular, the involvement of community-based park rangers and local *patronatos* played a key role in this (109:H15). They were reportedly often willing to look the other way in cases of genuine need, which defused some of the tension over enforcement of forestry laws (109:H15). In Costa Rica, a local park ranger supported a similar attitude and behaviors but complained that other park rangers who did not reside in the community often took a hard line in enforcing the law (89:CR11). Reflecting this harder line, Costa Rican respondents told about an organized community protest when one of their neighbors was jailed for felling young second growth (*tacotal*) to plant beans (88:CR9) and threatening to set fire to park forests if the rangers were too strict in enforcing conservation laws (87:CR7). There was also a sense in both countries that wealthy and well-connected landowners and loggers were more easily able to get permits than were local people with subsistence needs (150:CR3, 151:CR4, 176:H21, 178:H23). This conclusion is born out by our survey findings. About nine out of ten persons surveyed in both Costa Rica and Honduras agreed with the following statements:

- It is easier for rich owners of big farms to get permits to cut trees than it is for common or poor people.
- It should be easier for small farmers (*campesinos*) in this community to get permits to cut a tree for household use.

National parks. People in both countries associated the creation of the national parks with forest conservation and cited many of the same benefits for the park as they cited for forests, with an emphasis on broad, public benefits. Water availability was seen as a particularly important benefit of the parks, reflecting the fact that in Honduras the park was in the watershed of a major reservoir and in Costa Rica most local drinking water systems originated in the park or an adjacent protected zone (116:CR8, 122:CR13, 116:H10, 154:H7). Wildlife was clearly associated with the park in both countries and was discussed more often in relation to the park than it was in general discussions of forests (e.g., 113:CR14, 118:H3). The parks were also generally associated with "pure air" and "oxygen" (e.g., 1:CR16, 118:H3). People also valued the contacts that they had with outsiders as a result of the park (120:CR3, 126:H25).

The presence of the national parks was clearly associated with outside forces in both countries. Outside interests were seen as paying for the conservation in the parks to protect wood, wildlife, and water and for global oxygen production (113:CR14, 114:CR13, 118:H3, 121:H14). One interviewee in Costa Rica considered the park important because of the value of the timber being left unexploited, which was attributed to agreements with other countries for forest conservation (115:CR9). In Honduras, several respondents interpreted the level of outside funding to mean that the parks or their resources had been sold to other countries (e.g., 122:H17). Several comments in Honduras, one about having missed hearing about the park (123:H23) and one about having been told that the park was good for the village but having forgotten why (124:H5), reinforced the idea that people saw the park and conservation as being imposed on them by outside interests.

The park rangers and agencies receiving funds for managing the park were clearly seen as the most concrete beneficiaries in each country (e.g., 119:CR3, 150: H25). Yet local people also said that they received concrete benefits from the park, most significantly in terms of the availability of water and, to some extent, for air quality. There was a common belief that, without the park, all the forests would have been eliminated and that this would not have been a good thing for local people (116:CR8, 117:CR10, 118:CR18, 138:H15, 139:H13, 140:H24). Yet, many people expressed a level of frustration that the only benefits they received from the park were diffuse and long-term general benefits like air, water, and wildlife conservation (124:CR16, 153:H13). In the questionnaire, people generally saw themselves as benefiting from the park, but somewhat less than outsiders or those working for the park. Our survey findings from the question on "who benefits from the park" showed that a large proportion of the individuals interviewed in both Costa Rica and Honduras expected a wide range of benefits from the park (see figure 5.4).

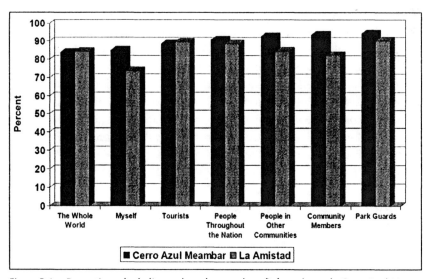

Figure 5.4.   Proportion who believe selected groups benefit from the park, Cerro Azul Meambar, Honduras, and La Amistad, Costa Rica

In Honduras, the situation was such that local people were living without electricity in an area where one reason for outside forest conservation efforts was protection of the watershed of a reservoir associated with a hydroelectric project. This situation produced one of our more interesting findings. When we talked to people about the possible unfairness of this situation, people recognized the imbalance in costs and benefits, but rather than complaining that others were getting more, they were trying to use this as justification for development aid and improvements in their own communities. Honduran interviewees tended to see the park as one of the few outside presences in the region and thought that this presence could be leveraged into obtaining better roads, electricity, water systems, and economic development opportunities through tourism and reforestation. As one said, " I hope and think that one day [the park] will make us better off in some way" (127:H18) There were also indications of this in Costa Rica (e.g., 124:CR16). People seemed to be indicating a willingness to accept the parks if they were associated with some development benefits.

The two parks have different management approaches, with the La Amistad International Park in Costa Rica being a strictly protected, "traditional" park where people live only outside the park boundaries and CAMNP in Honduras being a "zoned" park following more recent "parks-and-people" approaches that seeks to protect biodiversity while still allowing some resource use for rural people in some parts of the park. Zoned parks generally make more effort to meet local people's needs, and we have elsewhere addressed in detail the question of which model leads to greater expected benefits for local people, using these two case studies (Pfeffer et al. 2006). To summarize, we found that while in both cases people saw themselves as benefiting from the park, they also saw themselves as less likely to benefit than people living in other places, controlling for differences in the sociodemographic composition of the populations at the two study sites (figure 5.5). Yet, our Honduran respondents, who were experiencing a parks-and-people approach in the form of a zoned protected area and community park guards, were more likely than Costa Ricans to expect benefits for themselves because they had been closely integrated into park management, lived inside the park, and had access to some park resources. Costa Rican respondents tended to compartmentalize the park from their livelihoods, saying that the park was fine where it was but that it should stay out of the affairs of local landowners (155:CR17).

Hunting

Hunting, because it is often an illegal and clandestine activity, is a difficult subject for research. Costa Rican respondents were more likely to talk about hunting than Hondurans. They noted that hunting had once been prevalent but was now rare (126:CR4, 128:CR11). Respondents also indicated that wildlife was now more abundant than before and attributed this to the decline in hunting (127:CR20,

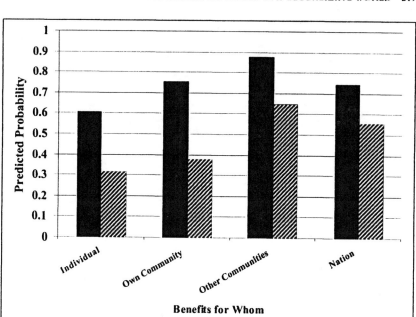

Figure 5.5.   Predicted probabilities of expected park benefits, Cerro Azul Meambar, Honduras, and La Amistad, Costa Rica

128:CR11). A clear antihunting norm was expressed, and hunters were called lazy (129:CR18, 131:CR24). In Honduras, a few people talked about their personal dislike for hunting (e.g., 158:H7), while indicating that hunting was still going on and that it was difficult stop it (157:H18, 159:H10). Our survey data indicated that most people disapproved of hunting for commercial purposes, although hunting for this purpose was slightly more acceptable in Honduras. As indicated in figure 5.6, about one in five Hondurans agreed that hunting animals is alright if one needs money, compared with less than 10 percent of the Costa Ricans. In contrast, more than half of both Hondurans and Costa Ricans agreed that hunting animals was acceptable if you need food. The patterns of responses in figure 5.6 show that people tended not to favor hunting but were more inclined to see it as acceptable if people were very poor and hungry.

The Nature and Development of Environmental Values

Local people living in or adjacent to these two national parks believed that forests provided many benefits. Water-related benefits (stream flow and rainfall) were the most frequently mentioned and were valued for their local importance, as well as the contribution that they made to regional and national water supplies

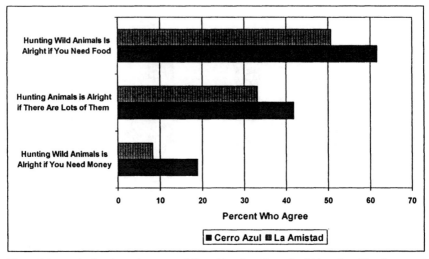

Figure 5.6.   Attitudes about the acceptability of hunting, Cerro Azul Meambar, Honduras, and La Amistad, Costa Rica

and power generation. Another important category of benefits related to air. At the broadest level, this was expressed by talking about the role of forests in "oxygen production." This value had a local element in discussions about desirable local climatic conditions, including fresh air and coolness, and was sometimes discussed in contrast to polluted urban areas. Wildlife was mentioned frequently in relation to forests and the national parks, often emphasizing the importance of future generations' being able to see wildlife species. In addition to very general statements about wildlife, as in the case of benefits related to water and air, local wildlife values were often discussed in terms of personal experiences of viewing and appreciating wildlife.

The socially constructed nature of these values manifested itself through the common and consistent terminology that people used to talk about water, air, and wildlife. For example, it is doubtful that anyone had actually noticed a decrease in oxygen, but statements about the role of tropical forests in oxygen production commonly appear in English-language environmental news articles and education materials.[2] We believe that this terminology came from social discourses of conservation emanating from core areas of the world. These have been experienced by local people in very specific and locally unique ways, through the media and through local arms of government conservation agencies, nongovernmental organizations (NGOs), and churches. Because of power imbalances between core and peripheral regions and facilitated by the fact that residents of the communities we studied were relatively recent agricultural colonists without deep experiences with forests, these new schemas of external origin have been widely adopted by local people and serve to structure much of people's discourse on forests and forest values, including opposition to conservation when it existed. Forest values also became integrated with a wide variety of social concerns and issues, including rural-urban tensions, religion, and gender relations, which reinforces our argument that environmental values are socially and culturally constructed. Many environmental values, rather than being a distinct domain, were intertwined with social concerns and values.

On the other hand, local people have had material relationships with forests through their uses of forest products and as beneficiaries of forest-related environmental services. Many of our interviewees gave specific examples of benefits of forests or the results of the forest degradation. These were in accord with global environmental discourse, but were illustrated with examples from their personal experiences living through periods of deforestation and, in some cases, reforestation. Forest products were widely used by rural people, and forests tended to be viewed through utilitarian perspectives. However, there were indications of growing appreciation of forests for their aesthetic and recreational values, with this perhaps being more deeply felt by people in Costa Rica. Hondurans were more dependent on subsistence resources than Costa Ricans, which may have contributed to what appeared to be a weaker norm against hunting, as well as a greater expectation of being able to continue household use of wood products and acceptance of the occasional necessity for forest clearing (at least in the qualitative interviews).

These findings on the development of forest beliefs and values confirm four of Steven R. Brechin and Willett Kempton's (1994) hypothesized sources of growing environmental values in lesser developed countries—diffusion of environmental values through mass media and personal communication, communication of environmental values and policies through organizations, direct observation of environmental problems, and a view of environmental quality as integral to development rather than as a luxury—and suggest that they operate in concert. Although local environmental values were derived from global environmentalism and confirmed by local experience, it is not clear that strong social norms had developed in local communities. Conservation laws were generally recognized as important and effective, although there were some complaints that they were insensitive to local livelihood needs and easily circumvented by powerful outsiders. While people discussed forest conservation with friends and family, it was still seen as a controversial subject at the community levels because of its potential to cause social discord and because they believed that powerful interests were behind much of the recent forest degradation and destruction. There was widespread support for retention of some managed forest patches and streamside forests on private lands to maintain local forest benefits. National parks were clearly seen as something of outside origin, and their perceived benefits were often broad and general. People expected and hoped to receive more tangible benefits from the parks in the future, believing that they might provide a stimulus for economic and infrastructure development. In Honduras, these expectations were higher, in part because the zoned park model and community park guards integrated local people and communities into the park more so than occurred in the strictly protected park in Costa Rica.

Environmental Values and Livelihood Values

As other research has shown (Kempton et al. 1995, Medin et al. 2006), environmental values are widespread today, and what really matters may be the meaning people ascribe to environmentalism and what happens when environmental values come into conflict with other values. In the rural communities where we conducted our research, land-based livelihoods easily conflict with forest conservation, and an important part of our analysis has been to understand how local people deal with these conflicts. In the previous section, we used two concepts from schema theory, verbal molecules and lip-service motivation (Strauss 1992, 1997, 2005), to suggest that people can state beliefs and values from dominant (global) social discourses about the environment but that these may have very little motivating force if they are compartmentalized from other values and not particularly salient in their everyday lives or sense of self. They may represent how people believe they should think in terms of outside social expectations, but in their daily interactions with people close to them, they may be exposed to different, yet more meaningful and motivating, beliefs and values. It was clear to us that some of the people that we interviewed were able to recite a standard litany of the benefits of forests but that these were compartmentalized and not integrated into their everyday land use decision making. Other people, on the other hand, had integrated environmental values with their livelihood values, and their talk showed changes in the nature and meaning of environmental beliefs and values and the emergence of unique local discourses of conservation, forests, and sustainable development.

Integrating Conservation and Livelihoods

In some cases, people seemed to have tried to find common ground between global conservation discourse and their livelihood values. One way they did this was by adjusting meanings to integrate across both value spheres. One such example can be found in the general beliefs and values about when it was acceptable and when it was not acceptable to fell trees or clear forests, which were similar in both of our study sites. This concept is exhibited in the first mediating discourse discussed in both Costa Rica and Honduras. In both countries, people rejected the earlier forest clearing of the past, in which trees were felled and burned or left to rot, as wasteful and done out of ignorance. They clearly considered this to be wrong. However, they thought of forests as something intended for use by humans and saw using trees for basic subsistence needs, like house construction and firewood, to be acceptable. Additional qualifications were often added, for example specifying that tree felling near streams or springs was not acceptable, that old and dying trees should be harvested to make room for new growth, and that the trees were a renewable resource, and when one was felled, new ones should be planted. This conception is similar to the utilitarian conservation that has characterized the forestry profession and different from the more preservation-oriented conservation that lies behind national parks in general and Costa Rican national parks in particular. This utilitarian conservation was not necessarily seen by local people as conflicting with wildlife conservation, recreational use of forests, and aesthetic appreciation of forested ecosystems, but it does place human needs first and allow for extractive forest use and management.

Redefinition or Appropriation

A second way that people adjusted meanings was by changing definitions and meanings of terms (Pfeffer et al. 2001). This is seen in the third mediating discourse from both study sites. One way this happened was by appropriating conservation definitions for activities that met their livelihood needs. For example, in both countries the presence of shade trees in coffee was seen to make it a conservation land use (192:CR8, 170:H21, 171:H22). In Honduras, this was taken further, with coffee often described as reforestation (173:H8, 217:H6). Similarly, people often associated planting fruit trees with reforestation and conservation, noting in some cases that it was dual purpose—providing the environmental benefits of trees while also providing products for the landowner (149:CR18, 188:CR10, 202: H18). At the landscape level, in Honduras in particular, people talked about clearing undergrowth and planting coffee under forest trees as a way of keeping forest benefits while getting the economic returns of agriculture (170:H21, 171:H22). This is seen in the second theme in the second mediating discourse from Honduras. Agroforestry land uses of this type do provide a mix of the environmental benefits of forests with livelihood benefits from marketable crops, but in most cases, the environmental benefits are reduced, and crop productivity may be as well (see Schelhas and Greenberg 1996, Schroth et al. 2004). Yet people appeared to gravitate toward these options because of their desire to engage in conservation while still meeting their livelihood needs. There were also definitional distinctions that place some trees and forests outside the category of forest, illustrated in the third mediating discourse from each country. Young second-growth forest in shifting cultivation systems, called *tacotal* or *charral* in Costa Rica and *guamil* in Honduras, were not considered trees and forests by local people, and they had few reservations about clearing them. It is true that young second growth can be considered a stage in agricultural systems, and if patches of second growth rotate around the landscape over time, they may provide ongoing conservation benefits (Schelhas and Greenberg 1996, Schroth et al. 2004). It is also true that some park guards or conservationists without rural livelihood experiences may not understand the role of woody fallows in agricultural systems. But what we observed and heard about went beyond this, with local people at times pushing the definition of woody fallows into what government conservation agencies and laws considered to be forest in an effort to retain their claim on agricultural land and make clearing justifiable. Disputes between forest guards and local people over what types of woody growth should be considered *tacotal* or *guamil* constituted one of the major sources of conflict at both sites.

Contesting Conservation with Other Values

Another way that people dealt with the conflict between livelihood values was by calling attention to other values, often values that were considered universal or globally powerful, and suggesting that these other values should take precedence over environmental values (Schelhas and Pfeffer 2005). People often used livelihood values in this way, as illustrated in the second mediating discourse from Honduras. For example, interviewees in Honduras pointed out their need to clear forest to plant crops, noting that, in Honduras, if you don't plant, you don't eat—no one is going to give you any food (168:H6, 169:H24, 191:H14). Another interviewee suggests that the Honduran government needs to pay attention to people in the park and what they need to live, in addition to thinking about conservation (133: H13). The interviewee goes on to say that it's not good to clear forest and that trees provide people with many benefits, but that the only choice they have is to cut trees. Similarly, interviewees in Costa Rica state that deforestation is a shame but that people have to eliminate some forest to plant something productive (12: CR7), that no one is going to give them money or a job if they don't grow crops (86:CR15, 87:CR7, 134:CR9), and that people who are "living under bridges and stealing" should be given land instead of dedicating it to forest conservation (11: CR26). One interviewee thinned the shade in his coffee without a permit and had some difficulties with forest guards but felt that what he did was urgent and necessary to protect his coffee (86:CR15). The significance of livelihood values and their expected power were revealed when Honduran interviewees, talking about their agriculture, said to us, "They have to give [a permit], right?" (180:H6) and "They can't keep us from planting beans or corn, how are we going to live?" (179: H21) (the fifth Honduran mediating discourse).

In Costa Rica we also heard appeals to property rights as a way of allowing people to meet their livelihood needs without interference from park rangers (Costa Rican mediating discourse five). In this case, people outside the park acknowledged that the government had a right to limit forest clearing in the park, which belonged to the government, but they also stated that they should be able to do what they need to do on their land because you shouldn't be able to tell your neighbor what to do on his or her land (155:CR17, 156:CR7). One of these individuals found a parallel with anti-Communism rhetoric, calling to mind "those other countries where they take away from you what you harvest" (157:CR17).

Contesting the Social Order

Parks and conservation, imposed from outside with imbalanced costs and benefits, make obvious the lack of power and resources of local people relative to urban and international interests (Pfeffer et al. 2001). Either because they recognized that the park has some benefits or because they felt powerless to confront it, they instead called attention to the issues of injustice that are made clear by the park and conservation and used these injustices as the basis for contesting the social order and to try to bring about changes that would address their needs and livelihoods. This was a common strategy and manifested itself in several ways.

One way was by apportioning greater blame for forest destruction to outside interests and loggers (the fourth mediating discourse in both Costa Rica and Honduras). It was common in both countries for people to argue that it was not local people who were destroying the forests—they had difficulties felling even a few trees for household use. Rather, they said, it was outside loggers who were destroying the forest for personal gain, leaving the local people to live with the results of both a lack of timber and a degraded environment (150:CR3, 151:CR4). They suggested that the government was not doing enough to stop this, casting doubt on the government's sincerity in terms of conservation (154:CR20) and validating their beliefs that the rich and powerful are generally able to circumvent laws (153: CR10). Even a park ranger acknowledged that this occurs (152:CR11).

Another way this was done involved accepting conservation but using it as leverage to obtain development assistance. This was most common in Honduras. One person talked about how a "proper park" would have good roads, telephones, and electricity (128:H18). As we discussed earlier, a number of interviewees in Honduras, when discussing the imbalance of local people having to take care of forests that were protecting watersheds for water and electricity projects, used this not to complain about injustice but to argue that similar services should be provided for local communities (155:H9, 156:H16). A number of people in Honduras also talked about the need for the government to create some employment options for local people to make up for the opportunities that they had to forgo due to conservation (181:H13, 182:H18, 183:H14, 184:H18, 186:H24) (Honduran mediating discourse six). In Costa Rica, perhaps because of the existence of programs of environmental services payments for people retaining forest on private lands, rather than arguing for employment opportunities, people said that if large amounts of forest were to be conserved on private land, monetary compensation was necessary (139:CR3, 140:CR16) (Costa Rican mediating discourse two).

Turning against Conservation

In Costa Rica, we encountered a few people who had turned against conservation. Several of the people who asked not have their interview recorded had land expropriated when the park was created and remained bitter. We also heard reports about people who had lost land when the park was created complaining about the speed and level of compensation and about the lost opportunities from the land they had claimed (113:CR14, 159:CR21). When this opposition was expressed, it was supported with a variety of ideas that we have already discussed. These included saying that some of the common ideas, or verbal molecules, used to justify conservation were not true ("We have plenty of oxygen" [10:CR27]) and/or arguing that that livelihood values were more important (for example, "Costa Rica has more forests than cultivated land . . . people are sleeping under bridges and stealing for lack of land to farm" [11:CR26]).

We are not certain why we did not encounter extensive oppositional discourses in Honduras, although there were some hints of opposition. One interviewee complained about the length of time—four years—for local people to learn that the park had been established (134:H14). Also, a number of people indicated that there was great concern when they learned about the park that local people were going to be forced out or not be able to work (134:H14, 135:H9, 136:H17). On the other hand, a number of park residents in Honduras felt that the park had not lived up to its potential. This sentiment was most pronounced in Cerro Azul, a community in a prime location to benefit from the park. In 1998, the village embarked on a campaign to lobby the park management to more actively pursue conservation efforts. Leaders of Cerro Azul, with strong agreement from village residents, felt they would benefit directly from conservation efforts by being well placed to attract tourists. Thus, residents of Cerro Azul did not oppose the park and its conservation goals but agitated for more vigorous development of it. Disappointment with the park set in when they realized that their hopes for potential benefits would at best be realized in the somewhat distant future. But, in general, any opposition to the park seemed to have been defused when the park established partnerships with local communities (134:H14) and, perhaps more importantly, because outside the core zone of the park people were allowed to continue to fell trees with permits and grow crops to meet their substance needs (136:H17, 137:H16). The combination of community involvement, being able to continue with their land use systems, and a feeling that the protected forests at the top of the mountain were important to the water supply seems to have made the park acceptable to local people.

Still, it is interesting in both these cases, considering the costs that park establishment had for local people in terms of lost opportunities for forest use, land clearing for agriculture, and hunting, that there wasn't greater opposition. There are several factors that appear to have contributed to this. One is that in both places local water supplies came from the park and these, perhaps along with other conservation benefits, were recognized as important. It is also possible that, to these relatively powerless local communities, internationally supported conservation seemed too difficult to resist overtly, and they could only contest with the everyday forms of resistance that James C. Scott (1985) has called "weapons of the weak." The relatively recent colonists in both sites had no other globally powerful social discourse (and related local NGO presence) to appeal to, such as indigenous rights or even a strong rural-development presence independent of conservation. To some extent, going along with conservation was the only game in town, and people instead engaged in the strategies we have discussed: going along with it when they could, recasting it to be more compatible with their interests, and trying to use it to leverage development assistance.

Influence of Environmental Beliefs and Values on Forest Behaviors

One of our key objectives was to learn more about how meanings, values, and beliefs about forests influenced forest-related behaviors. As we discussed in the introduction, most research on rural people's tree and forest behaviors in lesser developed countries has emphasized the role of material conditions and factors (e.g., Arnold and Dewees 1995). Within materialist research, there have been two broad approaches that theorize dynamic relationships between tree and forest cover and material conditions. One looks at intensification of land use with population growth, based on expansions of Ester Boserup's (1965) theory of agricultural intensification. This research has found that forests in frontier regions are often cleared and converted to extensive land uses, such as shifting agricultural and low-stocked pasture, but that as population increases, trees and forests are often integrated into the complex land use mosaics that develop (e.g., Schelhas 1996a, Tiffen et al. 1994). Using this model in our own research in the Honduran site (Pfeffer et al. 2005), we found that park creation, by decreasing the available land base, can drive land use change from shifting agriculture to intensive, permanent cropping, reducing forest cover and increasing coffee plantations. The second dynamic approach is the forest transition theory, which theorizes that industrialization and urbanization, again accompanying population growth, can result in increasing forest cover as agriculture becomes less important economically and forests are increasingly valued for environmental services, aesthetics, and recreation (Mather 1988, Palo and Vanhanen 2000, Rudel 2005). John Schelhas and Arturo Sanchez (2006) and Thomas K. Rudel et al. (2002) apply this to the Latin American tropics, both finding that while it can occur, it is not inevitable; "hollow frontiers" with low population and large cattle ranches occur instead in some cases.

We find confirmation in our results that material factors are important determinants of tree and forest decision making in our two sites, where land-based livelihoods dominate. But we do not believe that forest choices can be reduced to material factors; values, beliefs, and meanings are also important. As we have discussed, while people do think and talk about trees and forests in terms of the products and services that they get from them, their mental and cultural models of forests are deeply entwined with a variety of social and cultural values, including religion, urban-rural contrasts, and women's rights, and they are also influenced by global environmental values (transmitted by local actors). Furthermore, these mental and cultural models are also influenced by processes of cultural change originating from global social discourses on forests and conservation but influenced by local material conditions and social relationships in such a way that there can be broad changes over time in the way that forests are thought about and discussed. This, in turn, can change, for rural people, the morality associated with forest behaviors and the behaviors themselves, as we witness in the way that people's views of, and behaviors toward, forests have changed from the times when the forested frontiers were being settled to their current situation as neighbors or residents of national parks. R. Brian Ferguson (2006a, 2006b, 2007) suggests it is not possible to separate out or give priority to material or cultural factors in such cases; material and cultural processes operate through complex interrelationships over time, and we need to both identify material and political interests and understand how cultural identities, symbols, and values are employed. We think that people and forests need to be discussed in a similar way, in which people's mental and cultural models and material interests are understood to operate together.

When we showed people pictures of landscapes, they admired forests (e.g., 161: CR18, 162:CR3, 188:H2, 189:H15) but did not see a place for themselves or their communities in purely forested landscapes (163:CR15, 164:CR22, 165:CR21, 166:CR6, 190:H22, 191:H14). They showed a clear preference for landscapes that were mixes of agriculture, pasture, and forests (168:CR21, 169:CR11, 170:CR15, 192:H8, 193:H13, 194:H18). In their behaviors, they tended only to fell trees for local construction or to regulate shade over coffee and generally limited clearing to young second growth in shifting agricultural systems (199:H15, 202:H18, 204: H19, 205:H8). They left some patches of forest standing regardless of landholding size (176:CR3, 177:CR18, 207:H8, 208:H19). They planted trees, but their tree-planting behaviors tended toward fruit trees, living fences, agroforestry systems, and occasional plantations of timber trees (182:CR13, 184:CR2, 185:CR10, 186:

CR7, 187:CR18, 188:CR10, 189:CR17, 214:H13, 215:H22, 216:H11, 217:H6, 218:H17, 220:H11, 221:H20).

While material factors clearly influence land use decisions, forest values simultaneously exert influence. Early colonists placed little value on forest and cleared, according to the way this was described by our interviewees, too much forest. More recently, as trees and forests are more highly valued, people have been less likely to fell trees or clear forests (particularly in the absence of a strong livelihood need), more likely to object to the presence of outside loggers, and tended to conserve forest patches and plant trees when they could. In many cases, this involved planting only on field margins or in coffee and planting fruit trees, and for some landholders, this meant only planting a few trees for what appear to be largely symbolic reasons (because tree planting is considered a good thing to do) or planting fruit trees or coffee and thinking about this in conservation terms. Yet, overall, this change seems likely to result in more trees and forests in the landscape and in associated conservation benefits. Furthermore, if people are allowed to pursue these mosaic land use strategies where they live, the development of strong forest and environmental values appears to promote acceptance of nearby parks and protected areas.

Understanding Environmental Values in a Globalizing World

Our approach to environmental values, based on mental and cultural models, has some differences with social psychology approaches, which have dominated the natural resource fields (Pierce et al. 2001). Thomas Dietz et al. (2005), in reviewing social psychology approaches to values, emphasized the underlying stability of values across time and situations and research that has found environmental values positively correlated with humanistic and biospheric altruism and negatively correlated with self-interest values. Dietz et al. (2005) also discussed postmaterialist perspectives in social psychology (for example, Dunlap and Inglehart) that view environmental values as luxuries of concern only once material needs are met. Many of these approaches, such as Riley Dunlap's New Environmental Paradigm, develop a fixed listing of environmental values, often from environmental literature, and measure people's degree of agreement with certain sets of environmental values. This differs from cultural model approaches, which emphasize that meanings matter, vary cross-culturally and situationally, and need to be considered within dynamic cultural processes (Medin et al. 2006). Using a cultural model approach, we have found that the content of people's environmental values can vary widely and is subject to change and that forests can be valued for complex mixes of self-interest, humanistic altruism, and biospheric altruism. It is not clear to us what, exactly, people's responses mean when asked whether they agree with certain environmental values. On the one hand, if the statements used reflect preservationist and postmaterialist environmental values, people may not agree with them even if they value forests and the environment for other reasons. On the other hand, if people are asked questions that incorporate widely known verbal molecules, they may agree with these statements even when these values have little motivational force or are underlain by different, and perhaps much more complex, locally constructed values.

Second, social psychology approaches, with their emphasis on stable values with fixed meanings, seem to see a stronger or more predictable relationship (actually a hierarchy) among values, attitudes, beliefs, norms, and conservation behaviors than we find. This appears to often lead to an emphasis on transferring a fixed set of environmental values to people (often to young people, through environmental education) in the belief that raising awareness will change people's behaviors. Yet Dietz et al. (2005, 364–66) note that research in this area has generally lacked data on actual behavior and has still not adequately addressed the important question of how values are linked to behavior. Our research suggests that, in the sites where we worked, most people were aware of these environmental values, and people could talk about them—although with varying degrees of facility. Yet, in spite of this, the motivational force of values and the ways they were traded off with livelihood values varied greatly and was highly context dependent. Motivating environmental behaviors will require more attention to working to change contexts and situations to increase environmental motivation and to create situations that reduce conflict and increase compatibility of environmental values and livelihood values.

In another major approach to values, recent scholarship in anthropology and sociology has emphasized Foucauldian approaches to discourse, which we call, following Strauss (2005), social discourses. In this approach, a researcher identifies and deconstructs dominant discourses[3] associated with powerful interests and shows how they are used against the less powerful members of society. Researchers using these theories often study and support the effects of these discourses on rural or indigenous people, including the social movements and other social forms that sometimes arise to counter them. This is an important area of study that has revealed important links between environmental science and powerful political interests and shows how these can misdirect natural resource policies and management. While the idea of social discourses of global conservation is central to our analysis, we do, however, feel that in some cases this vein of scholarship overstates the polarization between powerful global conservation interests and local resistance to it in the interests of people's short-term livelihood needs. Our research suggests that local people tend to see benefits in conservation, especially if their livelihood needs can be accommodated, and that the local forms of global conservation that rural people actually interact with are less monolithic than they are often portrayed and often include efforts to accommodate conservation with local livelihood interests. Furthermore, we tend to agree with Coll Thrush (2003) that much of analysis of social discourses, while focusing attention on the concerns of people who bear the brunt of conservation initiatives, often gives those people very little voice. The complexity that we found in our interviewees' words has, we believe, led to a more nuanced story that can lead to better management and policy actions.

Finally, it is worth asking whether globalization is a central problem for conservation and for rural people's livelihoods. Globalization is a major force in the world today, and it appears to bring both threats and opportunities to local people. Globalization brings changes and is difficult to resist. But rural people at times find their interests aligned with global conservation in their efforts to resist global economic trends and powerful extractive interests. Even when global conservation threatens, successful resistance often involves appeal to, and alignment with, other global values (e.g., indigenous rights, livelihoods rights, property rights). There may be as much potential to find common ground between conservation and livelihood interests in the globalized world as there is (or was) in the isolation of a more fragmented world. A lot will depend on what actions are taken to balance different interests such as conservation and livelihoods, and this will require understandings of complex social and cultural processes.

Toward Fair and Effective Conservation

We began this book by talking about recurring conflicts in conservation philosophies and practices, particularly recent debates over protectionist approaches versus parks-and-people approaches. We will end by discussing some of the implications of our research for conservation practice, specifically efforts to effectively conserve biodiversity in ways that are fair to local people. There is little doubt that large, continuous areas of tropical forest are generally the most effective option for conserving biodiversity. But few, if any, parks are large enough to be sufficient for biodiversity conservation because they often are concentrated in habitats less suitable for agriculture and urban development (high mountains and the lowland tropics), because species migrate both locally and long distances, and because it is often not socially, economically, and politically feasible to make them large enough. Thus, conservation nearly always must involve some combination of protected areas, parks-and-people approaches, and promotion of forest conservation on private land. Of course, it is the details of this, where the lines are drawn and what combinations of management approaches are implemented, that determine success or failure.

We feel that it is important to recognize that the recent international increase in national parks is a phenomenon of globalization and that this often involves the imposition of new conservation practices and environmental values onto lo-cal people living in the remote areas where parks are generally established. While these new national parks have some broad public benefits that can be thought of as global (e.g., their role in preventing biodiversity loss and climate change), it is also true that few concrete benefits accrue to local people and that parks often impose great costs on local people in the form of lost land, diminished access to resources, and diminished autonomy as national governments and international organizations extend into local life in new ways. These changes have serious repercussions for local people, often threatening their livelihoods and well-being in significant ways. Because of the complex social contexts in which parks are embedded, as Katrina Brandon (1998, 416–17) notes, what some conservationists may see as simply establishing national parks or doing conservation ends up being large-scale social interventions. Because of this, conservation cannot be effective, let alone fair, if it does not address the ways that parks interface with existing social complexities. Environmental values are one important dimension of this.

Stark contrasts in approach, between parks-and-people versus strict protection, ignore many of the realities of conservation practice. Successful parks often include elements of both approaches, such as core areas and buffer zones. Furthermore, many strict parks, including those in the United States (which are often cited as the source of protectionist conservation—the "Yellowstone Model"), have made various adaptations and concessions to unique local needs and interests (Schelhas 2001a, Zube and Busch 1990). Effective conservation will never be about the im-position of fixed global conservation programs onto local people; rather, it requires the development of new forms of conservation at the global-local interface. Simi-larly, conservation cannot be about trying to transfer fixed, global environmental values to local people. We need to understand the complex processes of value change that can motivate behavioral change and the ways in which environmental values are traded off against other values.

While areas of continuous forest are most effective for conservation, we found that rural people did not see a place for themselves in these kinds of landscapes, even when they valued them for their beauty, environmental services, and biodi-versity. The people in the communities we studied were dependent on corn and beans, coffee, and livestock for their livelihoods. They did, however, value mixed landscapes that were mosaics of fields, pastures, and forests. They had ceased large-scale forest clearing, conserved streamside forests and other forest patches for diverse reasons, and were increasingly integrating trees into their farms in many different ways. Our results from Honduras indicate that when people were allowed to pursue their livelihoods in these mixed land use settings that include trees, they could also be willing to accept strictly protected conservation areas for their water-shed benefits and potential to stimulate economic development and assistance.

We found that global environmental values had a noticeable presence in the communities where we conducted our research, having arrived via media messages, government agencies, school environmental education programs, and NGOs. Nearly everyone we interviewed was able repeat to us some of the key phrases and concepts that they had heard. We argue that in a globalizing world with great power imbalances, global environmental messages carry considerable weight and force in remote rural regions. But we have endeavored to show that in many cases these global values take the form of verbal molecules that may not be motivating or have clear conflicts with livelihood values. Changes in environmental values that transform behaviors will require more than exposing people to new, global environmental values. It will also require addressing the question of how the content of values and the context in which they operate affect their motivating force.

Although there are examples in the literature where local people simply oppose conservation, we did not find this to be the case in the communities where we conducted our research. We found that local people valued forests for many reasons. But if conservation interventions are structured in such a way as to force people to choose between conservation and their land, livelihoods, and well-being, conflicts can be expected to emerge. People can oppose conservation in several ways. Because of the power of global environmental discourse, both in terms of the ideas and the institutions behind them, people may be able to mount large-scale, effective opposition by appealing to other globally important values and related institutions (e.g., indigenous rights, development needs, individual property rights). When these cannot be tapped into, people are likely to resort to "weapons of the weak," such as setting fires in forests and parks, illegal cutting, and noncooperation. But our results suggest some ways that such stark conflicts can be avoided.

We found that people recognized the importance and value of conservation. While many global environmental values, as packaged, were not particularly motivating, there was an ongoing process of interaction between these and local values that was producing a new set of unique local environmental values. Because this new set of values was more integrated with people's livelihood values, rather than being compartmentalized as a set of unfamiliar values with no connection to everyday life, these new values were more motivating. They did not motivate people to passively accept park imposition and restrictions on tree cutting and forest clearing, but they did motivate them to increase the tree and forest components of their land use and to be more likely to accept strictly protected areas and national parks if they are implemented in a way that makes a place for their livelihoods and/or are accompanied by development alternatives.

The second important point about these new values is that they emerged both through global-local interactions and through social interactions at the local level. That is, these new values emerge not from some nebulous process of absorption of global environmental values, but through interactions with specific media and actors that bring these values to local people and, in fact, often begin the process of adapting them to local conditions. Some local people are early adopters, and local conversations begin to take place that form the mechanisms through which these new values emerge. Because these values are shaped by and present in a wide variety of social interactions and are connected to other important cultural models outside of environmentalism, they become more motivating.

Thus, locally tailored conservation programs that include, but are not necessarily limited to, parks-and-people approaches influence environmental values and behaviors in at least two ways. (1) They create a social environment that allows unique local environmental values to emerge and to influence people's behaviors. These unique environmental values will be more integrated across individual mental models, as well as in cultural models and social worlds, making it less likely that they will see conservation in opposition to their interests and increasing the motivational force of environmental values. (2) Because environmental values will always be, to some extent, a separate value sphere from livelihood values, people will always be forced to make some trade-offs between them. But if the material context is altered, for example by presenting viable new options for livelihoods and development for local people, the way that these trade-offs are made can be altered, leading to greater local acceptance of conservation and more conservation behaviors.

Notes

1. In this chapter we use the following notation to indicate quotes from the previous two chapters: "number of quote in its respective chapter:interviewee." Thus, "10:CR27" refers to the tenth quote in the Costa Rican chapter, found in the transcribed interview of interviewee CR27.

2. Two examples: (1) A headline in the September 23, 1999, issue of the *Christian Science Monitor* about a Canadian action to forgive Honduran debt in exchange for forest conservation for carbon storage was headlined, "Buying Oxygen Is Polluted Countries' Latest Remedy." (2) A Rain Forest Alliance web resource on "tropical forests in our daily life" states that "By absorbing carbon dioxide from the air, storing the carbon and giving us fresh, clean oxygen, tropical forests act as the world's thermostat, regulating temperatures and weather patterns. More than 20 percent of the world's oxygen is produced by the Amazon rainforest" (www.rainforest-alliance.org/resources.cfm?id=daily_lives; accessed 3/5/2007).

3. A thorough review of this literature is beyond our scope here. Readers wanting more information may start with Dove (2003), Fairhead and Leach (2003), Haenn and Wilk (2006), Quinn (2005a), and Wilhusen (2003).

References

Abrahamson, Paul R. 1997. Postmaterialism and environmentalism: A comment on an analysis and a reappraisal. *Social Science Quarterly* 78(1): 21–23.

Agrawal, Arun. 2005. Environmentality: Community, intimate government, and the making of environmental subjects in Kumaon, India. *Current Anthropology* 46(2): 161–90.

Alcorn, Janis B. 1989. Process as resource: The traditional agricultural ideology of Bora and Huastec resource management and its implications for research. In: *Resource Management in Amazonia: Indigenous and Folk Strategies*, edited by D. A. Posey and W. Balée, pp. 63–77. Bronx, NY: New York Botanical Garden.

———. 1990. Indigenous agroforestry systems in the Latin American tropics. In: *Agroecology and Small Farm Development*, edited by M. A. Altieri and S. B. Hecht, pp. 203–18. Boca Raton, FL: CRC Press.

———. 1996. Forest use and ownership: Patterns, issues, recommendations. In: *Forest Patches in Tropical Landscapes*, edited by John Schelhas and Russell Greenberg, pp. 223–57. Washington, DC: Island Press.

———. 1998. Big conservation and little conservation: Collaboration in managing global and local heritage. In: *Local Heritage in the Changing Tropics: Innovative Strategies for Natural Resource Management and Control*, edited by Joseph A. Miller, pp. 13–30. Bulletin 98. New Haven, CT: Yale School of Forestry and Environmental Studies.

Allen, T. F. H., Joseph A. Tainter, and Thomas W. Hoekstra (eds.). 2003. *Supply-side Sustainability*. New York: Columbia University Press.

Angelson, A., and D. Kaimowitz. 1999. Rethinking the causes of deforestation: Lessons from economic models. *The World Bank Research Observer* 14(1): 73–98.

Arizpe, Lourdes, Fernanda Paz, and Margarita Velázquez. 1996. *Culture and Global Change: Social Perceptions of Deforestation in the Lacandona Rain Forest in Mexico*. Ann Arbor: University of Michigan Press.

Arnold, J. E. M., and P. A. Dewees. 1995. *Tree Management in Farmer Strategies: Responses to Agricultural Intensification*. Oxford: Oxford University Press.

Atran, Scott, Douglas Medin, Norbert Ross, Elizabeth Lynch, John Coley, Edilberto Ucan Ek', and Valentina Vapnarsky. 1999. Folkecology and commons management in the Maya lowlands. *Proceedings of the National Academy of Science* 96: 7598–603.

Atran, Scott, Douglas Medin, Norbert Ross, Elizabeth Lynch, Valentina Vapnarsky, Edilberto Ucan Ek', John Coley, Christopher Timura, and Michael Baran. 2002. Folkecology, cultural epidemiology, and the spirit of the commons: A garden experiment in the Maya lowlands, 1991–2001. *Current Anthropology* 43(3): 421–50.

Barton, W. A. 2001. Regulatory authority and participatory protected areas management at Cerro Azul Meambar National Park, Honduras. Ph.D. thesis, Development Sociology Department, Cornell University, Ithaca, New York.

Barucha, E. 1999. Cultural and spiritual values related to the conservation of biodiversity in the sacred groves of Western Ghats in Maharshtra. In: *Cultural and Spiritual Values of Biodiversity*, edited by Darrell Addison Posey, pp. 382–86. London: Intermediate Technology Publications.

Bilsborrow, R. E., and D. L. Carr. 2001. Population, agricultural land use and the environment in developing countries. In: *Tradeoffs or Synergies? Agricultural Intensification, Economic Development and the Environment*, edited by D. R. Lee and C. B. Barrett, pp. 35–36. Wallingford, UK: CABI Publishing.

Boserup, Ester. 1965. *The Conditions of Agricultural Growth: The Economics of Agrarian Change under Population Pressure.* New York: Aldine.

Boza, Mario. A. 1993. Conservation in action: Past, present, and future of the National Park System of Costa Rica. *Conservation Biology* 7(2): 239–47.

Brandon, Katrina. 1998. Perils to parks: The social context of threats. In: *Parks in Peril: People, Politics, and Protected Areas*, edited by Katrina Brandon, Kent H. Redford, and Steven E. Sanderson, pp. 415–39. Washington, DC: Island Press.

Brandon, Katrina, Kent H. Redford, and Steven E. Sanderson (eds.). 1998. *Parks in Peril: People, Politics, and Protected Areas.* Washington, DC: Island Press.

Brechin, Steven R. 1999. Objective problems, subjective values, and global environmentalism: Evaluating the postmaterialist argument and challenging a new explanation. *Social Science Quarterly* 80(4): 793–809.

Brechin, Steven R., and Willett Kempton. 1994. Global environmentalism: A challenge to the postmaterialist thesis? *Social Science Quarterly* 75(2): 245–69.

Brechin, Stephen R., Peter R. Wilshusen, Crystal L. Fortwangler, and Patrick C. West. 2003. *Contested Nature: Promoting International Biodiversity with Social Justice in the Twenty-first Century.* Albany: State University of New York Press.

Brockett, Charles D., and Robert R. Gottfried. 2002. State policies and the preservation of forest cover: Lessons from contrasting public policy regimes in Costa Rica. *Latin American Research Review* 37(1): 7–40.

Brosius, J. Peter. 1999. Analyses and interventions: Anthropological engagements with environmentalism. *Current Anthropology* 40(3): 277–309.

Brosius, J. Peter, Anna Lowenhaupt Tsing, and Charles Zerner (eds.). 2005. *Communities and Conservation: Histories and Politics of Community-Based Natural Resource Management.* Walnut Creek, CA: AltaMira Press.

Bruijneel, L. A. 2004. Hydrological functions of tropical forests: Not seeing the soil for the trees? *Agriculture, Ecosystems, & Environment* 104: 185–228.

Buck, Louise E., Charles C. Geisler, John Schelhas, and Eva Wollenberg. 2001. *Biological Diversity: Balancing Interests through Adaptive Collaborative Management.* Boca Raton, FL: CRC Press.

Burch, William, Jr. 1999. Gods of the forest—myth and ritual in community forestry. In: *Cultural and Spiritual Values of Biodiversity,* edited by Darrell Addison Posey, pp. 393–94. London: Intermediate Technology Publications.

Buttel, Frederick H. 1992. Environmentalism: Origins, processes, and implications for rural social change. *Rural Sociology* 57: 1–27.

Buttel, Frederick H., and Peter J. Taylor. 1992. Environmental sociology and global environmental change: A critical assessment. *Society and Natural Resources* 5: 211–30.

Calhoun, Craig. 2004. Cosmopolitans and locals (interview excerpt). *Anthropology News* 45(5): 5.

Campbell, Lisa M. 2002. Conservation narratives in Costa Rica: Conflict and co-existence. *Development and Change* 33: 29–56.

Campbell, Michael O'Neal. 2005. Sacred groves for forest conservation in Ghana's coastal savannas: Assessing ecological and social dimensions. *Singapore Journal of Tropical Geography* 26(2): 151–69.

Carrier, James G. (ed.). 2004. *Confronting Environments: Local Understanding in a Globalizing World.* Walnut Creek, CA: AltaMira Press.

———. 2004. Environmental conservation and institutional environments in Jamaica. In: *Confronting Environments: Local Understanding in a Globalizing World,* edited by James G. Carrier, pp. 119–41. Walnut Creek, CA: AltaMira Press.

Carrière, J. 1990. The political economy of land degradation in Costa Rica. *New Political Science* 18/19: 147–63.

Cary, John. 1993. The nature of symbolic beliefs and environmental behavior in a rural setting. *Environment and Behavior* 25(5): 555–76.

Ceballos, Gerardo, Paul R. Ehrlich, Jorge Soberón, Irma Salazar, John P. Fay. 2005. Global mammal conservation: What must we manage? *Science* 309: 603–607.

Chape, S., S. Blyth, L. Fish, P. Fox, and M. Spalding (compilers). 2003. *2003 United Nations List of Protected Areas.* Gland, Switzerland, and Cambridge, UK: IUCN, and Cambridge, UK: UNEP-WCMC.

Chape, S., J. Harrison, M. Spaulding, and I. Lysenko. 2005. Measuring the extent and effectiveness of protected areas as an indicator for meeting global biodiversity targets. *Philosophical Transactions of the Royal Society B.* 360: 443–55.

Clinnick, P. F. 1984. Buffer strip management in forest operations: A review. *Australian Forestry* 48(1): 34–45.

COHDEFOR–Administracion Forestal del Estado. 1994. Comunicado: Propuesto de Ampliación de Límites del Parque Nacional Cerro Azul Meambar. *La Tribuna,* Deciembre 23.

Congalton, R. G., and K. Green. 1999. *Assessing the Accuracy of Remotely Sensed Data: Principles and Practices.* New York: Lewis Publishers.

Cronon, William (ed.). 1996. *Uncommon Ground: Rethinking the Human Place in Nature.* New York: Norton.

D'Andrade, Roy. 1995. *The Development of Cognitive Anthropology.* Cambridge, UK: Cambridge University Press.

D'Andrade, Roy G., and Claudia Strauss (eds.). 1992. *Human Motives and Cultural Models.* Cambridge, UK: Cambridge University Press.

Daily, Gretchen C. (ed.). 1997. *Nature's Services: Societal Dependence on Natural Ecosystems.* Washington, DC: Island Press.

Diamond, Jared M. 2005. *Collapse: How Societies Choose to Fail or Succeed.* New York: Viking.

Dietz, Thomas, Amy Fitzgerald, and Rachel Shwom. 2005. Environmental values. *Annual Review of Environment and Resources* 30: 335–72.

DiMaggio, Paul. 2001. Why cognitive (and cultural) sociology needs cognitive psychology. In: *Culture in Mind: Toward a Sociology of Culture and Cognition*, edited by Karen A. Cerulo, pp. 274–81. New York: Routledge.

Dove, Michael R. 2003. Forest discourses in South and Southeast Asia: A comparison with global discourses. In: *Nature in the Global South: Environmental Projects in South and Southeast Asia*, edited by Paul Greenough and Anna Lownhaupt Tsing, pp. 103–23. Durham, NC: Duke University Press.

Dove, Michael R., Marina T. Campos, Andrew Salvador Mathews, Laura J. Meitzner Yoder, Anne Rademacher, Suk Bae Rhee, and Daniel Somers Smith. 2003. The global mobilization of environmental concepts: Rethinking the Western/non-Western divide. In: *Nature across Cultures: Views of Nature and the Environment in Non-Western Cultures*, edited by H. Selin, pp. 19–46. Dordrecht, the Netherlands: Kluwer.

Dugelby, Barbara, and Michelle Libby. 1998. Analyzing the social context at PIP sites. In: *Parks in Peril: People, Politics, and Protected Areas*, edited by Katrina Brandon, Kent H. Redford, and Steven E. Sanderson, pp. 63–75. Washington, DC: Island Press.

Dunlap, Riley. 1991. Trends in public opinion toward environmental issues: 1965–1990. *Society and Natural Resources* 4(3): 285–312.

Dunlap, Riley E., George H. Gallup, and Alec M. Gallup. 1993. Of global concern: Results of the health of the planet survey. *Environment* 35(9): 7–33.

Dunlap, Riley E., and Angela G. Mertig. 1997. Global environmental concern: An anomaly for postmaterialism. *Social Science Quarterly* 78(1): 23–29.

Einarrson, Niels. 1990. Of seals and souls: Changes in the position of seals in the worldview of Icelandic small-scale fishermen. *Maritime Anthropological Studies* 3(2): 35–48.

———. 1993. All animals are equal but some are cetaceans. In: *Environmentalism: The View from Anthropology*, edited by Kay Milton, pp. 73–84. London: Routledge.

Evans, Sterling. 1999. *The Green Republic: A Conservation History of Costa Rica.* Austin: University of Texas Press.

Fairhead, James, and Melissa Leach. 2003. *Science, Society and Power: Environmental Knowledge and Policy in West Africa and the Caribbean.* Cambridge, UK: Cambridge University Press.

Ferguson, R. Brian. 2006a. Archeology, cultural anthropology, and the origins and intensification of war. In: *The Archeology of Warfare: Prehistories of Raiding and Conquest*, edited by Elizabeth N. Arkush and Mark W. Allen, pp. 469–523. Gainesville: University Press of Florida.

————. 2006b. Tribal, "ethnic," and global wars. In: *The Psychology of Resolving Global Conflicts: From War to Peace*, edited by Mari Fitzduff and Chris E. Stout, pp. 41–69. Westport, CT: Praeger Security International.

————. 2007. Eight points on war. *Anthropology News* 49(2): 5–6.

Fisher, William H. 1994. Megadevelopment, environmentalism, and resistance: The institutional context of Kayapó indigenous politics in central Brazil. *Human Organization* 53(3): 220–32.

Frank, David John. 2002. The origins question: Building global institutions to protect nature. In: *Organizations, Policy and the Natural Environment: Institutions and Strategic Perspectives*, edited by A. J. Hoffman and M. J. Ventresca, pp. 41–56. Stanford, CA: Stanford University Press.

Frank, David John, Ann Hironka, and Evan Shofer. 2000. The nation-state and the natural environment over the twentieth century. *American Sociological Review* 65: 96–116.

Fransson, Niklas, and Tommy Gärling. 1999. Environmental concern: Conceptual definitions, measurement methods, and research findings. *Journal of Environmental Psychology* 19(4): 369–82.

Freese, Curtis H. (ed.). 1997. *Harvesting Wild Species: Implications for Biodiversity Conservation*. Baltimore: Johns Hopkins University Press.

Gamez, R., and A. Ugalde. 1988. Costa Rica's national park system and the preservation of biological diversity: Linking conservation and socio-economic development. In: *Tropical Rainforests: Diversity and Conservation*, edited by F. Almeda and C. M. Pringle, pp. 131–42. San Francisco: California Academy of Science and American Association for the Advancement of Science.

Geisler, Charles C. 2002. Endangered humans: How global land conservation efforts are creating a growing class of invisible refugees. *Foreign Policy* 130: 80–81.

Gerritsen, Peter, and Feerk Wiersum. 2005. Farmer and conventional perspectives on conservation in Western Mexico. *Mountain Research and Development* 25(1): 30–36.

Gezon, Lisa. 2005. Finding the global in the local: Environmental struggles in northern Madagascar. In: *Political Ecology across Spaces, Scales, and Social Groups*, edited by Susan Paulson and Lisa L. Gezon, pp. 135–53. New Brunswick, NJ: Rutgers University Press.

Giner, Salvador, and David Tábara. 1999. Cosmic piety and ecological rationality. *International Sociology* 14(1): 59–82.

Gomez, J. 1998. Detección de Cambios en la Cobertura Vegetal en Parque Nacional Cerro Azul Meambar. Programa Social Forestal (PSF), GTZ, Proyecto Profor Honduras, Siguatepeque, Honduras, 16 pp.

Greenough, Paul, and Anna Lowenhaupt Tsing (eds.). 2003. *Nature in the Global South: Environmental Projects in South and Southeast Asia*. Durham, NC: Duke University Press.

Grimes, Peter. 2000. Recent research on world-systems. In: *A World-Systems Reader: New Perspectives on Gender, Urbanism, Cultures, Indigenous Peoples, and Ecology*, edited by Thomas D. Hall, pp. 29–55. Lanham, MD: Rowman & Littlefield Publishers.

Grove, Richard H. 1995. *Green Imperialism: Colonial Expansion, Tropical Island Edens and the Origins of Environmentalism, 1600–1860*. Cambridge, UK: Cambridge University Press.

Haenn, Nora. 1999. The power of environmental knowledge: Ethnoecology and environmental conflicts in Mexican conservation. *Human Ecology* 27(3): 477–91.

————. 2005. *Fields of Power, Forests of Discontent: Culture, Conservation and the State in Mexico.* Tucson: University of Arizona Press.

Haenn, Nora, and Richard R. Wilk (eds.). 2006. *The Environment in Anthropology: A Reader in Ecology, Culture, and Sustainable Living.* New York: New York University Press.

Hannerz, Ulf. 1992. *Cultural Complexity: Studies in the Social Organization of Meaning.* New York: Columbia University Press.

Hannigan, J. A. 1995. *Environmental Sociology: A Social Constructionist Perspective.* New York: Routledge.

Hartup, B. K. 1994. Community conservation in Belize: Demography, resource use, and attitudes of participating landowners. *Biological Conservation* 69: 235–41.

Hernández-Mora, Nuria. 1995. Effects of policy reform on land use decisions and community forest management in Honduras: Four case studies. M.S. thesis, Department of Natural Resources, Cornell University, Ithaca, NY.

Hessel, Dieter T., and Rosemary Radford Ruether. 2000. *Christianity and Ecology.* Cambridge, MA: Harvard University Center for the Study of World Religions.

Heyman, Josiah. 2004. Conclusion: Understandings matter. In: *Confronting Environments: Local Understanding in a Globalizing World,* edited by James G. Carrier, pp. 183–95. Walnut Creek, CA: AltaMira Press.

Holl, Karen D., Gretchen C. Daily, and Paul R. Ehrlich. 1995. Knowledge and perceptions in Costa Rica regarding environment, population, and biodiversity issues. *Conservation Biology* 9(6): 1548–58.

Holland, D., and N. Quinn (eds.). 1987. *Cultural Models in Language and Thought.* Cambridge, UK: Cambridge University Press.

Igoe, Jim. 2004. *Conservation and Globalization: A Study of National Parks and Indigenous Communities from East Africa to South Dakota.* Belmont, CA: Wadsworth.

Inglehart, Ronald. 1995. Public support for environmental protection: Objective problems and subjective values in 43 societies. *PS: Political Science and Politics* 28(1): 57–72.

Jantzi, Terrence, John Schelhas, and James P. Lassoie. 1999. Environmental values and forest patch conservation in a rural Costa Rican community. *Agriculture and Human Values* 16: 29–39.

Kaimowitz, David. 1997. *Livestock and Deforestation in Central America in the 1980s and 1990s: A Policy Perspective.* Bogor, Indonesia: Center for International Forestry Research.

————. 2005. Useful myths and intractable truths: The politics of the link between forests and water in Central America. In: *Forests, Water and People in the Humid Tropics,* edited by M. Bonell and L. A. Bruijnzeel, pp. 86–98. Cambridge, UK: Cambridge University Press.

Kalberg, Stephen. 1990. The rationalization of action in Max Weber's sociology of religion. *Sociological Theory* 8(1): 58–84.

————. 1994. *Max Weber's Comparative Historical Sociology.* Chicago: University of Chicago Press.

————. 2004. The past and present influences of world views: Max Weber on a neglected sociological concept. *Journal of Classical Sociology* 4(2): 139–63.

Kappelle, M., M. Castro, A. Garita, H. Monge, and L. González. 2003. Ecosistemas del Área de Conservación La Amistad Pacífico. Santo Domingo de Heredia, Costa Rica: INBio.

Kempton, Willett, James S. Boster, and Jennifer A. Hartley. 1995. *Environmental Values in American Culture*. Cambridge, MA: MIT Press.

Kidd, Quentin, and Aie-Rie Lee. 1997. Postmaterialist values and the environment: A critique and reappraisal. *Social Science Quarterly* 78(1): 1–15.

Knight, John. 2000. Introduction. In: *Natural Enemies: People-Wildlife Conflicts in Anthropological Perspective*, edited by John Knight, pp. 1–35. London: Routledge.

Kramer, Randall, Carel van Schaik, and Julie Johnson (eds.). 1997. *Last Stand: Protected Areas and the Defense of Tropical Biological Diversity*. New York: Oxford University Press.

Krech, Shepard. 1999. *The Ecological Indian: Myth and History*. New York: W. W. Norton.

———. 2005. Reflections on conservation, sustainability, and environmentalism in indigenous North America. *American Anthropologist* 107(1): 78–86.

Laird, Sarah A. 1999. Forests, culture and conservation. In: *Cultural and Spiritual Values of Biodiversity*, edited by Darrell Addison Posey, pp. 347–58. London: Intermediate Technology Publications.

Laurance, William F., and Richard O. Bierregaard Jr. (eds.). 1997. *Tropical Forest Remnants: Ecology, Management, and Conservation of Fragmented Communities*. Chicago: University of Chicago Press.

Leach, Melissa, and James Fairhead. 2002. Anthropology, culture, and environment. In: *Exotic No More: Anthropology on the Front Lines*, edited by Jeremy MacClancy, pp. 209–26. Chicago: University of Chicago Press.

Lebbie, A., and M. S. Freudenberger. 1996. Sacred groves in Africa: Forest patches in transition. In: *Forest Patches in Tropical Landscapes*, edited by John Schelhas and Russell Greenberg, pp. 300–24. Washington, DC: Island Press.

Ledec, George, and Robert Goodland. 1988. *Wildlands: Their Protection and Management in Economic Development*. Washington, DC: The World Bank.

Leopold, Aldo. 1966. The land ethic. In: *A Sand County Almanac, with Essays on Conservation from Round River*, pp. 237–63. New York: Oxford University Press and Ballantine Books.

Lipschutz, R. D., and K. Conca. 1993. The implications of global ecological interdependence. In: *The State and Social Power in Global Environmental Politics*, edited by R. D. Lipschutz and K. Conca, pp. 327–44. New York: Columbia University Press.

Little, Paul. 1999. Environments and environmentalisms in anthropological research: Facing a new millennium. *Annual Review of Anthropology* 28: 253–84.

Lucas, P. H. C. 1984. How protected areas can help meet society's evolving needs. In: *National Parks, Conservation, and Development: The Role of Protected Areas in Sustaining Society*, edited by Jeffrey A. McNeely and Kenton R. Miller, pp. 72–77. Washington, DC: Smithsonian Institution Press.

Luke, T. W. 1996. Identity, meaning and globalization: Detraditionalization in postmodern space-time compression. In: *Detraditionalization*, edited by P. Heelas, S. Lash, and P. Morris, pp. 109–33. Cambridge, UK: Blackwell.

Mariñas Otero, Luis. 1962. *Las Constituciones de Honduras*. Madrid, Spain: Ediciones Cultura Hispanica.

Marvin, Garry. 2000. The problem of foxes: Legitimate and illegitimate killing in the English countryside. In: *Natural Enemies: People-Wildlife Conflicts in Anthropological Perspective*, edited by John Knight, pp. 189–211. London: Routledge.

Mather, A. S. 1998. The forest transition: A theoretical basis. *Area* 30: 117–24.

McNeely, Jeffrey A. 1990. The future of national parks. *Environment* 30(1): 16–20, 36–41.

———. 1995. *Expanding Partnerships in Conservation*. Washington, DC: Island Press.

McNeely, J. A., J. Harrison, and P. Dingwall. 1994. Introduction: Protected areas in the modern world. In: *Protecting Nature: Regional Reviews of Protected Areas*, edited by J. A. McNeely, J. Harrison, and P. Dingwall, pp. 1–28. Gland, Switzerland: IUCN.

Medin, Douglas L., Norbert O. Ross, and Douglas G. Cox. 2006. *Culture and Resource Conflict: Why Meanings Matter*. New York: Russell Sage Foundation.

Merrill, Tim L. 1995. *Honduras: A Country Study*. 3rd ed. Washington, DC: Federal Research Division, Library of Congress.

Milton, Kay. 1996. *Environmentalism and Cultural Theory*. London: Routledge.

———. 2000. Ducks out of water: Nature conservation as boundary maintenance. In: *Natural Enemies: People-Wildlife Conflicts in Anthropological Perspective*, edited by John Knight, pp. 229–46. London: Routledge.

———. 2002. *Loving Nature: Towards an Ecology of Emotion*. London: Routledge.

Nash, Roderick. 2001. *Wilderness and the American Mind*. New Haven, CT: Yale University Press.

National Research Council. 1999. *Human Dimensions of Global Environmental Change: Research Pathways for the Next Decade*. Committee on the Human Dimensions of Global Climate Change and the Committee on Global Change Research. Washington, DC: National Academy Press.

Neumann, Roderick P. 1995. Local challenges to global agendas: Conservation, economic liberalization and the pastoralists' rights movement in Tanzania. *Antipode* 27(4): 363–82.

———. 2001. Disciplining peasants in Tanzania: From state violence to self-surveillance in wildlife conservation. In: *Violent Environments*, edited by Nancy Lee Peluso and Michael Watts, pp. 305–27. Ithaca, NY: Cornell University Press.

Newmark, William D., Nancy Leonard, Hashim I. Sariko, and Deo-Gratis M. Gamassa. 1993. Conservation attitudes of local people living adjacent to five protected areas in Tanzania. *Biological Conservation* 63: 177–83.

Norton, Bryan G. 2003. *Searching for Sustainability: Interdisciplinary Essays in the Philosophy of Conservation Biology*. Cambridge, UK: Cambridge University Press.

Nygren, Anja. 1998. Environment as discourse: Searching for sustainable development in Costa Rica. *Environmental Values* 7: 201–22.

Oates, John F. 1999. *Myth and Reality in the Rain Forest: How Conservation Strategies Are Failing in West Africa*. Berkeley: University of California Press.

Oldfield, Margery L. 1984. *The Value of Conserving Genetic Resources*. Washington, DC: National Park Service.

Ortner, Sherry B. 1997. Thick resistance: Death and the cultural reconstruction of agency in Himalayan mountaineering. *Representations* 59: 135–62.

Palo, Matti, and Heidi Vanhanen (eds.). 2000. *World Forests from Deforestation to Transition?* Dordrecht, the Netherlands: Kluwer.

Paolisso, Michael. 1999. Toxic algal blooms, nutrient runoff, and farming on Maryland's Eastern Shore. *Culture and Agriculture* 21(3): 53–58.

———. 2002. Blue crabs and controversy on the Chesapeake Bay: A cultural model for understanding watermen's reasoning about blue crab management. *Human Organization* 61(3): 226–39.

Paolisso, Michael, and Erve Chambers. 2001. Culture, politics, and toxic dinoflagellate blooms: The anthropology of *Pfiesteria. Human Organization* 60(1): 1–12.

Paolisso, Michael, and R. Shawn Maloney. 2000a. Recognizing farmer environmentalism: Nutrient runoff and toxic dinoflagellate blooms in the Chesapeake Bay region. *Human Organization* 59(2): 209–21.

———. 2000b. Farmer morality and Maryland's nutrient management regulations. *Culture and Agriculture* 22(3): 32–39.

Parajuli, Pramod. 1999. Peasant cosmovisions and biodiversity: Some reflections from South Asia. In: *Cultural and Spiritual Values of Biodiversity,* edited by Darrell Addison Posey, pp. 385–88. London: Intermediate Technology Publications.

Peluso, Nancy Lee. 1992. *Rich Forests, Poor People: Resource Control and Resistance in Java.* Berkeley: University of California Press.

Pfeffer, Max J., and J. Mayone Stycos. 2002. Immigrant environmental behavior in New York City. *Social Science Quarterly* 83(1): 64–81.

Pfeffer, Max J., John W. Schelhas, and Leyla Day. 2001. Forest conservation, value conflict, and interest formation in a Honduran national park. *Rural Sociology* 66(3): 382–402.

Pfeffer, Max J., John W. Schelhas, Stephen D. DeGloria, and Jorge Gomez. 2005. Population, conservation, and land use change in Honduras. *Agriculture, Ecosystems, and Environment* 110(1–2): 14–28.

Pfeffer, Max J., John Schelhas, and Catherine Meola. 2006. Environmental globalization, organizational form, and expected benefits from protected areas in Central America. *Rural Sociology* 71(3): 429–50.

Pierce, Cynthia L., Michael J. Manfredo, and Jerry J. Vaske. 2001. Social science theories in wildlife management. In: *Human Dimensions of Wildlife Management in North America,* edited by D. Decker, T. Brown, and W. F. Siemer, pp. 39–56. Bethesda, MD: Wildlife Society.

Pinedo-Vasquez, Miguel, and Christine Padoch. 1996. Managing forest remnants and forest gardens in Peru and Indonesia. In: *Forest Patches in Tropical Landscapes,* edited by John Schelhas and Russell Greenberg, pp. 327–42. Washington, DC: Island Press.

Potter, D., and A. Taylor. 1996. Introduction. In: *NGOs and Environmental Policies: Asia and Africa,* edited by D. Potter, pp. 1–8. Portland, OR: Frank Cass.

Power, A. G. 1996. Arthropod diversity in forest patches and agroecosystems of tropical landscapes. In: *Forest Patches in Tropical Landscapes,* edited by John Schelhas and Russell Greenberg, pp. 91–110. Washington, DC: Island Press.

Price, M. F. 1996. People in biosphere reserves: An evolving concept. *Society and Natural Resources* 9: 645–54.

Pulido, Laura. 1996. *Environmentalism and Economic Justice: Two Chicano Struggles in the Southwest.* Tucson: University of Arizona Press.

Quinn, Naomi. 2005a. Introduction. In: *Finding Culture in Talk: A Collection of Methods,* edited by Naomi Quinn, pp. 1–34. New York: Palgrave Macmillan.

———. 2005b. How to reconstruct schemas people share, from what they say. In: *Finding Culture in Talk: A Collection of Methods,* edited by Naomi Quinn, pp. 35–81. New York: Palgrave Macmillan.

Raven, Peter H., and Jeffrey A. McNeely. 1998. Biological extinction: Its scope and meaning for us. In: *Protection of Global Biodiversity: Converging Strategies,* edited by Lakshman D. Guruswamy and Jeffrey A. McNeely, pp. 13–32. Durham, NC: Duke University Press.

Redclift, Michael. 1984. *Development and the Environmental Crisis: Red or Green Alternatives.* London: Methuen.

Redford, Kent. H. 1992. The empty forest. *BioScience* 42: 412–22.

Redman, Charles L. 1999. *Human Impact on Ancient Environments.* Tucson: University of Arizona Press.

Ritzer, George. 1996. *The McDonaldization of Society: An Investigation of Contemporary Social Life.* Thousand Oaks, CA: Pine Forge Press.

Robbins, Paul. 2000. The practical politics of knowing: State environmental knowledge and local political economy. *Economic Geography* 76(2): 126–44.

Robbins, Paul, and Alistair Fraser. 2003. A forest of contradictions: Producing the landscapes of the Scottish Highlands. *Antipode* 35(1): 95–118.

Robinson, John G. 1996. Hunting wildlife in forest patches: An ephemeral resource. In: *Forest Patches in Tropical Landscapes,* edited by John Schelhas and Russell Greenberg, pp. 111–30. Washington, DC: Island Press.

Rocheleau, D., and L. Ross. 1995. Trees as tools, trees as text: Struggles over resources in Zambrana-Chacuey, Dominican Republic. *Antipode* 27: 407–28.

Rockwell, R. C. 1994. Culture and global change. In: *Changes in Land Use and Land Cover: A Global Perspective,* edited by W. B. Meyer and B. L. Turner II, pp. 357–82. Cambridge, UK: Cambridge University Press.

Rudel, Thomas K. 2005. *Tropical Forests: Regional Paths of Destruction and Regeneration in the Late Twentieth Century.* New York: Columbia University Press.

Rudel, Thomas K., D. Bates, and R. Machinguiashi. 2002. A tropical forest transition? Agricultural change, out-migration, and secondary forests in the Ecuadorian Amazon. *Annals of the Association of American Geographers* 92: 87–102.

Rudel, Thomas K., Oliver T. Coomes, Emilio Moran, Frederic Achard, Arild Angelsen, Jianchu Xu, and Eric Lambin. 2005. Forest transitions: Towards a global understanding of land use change. *Global Environmental Change* 15: 23–31.

Rudel, Thomas K., K. Flesher, D. Bates, S. Baptista, and P. Holmgren. 2000. Tropical deforestation literature: Geographical and historical patterns. *Unasylva* 51 (203): 11–18.

Runte, Alfred. 1997. *National Parks: The American Experience.* Lincoln: University of Nebraska Press.

Sahlins, Marshall. 1994. Goodbye to the tristes tropes: Ethnography in the context of modern world history. In: *Assessing Cultural Anthropology*, edited by Robert Borofsky, pp. 377–95. New York: McGraw-Hill.

Satterfield, Terre, and Linda Kalof. 2005. Environmental values: An introduction—relativistic and axiomatic traditions in the study of environmental values. In: *The Earthscan Reader in Environmental Values*, edited by Linda Kalof and Terre Satterfield, pp. xxi–xxxiii. London: Earthscan.

Schelhas, John. 1996a. Land use choice and change: Intensification and diversification in the lowland tropics of Costa Rica. *Human Organization* 55: 298–306.

———. 1996b. Land use choice and forest patches in Costa Rica. In: *Forest Patches in Tropical Landscapes*, edited by John Schelhas and Russell Greenberg. Washington DC: Island Press.

———. 2001a. The U.S.A. national parks in international perspective: Have we learned the wrong lesson? *Environmental Conservation* 28(4): 300–304.

———. 2001b. Ecoregional management in southern Costa Rica: Finding a role for adaptive collaborative management. In: *Biological Diversity: Balancing Interests through Adaptive Collaborative Management*, edited by L. E. Buck, C. G. Geisler, J. Schelhas, and E. Wollenberg, pp. 245–59. Boca Raton, FL: CRC Press.

Schelhas, John, Louise E. Buck, and Charles C. Geisler. 2001. Introduction: The challenge of adaptive collaborative management. In: *Biological Diversity: Balancing Interests through Adaptive Collaborative Management*, edited by L. E. Buck, C. G. Geisler, J. Schelhas, and E. Wollenberg, pp. xix–xxxv. Boca Raton, FL: CRC Press.

Schelhas, John, and Russell Greenberg (eds.). 1996. *Forest Patches in Tropical Landscapes*. Washington, DC: Island Press.

Schelhas, John, and Max J. Pfeffer. 2005. Forest values of national park neighbors in Costa Rica. *Human Organization* 64(4): 385–97.

Schelhas, John, and Arturo Sanchez. 2006. Post-frontier forest change adjacent to Braulio Carrillo National Park, Costa Rica. *Human Ecology* 43(3): 407–31.

Schmink, M. 1994. The socioeconomic matrix of deforestation. In: *Population and Environment: Rethinking the Debate*, edited by L. Arizpe, M. P. Stone, and D. C. Major, pp. 253–75. Boulder, CO: Westview Press.

Schroth, Götz, Gustavo A. B. da Fonseca, Celia Harvey, Claude Gascon, Heraldo L. Vasconcelos, and Anne-Marie N. Izac (eds.). 2004. *Agroforestry and Biodiversity Conservation in Tropical Landscapes*. Washington, DC: Island Press.

Scott, James C. 1985. *Weapons of the Weak: Everyday Forms of Peasant Resistance*. New Haven, CT: Yale University Press.

Selin, H. (ed.). 2003. *Nature across Cultures: Views of Nature and the Environment in Non-Western Cultures*. Dordrecht, the Netherlands: Kluwer.

Sellars, Richard W. 1999. *Preserving Nature in the National Parks: A History*. New Haven, CT: Yale University Press.

Shanahan, James, Lisa Pelstring, and Katerine McComas. 1999. Using narratives to think about environmental attitude and behavior: An exploratory study. *Society and Natural Resources* 12(5): 405–20.

Sharma, Uday R., and William W. Shaw. 1993. Role of Nepal's Royal Chitwan National Park in meeting the grazing and fodder needs of local people. *Environmental Conservation* 20(2): 139–42.

Shore, Bradd. 1996. *Culture in Mind: Cognition, Culture, and the Problem of Meaning.* New York: Oxford University Press.

Slater, Candace (ed.). 2003. *In Search of the Rain Forest.* Durham, NC: Duke University Press.

Smith, Joyotee, José Vicente Cadavid, Alvaro Rincón, and Raúl Vera. 1997. Land speculation and intensification at the frontier: A seeming paradox in the Colombian savanna. *Agricultural Systems* 54(4): 501–20.

Smith, Neil. 1996. The production of nature. In: *FutureNatural: Nature, Science, and Culture,* edited by George Robertson, Melinda Mash, Lisa Tickner, Jon Bird, Barry Curtis, and Tim Putnam, pp. 35–54. London: Routledge.

Song, S. Hoon. 2000. The great pigeon massacre in a deindustrializing American region. In: *Natural Enemies: People-Wildlife Conflicts in Anthropological Perspective,* edited by John Knight, pp. 212–28. London: Routledge.

Stern, Paul C., Thomas Dietz, and Linda Kalof. 1993. Value orientations, gender and environmental concern. *Environment and Behavior* 25: 227–45.

Stokes, William S. 1947. The land laws of Honduras. *Agricultural History* 21: 148–54.

Strauss, Claudia. 1992. What makes Tony run? Schemas as motives reconsidered. In: *Human Motives and Cultural Models,* edited by Roy D'Andrade and Claudia Strauss, pp. 197–224. Cambridge, UK: Cambridge University Press.

———. 1997. Partly fragmented, partly integrated: An anthropological examination of "postmodern fragmented subjects." *Cultural Anthropology* 12(3): 362–404.

———. 2005. Analyzing discourse for cultural complexity. In: *Finding Culture in Talk: A Collection of Methods,* edited by Naomi Quinn, pp. 203–42. New York: Palgrave Macmillan.

Strauss, Claudia, and Naomi Quinn. 1997. *A Cognitive Theory of Cultural Meaning.* Cambridge, UK: Cambridge University Press.

Taylor, Peter J., and Frederick H. Buttel. 1992. How do we know we have global environmental problems? Science and the globalization of environmental discourse. *Geoforum* 23(3): 405–16.

Terborgh, John, Carel van Schaik, Lisa Davenport, and Madhu Rao (eds.). 2002. *Making Parks Work: Strategies for Preserving Tropical Nature.* Washington, DC: Island Press.

Thacher, Thomas A., David Lee, and John Schelhas. 1997. Farmer participation in government sponsored reforestation incentive programs in Costa Rica. *Agroforestry Systems* 35: 269–89.

Theodossopoulos, Dimitrios. 2004. "Working in nature," "caring for nature": Diverse views of the environment in the context of an environmental dispute. In: *Confronting Environments: Local Understanding in a Globalizing World,* edited by James G. Carrier, pp. 49–70. Walnut Creek, CA: AltaMira Press.

Thomas, C. 1994. Beyond UNCED: An introduction. In: *Rio: Unraveling the Consequences,* edited by C. Thomas, pp. 1–27. Portland, OR: Frank Cass.

Thrush, Coll. 2003. Review of David G. Anderson and Eeva Berglund, eds., *Ethnographies of Conservation: Environmentalism and the Distribution of Privilege,* H-Environment,

H-Net Reviews, December 2003, available at www.h-net.msu.edu/reviews/showrev .cgi?path=136761077591757.

Thurston, H. David, Margaret Smith, George Abawi, and Steve Kearl. 1994. *TA-PADO Slash/Mulch: How Farmers Use It and What Researchers Know about It.* Ithaca, NY: Cornell International Institute for Food, Agriculture and Development (CIIFAD).

Tiffen, Mary, Michael Mortimore, and Francis Gichuki. 1994. *More People, Less Erosion: Environmental Recovery in Kenya.* Chichester, UK: John Wiley.

Tsing, Anna Lowenhaupt. 2005. *Friction: An Ethnography of Global Connection.* Princeton, NJ: Princeton University Press.

Turner, B. L., II, D. Skole, S. Sanderson, G. Fischer, L. Fresco, and R. Leemans. 1995. *Land Use and Land Cover Change: Science/Research Plan.* Stockholm, Sweden, and Geneva, Switzerland: International Geosphere-Biosphere Programme of the International Council of Scientific Unions and Human Dimensions of Global Change Programme of the International Social Science Research Council.

United National Development Programme, United Nations Environment Programme, The World Bank, and World Resources Institute. 2003. *World Resources 2002–2004.* Washington, DC: World Resources Institute.

United Nations, Department of Economic and Social Affairs, Population Division. 2001. *Abortion Policies: A Global Review.* New York: United Nations.

Utting, Peter. 1994. Social and political dimensions of environmental protection in Central America. *Development and Change* 25: 231–59.

Vallejo, Antonio R. 1911. *Guía de Agrimensores, o sea Recopilación de Leyes Agrarias.* Tegucigalpa, Honduras: Tipografía Nacional.

Vivanco, Luis A. 2001. Spectacular quetzals, ecotourism, and environmental futures in Monte Verde, Costa Rica. *Ethnology* 40(2): 79–92.

Watson, James L. 1997. *Golden Arches East: McDonald's in East Asia.* Stanford, CA: Stanford University Press.

Watson, V., S. Cervantes, C. Castro, L. Mora, M. Solis, I. T. Porras, and B. Cornejo. 1998. Making space for better forestry. Costa Rica Country Study. Policy That Works for Forests and People Series 6. San José, Costa Rica, and London: Centro Científico Tropical and International Institute for Environment and Development.

Wear, David N., and David H, Newman. 2004. The speculative shadow over timberland values in the U.S. South. *Journal of Forestry* 102(8): 25–31.

Wells, M., and K. Brandon. 1992. *People and Parks: Linking Protected Area Management with Local Communities.* Washington, DC: World Bank.

West, P., and S. Brechin (eds.). 1991. *Resident Peoples and National Parks: Social Dilemmas and Strategies in International Conservation.* Tucson: University of Arizona Press.

West, Paige, and Dan Brockington. 2006. An anthropological perspective on some unexpected consequences of protected areas. *Conservation Biology* 20(3): 609–16.

West, Patrick C. 1991. Introduction. In: *Resident Peoples and National Parks: Social Dilemmas and Strategies in International Conservation,* edited by Patrick C. West and Steven R. Brechin, pp. xv–xxiv. Tucson: University of Arizona Press.

Western, David, and R. Michael Wright (eds.). 1994. *Natural Connections: Perspectives in Community-Based Conservation.* Washington, DC: Island Press.

Wilhusen, Peter R. 2003. Exploring the political contours of conservation: A conceptual view of power in practice. In: *Contested Nature: Promoting International Biodiversity Conservation with Social Justice in the Twenty-first Century.* Albany: State University of New York Press.

Wilshusen, P., S. R. Brechin, C. L. Fortwangler, and P. West. 2002. Beyond the square wheel: Toward a more comprehensive understanding of biodiversity conservation as social and political process. *Society and Natural Resources* 15: 41–64.

Wilk, Richard. 1994. Consumer goods as dialogue about development: Colonial time and television time in Belize. In: *Consumption and Identity*, edited by Jonathan Friedman, pp. 97–118. Chur, Switzerland: Harwood Academic Publishers.

———. 2006. *Home Cooking in the Global Village: Caribbean Food from Buccaneers to Ecotourists.* Oxford: Berg.

World Resources Institute. 1994. *World Resources 1994–95.* New York: Oxford University Press.

Yearley, Steven. 1996. *Sociology, Environmentalism, Globalization: Reinventing the Globe.* London: Sage.

Zerner, Charles. 1994. Through a green lens: The construction of customary environmental law and community in Indonesia's Maluku Islands. *Law and Society Review* 28(5): 1079–1122.

Zube, Ervin H., and Miriam L. Busch. 1990. Park-people relationships: An international review. *Landscape and Urban Planning* 19: 117–31.

Data Collection
and Processing

Appendix A

W E COLLECTED A VARIETY OF DATA for this study, and we also processed available satellite imagery to create maps of our study sites. This appendix provides a brief description of various data that have been presented throughout this book.

Semistructured Interviews

We conducted a set of semistructured qualitative interviews with fifty-four individuals in five villages within the Cerro Azul Meambar National Park (CAMNP) (completed in 1999) and sixty-seven persons in five villages within five kilometers of La Amistad International Park's (LAIP) southern perimeter (completed in 2000). The villages we selected were geographically dispersed. We selected respondents purposefully, typically making initial contacts in the villages through park guards or other local informants, targeting community leaders for interviews. About half of the interviews resulted from cold calls that initiated contacts with individuals we felt were missed in the introductions provided by park guards or informants.

We engaged respondents in semistructured interviews of between one and two hours duration. Our questioning was based on an interview guide consisting of a variety of open-ended questions about attitudes and behaviors related to forests and the park. Specifically, we asked respondents what they thought the benefits of the park were, who benefited from the park, if they felt the distribution of benefits was fair, and if they thought there were any problems associated with the park. The responses were open-ended and allowed us to capture the respondents' sentiments in their own words. We used these qualitative data to select content for our survey questionnaires and to verify and interpret the results of our quantitative analyses.

Our analysis of the qualitative data began with a simple reading of field notes and interview transcripts. We looked for patterns of responses to our questioning. For the purposes of this book, we focused on a subset of the patterns or themes related to benefits from the park and looked for consistency of responses across the interviews. We present selected quotations to support and elaborate the findings of our quantitative analysis. Our interview guide is found in appendix B.

Surveys

In 1999, with the assistance of students and faculty at the Honduran National Forestry School, we interviewed 601 randomly selected household heads living in eight communities in or near CAMNP. In 2000 we conducted a similar survey of 523 randomly selected households in eight villages within five kilometers of the southern border of LAIP with the assistance of faculty and students from the National University of Costa Rica. The communities were purposefully selected to provide a complete geographic coverage within the CAMNP buffer zone in Honduras and along the southern boundary of the LAIP. In both cases, our sampling frames were complete lists of all households in our selected communities. We targeted household heads after discovering in earlier qualitative interviewing that they were much more informed about land use decisions than other household members. When household heads were not available, we interviewed their spouses. Thirty-eight percent of our Honduran and 36 percent of our Costa Rican respondents were female.

The wide-ranging survey interviews included questions about attitudes toward natural resources, especially forests and the park; land use, including agricultural production and de- and reforestation; sources of information about forests and the environment; expected benefits from the park; and a variety of sociodemographic characteristics like income, income sources, age, education, and household composition. Complete copies of the questionnaires with summary statistics are presented in appendixes C and D.

Satellite Imagery

The Costa Rica land cover map was made by Guillermo Duran Sanabria from data from a land cover analysis by INBio. Details on data and procedures used can be found in M. Kappelle et al. (2003).

Satellite data were used to evaluate changes in land use in Honduras. Land use maps were developed for February 1993 and January 1998 based on Landsat Thematic Mapper satellite images.[1] Based on information on land use from the qualitative interviews and previous experience (Gomez 1998), a classification scheme was developed based on four land use types: forest, fallow, coffee, and agriculture. To create the maps using a supervised classification approach, an average of twenty global positioning system (GPS) readings were acquired for each land use type throughout the park's buffer zone.

Differentiation of coffee from forest presented the greatest challenge. To aid in locating coffee plantations, a 1999 Indian Remote Sensing (IRS) satellite image was used. Land cover for the region was mapped using spectral data acquired by Linear Imaging Self-Scanning Sensor (LISS-3) aboard the Indian remote sensing satellite IRS-1C. The LISS-3 acquired spectral data for our study site in January 1999 using four spectral bands with spatial resolution of 23.7 meters. The high spatial resolution of this image facilitated identification of roads that usually led to land parcels where coffee was the dominant land use. In contrast, forested land is seldom marked by roads. The 1999 image was used as a guide to identify coffee plantations, to take GPS readings in 1999, and to make supervised classifications.

Accuracy of the classification was assessed in three ways: (1) visual inspection of the map for patterns consistent with direct observations, (2) comparison of the land use classification with land use data derived from the social survey, and (3) construction of an error matrix based on the comparison of a sample of direct observations with the land use classification. The land use classification was found to be reasonably satisfactory.

Visual inspection of the map indicated that the land use patterns mapped were consistent with direct observations and extensive feedback from consultations with park personnel and residents. When land use reported by farmers was compared with the GIS classification, the overall patterns were very similar to coffee and agriculture (see table A.1).

Table A.1.   Land Use Classification Error Matrix

Land Use (Predicted)	Land Use (Observed)					Percentage Error
	Coffee	Agriculture	Fallow	Forest	Total	
Coffee	11	0	0	6	17	35.3
Agriculture	10	22	3	1	36	38.9
Fallow	0	1	0	3	4	100.0
Forest	2	1	0	7	10	30.0
Total	23	24	3	17	67	—
Percentage Correct	47.8	91.7	0.0	41.2	—	—

Overall accuracy (%) = 59.7
Kappa Statistic = .407
Sources: Field observations (observed) and satellite images (predicted)

We verified the land use classification with sixty-seven georeferenced ground observations (Congalton and Green 1999). This method of accuracy assessment identified some errors. Overall accuracy was 60 percent (Kappa Statistic = 0.407). These statistics might have been higher if the sample of ground observations had been larger and better distributed across the land use classes. Two patterns of errors were most common. One type of error was to confuse coffee and agriculture. This occurred most frequently in areas recently planted to coffee. The other common error was to confuse coffee and forest, and this was most often done in areas of mature shade coffee (see Pfeffer et al. 2005 for details).

Since no direct assessment could be made of land use in 1993, local people were interviewed and questions posed about the age of specific coffee plantations and other significant land use changes, and this information was then used to evaluate the quality of the 1993 classification.

Note
1. We processed the images with Erdas Imagine 8.2 for PC.

Qualitative Interview Guide   # Appendix B

Fotografías

¿Que es lo que ve en esta foto? . . . ¿y en ésta? (If no response, see probes below.)

¿Cuál de estas fotos se parecen más a sus tierras? ¿Cómo?

¿Cómo llegó a ser así?

¿Cuál de estas fotos representa como le gustaría que sean sus tierras? . . . ¿por que?
¿Es posible que puedan llegar a ser así? ¿Que tendría que hacer para que sean así?

[*Probe: ¿Cree usted que los bosques son importantes? ¿Por qué?*
¿Los bosques son importantes para usted?
¿Los bosques son importantes para la comunidad?
. . . ¿para los animales? . . . ¿para las plantas? . . . ¿para quién más son importantes los bosques?
¿Qué me puede usted decir de los árboles? ¿Por qué cree usted que están ahí?
¿Usted cree que son importantes?
¿Qué me dice usted de la pastura?]

Bosques—preguntas generales

1. ¿Cuando usted piensa en los bosques y en los árboles, qué es lo que usted piensa primero—cuál es el primer pensamiento que le viene a la mente?

[*Probes: ¿Considera usted a los bosques y a los árboles como parte de la naturaleza? ¿como parte de su comunidad? ¿como parte de su rancho? ¿propiedad? ¿granja?*]

2. ¿Usted piensa que los bosques y los árboles son importantes o no? . . . ¿Por qué?

Bosques en la comunidad y en la región

Primero nos gustaría hablar acerca de los bosques que hay en su comunidad y en las áreas cercanas. Después nos gustaría hablar de los bosques que hay dentro de su propiedad.

3. ¿Cómo han cambiado los bosques y los árboles en su comunidad y en el área que le rodea desde que usted empezó a sembrar y trabajar en esta área?

4. ¿Por qué cree usted que ha habido estos cambios?
[*Probe: ¿Provocados por la naturaleza? ¿provocados por los hombres?*]

5. ¿Quiénes han hecho estos cambios?
[*General probe: ¿Hay aquí algún grupo de personas, o alguna organización local o en la región que sea responsable de estos cambios?*]

6. ¿Cuáles han sido los resultados de estos cambios?
[*Probe: ¿Ha afectado (impactado) al medio ambiente; ha afectado a la comunidad; ha tenido un impacto en la economía del lugar?*]

7. ¿A usted le gustaría tener más montaña (monte) o árboles en su comunidad, y en las áreas cercanas, o los bosques y árboles que hay ahora es suficiente? . . . ¿Por qué?

Nos gustaría hablar un poco sobre la corta de árboles

8. ¿Considera usted que a veces es bueno cortar árboles? . . . ¿Por qué?

9. ¿Considera usted que a veces es malo cortar árboles? . . . ¿Por qué?
10. ¿Qué cree usted que pasaría si alguien en la comunidad se pone a cortar árboles?

11. *[Probe: ¿Cómo reaccionaría la comunidad?]*

12. (Farmers) ¿Ha cortado árboles en las tierras que usted trabaja?

13. ¿Cuáles han sido los resultados?

14. ¿Qué partes de estos resultados fueron positivos? . . . ¿Por qué?

15. ¿Qué partes de estos resultados fueron negativos? . . . ¿Por qué?

Descombrar bosque

16. ¿Considera usted que a veces es bueno descombrar areas con árboles, como bosques o montañas? . . . ¿Por qué?

17. ¿Considera usted que a veces es malo descombrar areas con árboles, como bosques o montañas? . . . ¿Por qué?

18. ¿Qué cree usted que pasaría si alguien en la comunidad se pone a descombrar áreas con árboles, como bosques, o montaña?
[Probe: ¿Cómo reaccionaría la comunidad?]

19. ¿Ahora tiene usted en su propiedad mas o menos la misma cantidad de bosques ó árboles, que cuando usted empezó a trabajar aquí?

20. (Farmers) ¿Ha descombrado áreas con árboles como bosques o montañas en las tierras que usted trabaja?

21. ¿Cuáles han sido los resultados?

22. ¿Qué partes de estos resultados fueron positivos? . . . ¿Por qué?

23. ¿Qué partes de estos resultados fueron negativos? . . . ¿Por qué?

Ahora nos gustaría hablar acerca de plantar árboles

24. ¿Usted considera que es algo bueno plantar árboles? . . . ¿Por qué?

25. ¿Usted cree que hay algo malo en ponerse a plantar árboles? . . . ¿Por qué?

26. (Farmers) ¿Ha plantado árboles en las tierras que usted trabaja?

27. ¿Cuáles han sido los resultados?

28. ¿Cuáles fueron los beneficios de plantar árboles? . . . ¿Como cuáles?

29. ¿Cuáles son los costos de plantar árboles? . . . ¿Como cuáles?

Ahora nos gustaría hablar acerca de dejar los bosques en vivo

30. ¿Usted considera que es algo bueno dejar los bosques en vivo? . . . ¿Por qué?

31. ¿Usted cree que hay algo malo en dejar los bosques en vivo? . . . ¿Por qué?

32. (Farmers) ¿Usted ha dejado bosques en vivo en sus tierras?

33. ¿Cuáles han sido los resultados?

34. ¿Qué partes de estos resultados fueron positivos? . . . ¿Por qué?

35. ¿Qué partes de estos resultados fueron negativos? . . . ¿Por qué?

Montaña dentro de la comunidad

36. ¿A usted le gustaría tener más bosques ó árboles en su comunidad? . . . ¿Por qué?

37. ¿A usted le gustaría tener menos bosques ó árboles en su comunidad? . . . ¿Por qué?

38. ¿Quién tiene la responsabilidad de cuidar los bosques y los árboles? (¿un ejemplo?)

39. ¿En esta comunidad? (if they don't specify)

40. ¿Usted habla (discute?) con otras personas acerca de los bosques y los árboles?

41. ¿Quién tiene la responsabilidad de cuidar los bosques y los árboles? (¿un ejemplo?)

42. ¿En esta comunidad? (if they don't specify)

43. ¿Usted habla (¿discute?) con otras personas acerca de los bosques y los árboles?

44. Deme un ejemplo de una situación.

45. ¿De quién aprendió lo que usted sabe sobre los bosques y los árboles?
[*Probe: ¿aprendió usted de . . . otros miembros de la comunidad? . . . ¿de sus padres? . . . ¿de los guardias del parque? . . . ¿de los trabajadores de desarrollo? (¿extensionistas? ¿técnicos?) . . . ¿de la iglesia? . . . ¿la radio? . . . ¿la televisión? . . . ¿los periódicos?*]

Parques forestales

46. ¿Ha oído hablar usted del Parque Nacional Cerro Azul-Meambar?

47. ¿Por qué existe el Parque? (¿para qué sirve?)

48. ¿Qué cree usted que le pasaría a los bosques y a los árboles si el Parque fuera eliminado?

49. ¿Cuáles son los beneficios de tener el Parque?

50. ¿Quién se beneficia del Parque?
[*Probe: . . . ¿usted? . . . ¿la comunidad? . . . ¿otra gente? ¿como quiénes? . . . ¿la naturaleza?*

51. ¿Usted cree que es justo o injusto que <u>(beneficiario)</u> reciba tal beneficio por el Parque?

52. ¿Cuáles son los daños o problemas en tener un parque?

53. ¿A quién le perjudica el Parque?
[*Probe: ¿a usted? . . . ¿a la comunidad? . . . ¿a la naturaleza?*]

54. ¿Usted cree que es justo o injusto (¿que está bien?) que esto le pase a _(persona perjudicada)_?

Características del entrevistado

Hemos terminado, ahora solo unas preguntas sobre usted.

55. Edad   _____

56. Género (por observación):
    Masculino   _____
    Femenino   _____

57. ¿Cuánto tiempo lleva viviendo en esta comunidad?   _____

58. Ocupación   _____

59. Número de años escolares   _____

60. Religión   _____

61. ¿Está usted activo en su religión?   SI_____   NO_____

Appendix C

**Costa Rica
Questionnaire with
Summary Data**

Encuesta: Colaboración UNA-OTS-Cornell

Nombre del entrevistador: Ocho comunidades en del Parque Internacional
La Amistad

Fecha: 6–20 Enero 2000

Numero entravistas: 518

Este documento resume los resultados de la encuesta realizada en ocho comunidades localizadas dentro del Parque Internacional La Amistad. Este reporte presenta los resultado del estudio sobre los conocimientos y las actitudes que las personas tienen sobre el bosque y el parque. Maestos y estudiantes de la Escuela Nacional de Forestería condujeron esta encuesta durante mese de enero de 2000. Este estudio no se hubiera podido realizar sin el generoso apoyo de los lideres de la comunidad y sus residentes.

Es el sincero deseo de los directores de este estudio, que estos resultados sean de utilidad para las comunidades, los líderes y los oficiales de gobierno para mejorar tanto las condiciones de los habitantes del Parque Internacional La Amistad, como para la proteccion ambiental del parque.

Voy a leerle algunos comentarios que la gente hace sobre los bosques. Por favor dígame si usted está de acuerdo, en desacuerdo, si no está de acuerdo ni en desacuerdo con el comentario, porque le es indiferente, o si no sabe dígame no sé.

LA GENTE PIENSA QUE	De acuerdo (%)	En des- acuerdo (%)	Ni de acuerdo, ni en des- acuerdo (me es indiferente) (%)	No sé (%)
1. Más que para ninguna otra cosa, el bosque existe para dar leña y madera.	32.6	64.7	1.2	1.5
2. Está bien cortar los árboles que no producen buena madera.	25.9	67.2	3.5	3.5
3. Es de suma importancia cuidar los árboles que nos dan madera y frutos.	99.0	0.6	0.4	—
4. Está bien cortar los árboles viejos o árboles muertos.	67.2	24.9	4.6	3.3
5. La caza de animales está bien, cuando existen muchos de ellos en el lugar.	33.2	61.8	1.5	3.5
6. Lo más importante acerca de los árboles es hacer dinero con ellos.	16.4	79.2	2.5	1.9
7. Tenemos que cuidar mucho nuestros bosques si queremos que el turismo crezca y nos traiga dinero.	95.9	2.1	0.6	1.4
8. Sin bosques, nuestra comunidad no tendría agua suficiente.	97.3	2.5	0.2	—
9. Los bosques en nuestra comunidad son fuente de agua para los que viven en otra parte del país.	89.9	3.5	—	6.6
10. Los árboles que crecen en las orillas de los ríos y quebradas nunca se deberían de cortar.	95.7	4.1	0.2	—
11. Sin bosques, no tendríamos suficiente oxígeno para respirar.	98.3	1.2	—	0.6
12. Debemos conservar los bosques porque son muy importantes para producir electricidad.	86.9	2.1	0.2	10.8
13. Los bosques por aquí, ayudan a mantener el clima fresco.	100.0	—	—	—

14. Está bien cortar un árbol si plantas uno nuevo.	80.4	16.4	1.2	1.7
15. Está bien cortar unos cuantos árboles grandes para que los árboles nuevos puedan crecer.	72.2	20.1	2.5	5.2
16. La quema puede ayudar a que los cultivos crezcan mejor.	18.7	74.1	1.7	5.4
17. Está bien cortar los bosques, porque fácilmente vuelven a crecer.	14.1	82.8	0.6	2.5
18. Si hay demasiado bosque, la tierra estaría muy húmeda para poder cultivar por ahí.	68.9	22.8	2.9	5.4
19. Las plagas y enfermedades que vienen de los bosques pueden dañar nuestros cultivos.	44.1	42.6	1.4	12.0
20. Deberíamos tener por aquí muchos bosques porque son tan hermosos.	97.3	1.4	0.8	0.6
21. La gente joven debería estar enojada con las generaciones anteriores por el daño que han hecho a los bosques por aquí.	70.3	24.7	1.7	3.3
22. Los potreros deberían tener algunos árboles.	94.8	4.6	0.2	0.4
23. No es bueno tener árboles cerca de los cultivos.	51.9	37.1	5.4	5.6
24. Porque Dios creó los bosques, está mal abusar de ellos.	83.0	11.8	1.9	3.3
25. Los bosques son una parte importante de nuestro patrimonio nacional.	99.2	—	—	0.8
26. Todas las cosas vivas, incluyendo los animales, los pájaros y los árboles, tienen también derecho a la vida.	99.8	—	—	0.2
27. Siempre está bien cazar o matar animales silvestres.	9.5	87.2	2.3	1.0
28. Son nuestros hijos quienes se beneficiarán de los árboles y bosques que nosotros protejamos.	99.0	0.4	0.2	0.4

29. ¿Qué es más hermoso?

☐	LAS ÁREAS SEMBRADAS	11.8%
☐	LOS BOSQUES	36.5
☐	*[LOS DOS IGUAL]*	50.2
☐	*[NINGUNO]*	—
☐	*NO SÉ*	1.5

30. ¿Con qué piensa usted que uno puede hacer más dinero?

☐	UNA HECTÁREA DE CAFÉ	61.8%
☐	UNA HECTÁREA DE BOSQUE	10.0
☐	*[LOS DOS IGUAL]*	17.8
☐	*[NINGUNA]*	0.4
☐	*NO SÉ*	5.2

31. ¿Con qué piensa usted que uno puede hacer más dinero?

☐	UNA HECTÁREA DE PASTO	22.2%
☐	UNA HECTÁREA DE BOSQUE	43.2
☐	*[LOS DOS IGUAL]*	15.1
☐	*[NINGUNA]*	4.4
☐	*NO SÉ*	15.1

32. ¿Cuál es mejor para el ambiente?

☐	UNA HECTÁREA DE CAFÉ O	63.4%
☐	UNA MANZANA DE PASTO	9.1
☐	*[LOS DOS IGUAL]*	14.9
☐	*[NINGUNA]*	6.6
☐	*NO SÉ*	6.0

33. ¿Cuál es mejor para el ambiente?

☐	UNA HECTÁREA DE CAFÉ	9.5%
☐	UNA HECTÁREA DE BOSQUE	67.5
☐	*[LOS DOS IGUAL]*	19.1
☐	*[NINGUNA]*	0.2
☐	*NO SÉ*	3.7

34. ¿Cuál es mejor para el ambiente?

☐	UNA HECTÁREA DE BOSQUE	78.4%
☐	UNA HECTÁREA DE PASTO	3.9
☐	*[LOS DOS IGUAL]*	13.3
☐	*[NINGUNA]*	0.6
☐	*NO SÉ*	3.9

35. ¿Pensando en los árboles que hay en su propio terreno o finca, usted piensa que hay . . .?

☐	DEMASIADOS ÁRBOLES	9.0%
☐	EXACTAMENTE LOS NECESARIOS	32.8
☐	NO HAY SUFICIENTES ÁRBOLES	51.9
☐	*NO SÉ*	6.3

Ahora quisiera que usted me dijera de quién aprendió lo que usted sabe de los árboles y de los bosques.

APRENDIÓ SOBRE LOS BOSQUES	SI (%)	NO (%)	NO SÉ (%)
36. ¿De sus padres?	56.0	43.2	0.8
37. ¿De sus vecinos?	53.3	45.8	1.0
38. ¿De trabajar la tierra?	83.4	15.1	1.5
39. ¿En la iglesia?	49.0	50.2	0.8
40. ¿De los turistas?	48.8	49.8	1.4
41. ¿Escuchando la radio?	84.9	14.9	0.2
42. ¿Viendo televisión?	86.1	13.5	0.4
43. ¿De los guarda parques?	72.0	27.4	0.6
44. ¿De los agentes de extensión o extensionistas que trabajan con alguna organización?	46.9	51.4	1.7
45. ¿Charlas a las que usted ha asistido?	45.9	53.7	—
46a. ¿Del patronato o líderes locales?	30.3	69.1	0.6

46b. ¿En la escuela o colegio?	61.1	38.7	0.2
46c. ¿De sus propias experiencias con el bosque?	90.5	8.3	1.2

47. ¿De todas estas fuentes de información acerca del bosque [*léale las respuestas afirmativas*], cuál de éstas es la más importante para usted?

    <u>Propias experiencias (29.3%)</u> LA MÁS IMPORTANTE *(# de la tabla anterior)*

48. ¿Después de cuántos años el charral o tacotal se convierte en bosque?

    <u>14.7 AÑOS</u> *[promedio]*

☐   *NO SÉ*

49. ¿Cuántos años tarda el charral o tacotal en crecer antes de que usted lo pueda volver a cortar o quemar para plantar un cultivo nuevo?

    <u>3.0 AÑOS</u> *[promedio]*

☐   *NO SÉ*

Ahora voy a leerle algunas afirmaciones. Por favor dígame si está usted de acuerdo, en desacuerdo, o indiferente con cada una de ellas.

LA GENTE ASEGURA QUE	De acuerdo (%)	En des- acuerdo (%)	Ni de acuerdo, ni en desacuerdo (me es indiferente) (%)	No sé (%)
50. Está bien quemar charral o tacotal si se va a cultivar ahí.	29.9	65.4	2.5	2.1
51. Cuando el charral o tacotal crece muy grande se convierte en bosque.	89.6	7.1	1.0	2.3
52. Está permitido cortar o botar bosque.	7.7	89.4	0.8	2.1

53. Las plantas de café son un tipo de árbol.	54.9	36.8	0.8	7.5
54. Es más fácil para los dueños ricos de grandes fincas conseguir permisos para cortar árboles, que para la gente común o pobre.	90.5	5.4	0.2	3.9
55. Si el charral o tacotal se convierte en bosque, el gobierno no lo deja cultivar más esa tierra.	75.3	16.0	0.4	8.3
56. Está permitido limpiar o botar charral o tacotal.	54.2	35.1	2.7	7.9
57. Los árboles frutales son tan árboles como lo son los árboles maderables.	80.3	17.2	0.8	1.7
58. Debería ser más fácil para el campesino de esta comunidad conseguir el permiso para cortar un árbol para uso en la casa.	85.9	10.2	0.2	3.7
59. Los árboles pertenecen al gobierno.	42.2	42.8	1.7	13.2
60. Está permitido limpiar o botar montaña.	7.1	90.3	1.0	1.5
61. Pequeños propietarios pueden conseguir permisos para cortar árboles tan fácilmente como los demás.	23.7	64.4	0.8	8.1
62. Si no tuviéramos leyes que protegen a los bosques, tendríamos muchos menos árboles.	99.2	0.6	0.2	—
63. Si a la gente se le permitiera cortar todos los árboles que quieran, no sabrían cuando parar.	94.8	3.7	0.4	1.2

64. La gente no hace quemas en sus tierras de cultivo porque tienen miedo del gobierno.	74.9	18.7	2.9	3.5
65. Debería ser más fácil para los dueños de tierra en esta comunidad conseguir un permiso para cortar árboles para su venta comercial.	39.4	53.7	1.2	5.8
66. Es la responsabilidad del gobierno de cuidar los árboles.	84.4	12.9	1.4	1.4
67. El gobierno no puede por si solo cuidar a los árboles y a los bosques, la gente de la comunidad debe ayudar también.	98.6	1.2	—	0.2
68. La mayoría de la gente que vive por aquí no le importa si se cortan los árboles.	44.0	45.2	2.7	0.1
69a. La gente en esta comunidad puede, sin la ayuda del gobierno, cuidar los árboles.	57.6	39.7	0.8	1.9
69b. Por la falta de empleo, a veces es necesario talar o cortar árboles.	54.4	39.0	0.8	5.8
69c. Por la falta de empleo, a veces es necesario montear.	21.2	73.6	1.0	4.2
69d. Está bien matar a las culebras u otros animales que puedan causar daño a la gente o los animales domésticos.	65.6	29.0	3.5	1.9

69e. La gente de la comunidad no tiene la responsabilidad de denunciar a sus vecinos por la tala de árboles o porque montean. Eso es deber de los funcionarios del MINAE o de las patrullas de vigilancia del MINAE.	36.1	60.0	0.8	3.1

Ahora quiero hacerle unas preguntas acerca de sus tierras.

TRABAJA USTED ALGUNA TIERRA EN ESTAS CONDICIONES	SI (%)	NO (%)	COMO CUÁNTAS HECTÁREAS TIENE USTED EN [promedio]	NO LO SÉ
70. ¿Con bosque o montaña?	33.1	66.9	3.8	—
71. ¿Con charral o tacotal?	43.6	56.4	1.6	—
72. ¿Con café?	86.6	13.4	3.1	—
73. ¿Con potrero?	41.2	58.8	5.3	—
74. ¿Con hortalizas?	7.6	92.4	0.19	—
75. ¿Con cultivos como maíz, frijol o tubérculos?	30.9	69.1	1.9	—
76. ¿En otras condiciones? Especifique.	13.5	86.5	0.8	—
77. TOTAL. (Entonces, considerando todas sus tierras, usted tiene como (#) _____ hectáreas, cierto? [Si no, revise las preguntas y reconfirme las hectáreas en cada categoría.]			14.7	

Ahora le voy a preguntar sobre la plantación de árboles o reforestación:

HA SEMBRADO USTED	NO (%)	SÍ, EN MI PROPIA TIERRA (%)	SÍ, EN TIERRAS DE OTROS (%)	SI, EN MI PROPIA TIERRA Y EN TIERRAS DE OTROS (%)
78. ¿Amarillones?	55.0	26.3	15.6	3.1
79. ¿Otros árboles maderables?	55.7	28.5	13.4	2.3
80. ¿Árboles frutales?	7.9	72.3	11.2	8.5
81. ¿Otros?	73.9	19.9	4.2	2.0

[Si ha sembrado árboles:]

HA SEMBRADO USTED ÁRBOLES	SI (%)	NO (%)	NO SÉ (%)
82. ¿A lo largo de quebradas y ríos?	38.7	60.9	0.4
83. ¿A lo largo de las orillas de los cultivos?	46.5	53.3	0.2
84. ¿En potreros?	37.5	62.4	0.2
85. ¿En el cafetal?	70.2	29.6	0.2
86. ¿Alrededor de la casa?	72.1	27.5	0.4
87. ¿A lo largo del camino?	46.3	53.3	0.4

88. ¿Ha conservado usted bosques en su propia tierra?

☐   SI   39.4%   ==> 89. ¿Cómo cuántas hectáreas ha conservado usted? <u>4.6</u> HECTÁREAS

☐   NO   58.1

☐   *NO SÉ*   2.5

90. ¿Ha cortado alguna vez árboles, o ha arralado o botado bosques, en su propiedad?

☐   SI   38.8%
☐   NO   61.0   ==> pase a la pregunta 92
☐   *NO LO SÉ*   0.2   ==> pase a la pregunta 92

91. *[Si cortó árboles]* Cortó usted estos árboles para *(marque todas las opciones que sean válidas)*:

☐   LIMPIAR BOSQUE PARA CULTIVAR LA TIERRA   78.3%
☐   PARA TENER MADERA PARA CONSTRUIR SU CASA   72.2
☐   PARA VENDER   18.7
☐   PARA LEÑA   63.1
☐   PARA RECLAMAR O ESTABLECER DERECHOS
      SOBRE LA TIERRA   16.2
☐   OTRO, ESPECIFIQUE _____   16.2

Voy a leerle más comentarios que la gente hace sobre los bosques. Por favor dígame si **usted** está de acuerdo, en desacuerdo, o si el comentario le es indiferente.

LA GENTE PIENSA QUE	De Acuerdo (%)	En desacuerdo (%)	Ni de acuerdo, ni en desacuerdo (me es indiferente) (%)	No sé (%)
92. Debemos pensar en las generaciones futuras cuando tomamos decisiones respecto al uso de nuestros bosques.	97.1	1.2	0.2	1.5
93. En estos días la gente de esta comunidad tiene más cuidado con los bosques que antes.	94.4	3.7	0.6	1.4
94. Cuando alguien corta un árbol, aunque lo corte en su propia tierra, nos perjudica a todos.	89.6	5.2	1.7	3.5
95. Cazar o matar animales silvestres está bien, si usted lo hace para alimentarse.	50.7	45.6	1.9	1.7

96. Las compañías madereras destruyen más bosque que la gente que vive en esta comunidad.	95.8	2.3	0.6	1.4
97. Los bosques por aquí benefician más a gente de afuera, como por ejemplo, científicos y turistas, que a la gente que vive aquí en esta comunidad.	47.7	44.2	2.7	5.4
98. Necesitamos primero alimentos y dinero antes de poder empezar a preocuparnos de cuidar los bosques.	58.2	33.6	4.4	3.5
99. Los seres humanos tienen que cortar árboles para poder vivir.	29.3	64.5	2.9	3.3
100. Es mejor usar la tierra para producir alimentos que dejarla así como bosque.	44.0	36.2	15.5	4.3
101. Por aquí estaríamos mejor económicamente si tuviéramos menos árboles.	12.0	80.3	1.7	6.0
102. Es muy importante que nuestros niños tengan la oportunidad de poder disfrutar de los bosques y los animales silvestres.	98.5	1.0	—	0.6
103. Se le debería permitir a la gente vender los árboles que están en su propia tierra sin ninguna restricción por parte del gobierno.	13.7	81.7	1.2	3.5
104. Cazar o matar animales silvestres está bien, si usted necesita dinero.	8.3	88.9	0.8	1.9
105. Costa Rica está ayudando al resto del mundo preservando sus bosques.	89.8	1.7	0.4	8.1
106. Se le debería permitir a la gente limpiar o botar bosque para cultivar o sembrar café sin ninguna restricción de parte del gobierno.	24.9	68.1	1.7	5.2

107. Si hay mucho bosque por aquí los animales que viven en el bosque pueden dañar mis cultivos o mis animales.	50.4	45.9	1.5	2.1
108. El gobierno debería prohibir a la gente el corte de árboles para vender la madera.	67.8	23.2	3.9	5.2
109. Se le debería permitir a la gente que corte árboles para construir su casa sin ninguna restricción por parte del gobierno.	59.3	37.1	1.4	2.3
110. Se le debería permitir a la gente hacer lo que quieran con los árboles que se encuentran en su tierra.	8.3	89.9	0.6	1.2
111. Si nosotros fuéramos a conservar bosques por aquí, tenemos menos oportunidad de ganar dinero.	38.5	50.1	1.9	9.5
112. Nuestra comunidad estaría mejor a largo plazo si conservamos nuestros bosques en vez de cortarlos.	87.8	5.8	1.5	4.8
113. Hay muchas maneras de aprovechar nuestros bosques y hacer dinero, sin tener que cortarlos.	80.5	11.0	0.8	7.7
114. El gobierno debería prevenir que la gente corte bosque para cultivar café.	56.0	34.2	2.5	7.3

115. ¿Ha sido castigado o multado por acciones en contra de las leyes o sus reglamentos?

☐   SI   3.7%
☐   NO   95.8
☐   NO SÉ   0.6
☐   REHUSÓ   —

Ahora quiero hacerle algunas preguntas acerca del Parque Internacional La Amistad.

116. ¿Es bueno vivir cerca de un parque nacional?

☐   SI   84.7%
☐   NO   6.0
☐   *INDECISO*   2.1
☐   *NO LO SÉ*   7.2

¿Cuál de los siguientes grupos de gente se benefician del parque [*cheque todos los que se mencionen*]?

SE BENEFICIAN DEL PARQUE	SI (%)	NO (%)	NO SÉ (%)
117. ¿Usted mismo?	73.7	19.35	6.38
118. ¿Gente en la comunidad?	82.2	9.3	8.5
119. ¿Los guardas del parque?	90.3	2.1	7.5
120. ¿Turistas?	89.6	3.5	6.9
121. ¿Gente de todo el país?	88.6	5.2	6.2
122. ¿Gente en otras comunidades?	84.4	5.2	10.4
123. ¿Todo el mundo?	84.2	6.9	8.9

124. ¿Quién de ellos [*léale las respuestas afirmativas*] se beneficia más?

Todo el mundo (34.7%) BENEFICIA MÁS (*# de la tabla anterior*).

Dígame si usted piensa que el Parque es *muy importante, importante,* o *no es importante* para lo siguiente:

EL PARQUE	MUY IMPOR-TANTE (%)	IMPOR-TANTE (%)	NO ES IMPOR-TANTE (%)	NO SABE (%)
125. ¿Proteger los bosques y los árboles?	58.7	39.8	0.4	1.2

126. ¿Proteger fuentes de agua para tener una buena calidad y cantidad de agua?	70.3	29.2	0.2	0.4
127. ¿Proteger la diversidad de plantas y animales (biodiversidad) y los recursos genéticos?	62.2	36.7	0.4	0.8
128. ¿Proteger vida silvestre?	62.0	37.1	—	1.0
129. ¿Proteger los suelos para evitar la erosión?	64.5	2.0	1.4	2.1
130. ¿Fomentar el desarrollo nacional?	50.6	37.3	2.3	9.8
131. ¿Fomentar turismo?	56.2	40.3	1.2	2.3
132. ¿Fomentar el desarrollo comunitario?	51.4	40.5	3.3	4.8
133. ¿Ciencia e investigaciones?	55.0	37.6	6.0	6.8
134. ¿Bajar impactos al ambiente?	57.7	35.1	1.9	5.2

Por último le voy a hacer algunas preguntas sobre usted:

135. [*Marque el género de la persona que entrevista por observación*]

☐   HOMBRE   63.2%
☐   MUJER   36.8

136. ¿En que año nació usted? 19_60_AÑO [*promedio*]

☐   NO SÉ
☐   *REHUSÓ*

137. ¿Usted nació en _____ [*mencione el nombre de la comunidad donde está llevando a cabo la entrevista*]?

□   SI   6.6%
□   NO   93.2 ==>138. ¿En que año llegó usted a ésta comunidad
                por primera vez? 19_82_AÑO
□   *NO SÉ*   —
□   *REHUSÓ*   —

139. ¿Cuántos años asistió usted a la escuela o colegio?

     4.0 AÑOS DE PRIMARIA
     0.5 AÑOS DE SECUNDARIA
     0.1 OTRO _____ (ESPECIFIQUE)

□   *NO SÉ*
□   *REHUSÓ*

140. ¿Qué religión practica usted?

□   CATÓLICA   74.5%
□   EVANGÉLICO   16.4
□   OTRA _____ (ESPECIFIQUE)   7.2
□   *NO SÉ*   1.2
□   *REHUSÓ*   0.8

141. ¿Más o menos, cuál fue su ingreso total de la casa durante el año pasado?

□   MENOS DE ₡600.000   (50.000 por mes)   50.5%
□   ENTRE ₡600.001 y   (más de 50.000 y hasta   11.5
    ₡1.080.000   90.000 por mes)
□   ENTRE ₡1.080.001 y   (más de 90.000 y hasta   4.7
    ₡1.800.000   150.000 por mes)
□   ENTRE ₡1.800.001 y   (más de 150.000 y hasta   1.2
    ₡2.400.000   200.000 por mes)
□   MÁS DE ₡2.400.001   (más de 200.000 por mes)   1.6
□   *NO SÉ*   30.1
□   *REHUSÓ*   0.4

142. Por favor dígame si usted o alguien en su familia recibe dinero. Por ejemplo de [*marque todos los que mencione*]:

☐	AGRICULTURA	46.7%
☐	NEGOCIOS COMO TIENDA O PULPERÍA	6.9
☐	SALARIO DE OBRERO, JORNALERO	43.8
☐	RECOGIENDO CAFÉ	85.1
☐	ALGUN FAMILIAR QUE VIVE AQUI EN EL PAÍS PERO NO EN LA CASA	10.0
☐	ALGUN FAMILIAR QUE VIVE FUERA DE COSTA RICA	5.4
☐	OTRO _____	14.3%
☐	*NO SÉ*	—
☐	*REHUSÓ*	—

143. ¿De todas estas fuentes de dinero [*léale las respuestas afirmativas*], cuál de éstas es la más importante para su casa?

Recogiendo café (57.1%) LA MÁS IMPORTANTE

144. ¿Cuántos hijos tiene usted (o el padre de la familia)?

4.2 HIJOS *[promedio]*

145. ¿Cuántas personas viven en esta casa?

4.7 PERSONAS *[promedio]*

146. ¿Usted se siente satisfecho con lo que gana en actualidad?

☐	SI	51.5%
☐	NO	45.9
☐	*NO SÉ*	2.5

147. ¿Cómo cree usted que su situación económica ha cambiado en los últimos 5 años?

☐	HA MEJORADO	43.8%
☐	SE HA PUESTO PEOR	26.4
☐	QUEDA IGUAL COMO ANTES	27.6
☐	*NO SÉ*	2.1

148. ¿En comparación a los otros de su comunidad, usted diría que sus ganancias económicas son . . .?

☐ ENTRE LO NORMAL	53.9%
☐ MÁS QUE OTROS	9.7
☐ MENOS QUE OTROS	23.4
☐ NO SÉ	13.1

149. ¿Actualmente, usted se siente satisfecho con el bienestar de su núcleo familiar?

☐ SI	90.3%
☐ NO	8.9
☐ NO SÉ	0.8

150. ¿Cómo cree usted que el bienestar de su núcleo familiar ha cambiado en los últimos 5 años?

☐ HA MEJORADO	58.9%
☐ SE HA PUESTO PEOR	7.5
☐ QUEDA IGUAL COMO ANTES	29.9
☐ NO SÉ	3.7

151. ¿En comparación a los otros de su comunidad, usted diría que el bienestar de su nucleo familiar es . . .?

☐ ENTRE LO NORMAL	66.8%
☐ MEJOR QUE OTROS	17.4
☐ PEOR QUE OTROS	4.6
☐ NO SÉ	11.2

152. ¿Si usted pudiera ganar más dinero, sea con el turismo u otra ocupación, como cree que lo gastaría [marque todos que se mencione]?

☐ MANTENER A LA FAMILIA (COMPRAR COMIDA, ROPA)	93.6%
☐ PAGAR LA EDUCACIÓN DE USTED Y SUS HIJOS	90.9
☐ CURARSE LA SALUD (SUYA Y DE SUS HIJOS)	95.6
☐ MEJORAR (O CONSTRUIR) LA CASA	92.7
☐ COMPRAR GANADO	34.7
☐ COMPRAR TIERRA	67.8
☐ CONTRATAR A OTROS PARA QUE TRABAJEN SU FINCA	67.4

☐   COMPRAR MAQUINARIA PARA LA AGRICULTURA
O GANADERÍA   50.8
☐   COMPRAR MAQUINARIA PARA LIMPIAR MONTAÑA   9.9
☐   COMPRAR UN CARRO   69.1
☐   VIAJAR   59.8
☐   AHORRAR PARA EL FUTURO   95.6
☐   IRSE A OTRO SITIO   20.8
☐   OTRO (especificar)   13.9

153. ¿De todos estos *[léale las respuestas afirmativas]*, cuál sería la prioridad principal?
<u>Mantener a la familia (32.9%)</u>

Hora de finalización: _____

Estas son todas mis preguntas. Muchas gracias por su ayuda.

Tendría usted otro comentario que agregar.

[Anote el comentario]

Le agradecemos mucho su colaboración. Que pase buen día.

Appendix D

Encuesta: Colaboración ESNACIFOR-Cornell

Nombre de la comunidad: <u>Ocho Comunidades en el Parque Nacional</u>
<u>Cerro Azul Meambar</u>

Fecha: <u>Julio–Agosto 1999</u>

Número de entrevistas: <u>601</u>

Este documento resume los resultados de la encuesta realizada en ocho comunidades localiza-das dentro del Parque Nacional Cerro Azul Meambar. Este reporte presenta los resultados del estudio sobre los conocimientos y las actitudes que las personas tienen sobre el bosque y el parque. Maestos y estudiantes de la Escuela Nacional de Forestería condujeron esta encuesta durante los meses de julio y agosto de 1999. Este estudio no se hubiera podido realizar sin el generoso apoyo de los líderes de la comunidad y sus residentes.

Es el sincero deseo de los directores de este estudio, que estos resultados sean de utilidad para las comunidades, los líderes y los oficiales del gobierno para mejorar tanto las condiciones de los habitantes del Parque Nacional Cerro Azul Meambar, como para la protección ambiental del parque.

Voy a leerle algunos comentarios que la gente hace sobre los bosques. Por favor dígame si usted está de acuerdo, en desacuerdo, o si el comentario le es indiferente.

LA GENTE PIENSA QUE	De acuerdo (%)	En desacuerdo (%)	Ni de acuerdo, ni en desacuerdo (me es indiferente) (%)	No sé (%)
1. Más que para ninguna otra cosa, el bosque existe para dar leña y madera.	33.6	64.7	1.3	0.3
2. Está bien cortar los árboles que no producen buena madera.	40.4	54.1	4.5	1.0
3. Es de suma importancia cuidar los árboles que nos dan madera y frutos.	97.0	2.7	0.2	0.2
4. Está bien cortar los árboles viejos o árboles muertos.	81.2	13.1	5.0	0.7
5. La caza de animales está bien, cuando existen muchos de ellos en el lugar.	41.8	52.8	2.8	2.5
6. Lo más importante acerca de los árboles es hacer dinero de ellos.	28.2	65.9	3.8	2.0
7. Tenemos que cuidar mucho nuestros bosques si queremos que el turismo crezca y nos traiga dinero.	96.5	2.7	0.7	0.2
8. Sin bosques, nuestra comunidad no tendría agua suficiente.	98.5	1.5	—	—
9. Los bosques en nuestra comunidad son fuente de agua para los que viven en otra parte del país.	96.0	3.7	0.3	—
10. Los árboles que crecen en las orillas de los ríos y quebradas nunca se deberían de cortar.	93.2	4.5	0.2	2.2

11. Sin bosques, no tendríamos suficiente oxígeno para respirar.	99.5	0.3	0.2	—
12. Debemos conservar los bosques porque son muy importantes para producir electricidad.	94.3	0.5	0.2	0.5
13. Los bosques por aquí, ayudan a mantener el clima fresco.	99.8	0.2	—	—
14. Está bien cortar un árbol si plantas uno nuevo.	93.3	6.2	0.2	0.3
15. Está bien cortar unos cuantos árboles grandes para que los árboles nuevos puedan crecer.	84.4	10.0	3.0	2.5
16. La quema puede ayudar a que los cultivos crezcan mejor.	34.1	58.5	5.0	2.3
17. Está bien cortar los bosques, porque fácilmente vuelven a crecer.	21.1	73.4	3.0	2.5
18. Si hay demasiado bosque, la tierra estaría muy húmeda para poder cultivar por ahí.	78.1	17.7	1.5	2.7
19. Las plagas y enfermedades que vienen de los bosques pueden dañar nuestros cultivos.	66.4	26.5	2.2	4.8
20. Deberíamos tener por aquí muchos bosques porque son tan hermosos.	98.5	0.7	0.5	0.3
21. La gente joven debería estar enojada con las generaciones anteriores por el daño que han hecho a los bosques por aquí.	77.5	16.4	3.5	2.7
22. Las pasturas deberían tener algunos árboles.	97.0	1.8	0.3	0.8
23. No es bueno tener árboles cerca de los cultivos.	52.3	36.7	8.8	2.2

24. Porque Dios creo los bosques, está mal abusar de ellos.	88.5	10.0	0.8	0.7
25. Los bosques son una parte importante de nuestro patrimonio nacional.	97.3	0.2	0.5	2.0
26. Todas las cosas vivas, incluyendo los animales, los pájaros y los árboles, tienen también derecho a la vida.	99.8	—	0.2	—
27. Siempre está bien cazar o matar animales silvestres.	14.3	81.2	4.0	0.5
28. Son nuestros hijos quienes se beneficiarán de los árboles y bosques que nosotros protejamos.	99.5	0.2	0.3	—

29. ¿Cuáles son mas hermosos?

☐   LOS SEMBRADOS   09.0%
☐   LOS BOSQUES   26.9
☐   [LOS DOS IGUAL]   63.6
☐   [NINGUNA]   —
☐   NO SÉ   0.8

30. ¿Con qué piensa usted que uno puede hacer mas dinero?

☐   UNA MANZANA DE CAFÉ QUE CON   45.1%
☐   UNA MANZANA DE BOSQUE   20.1
☐   [LOS DOS IGUAL]   30.1
☐   [NINGUNA]   0.2
☐   NO SÉ   4.5

31. ¿Con qué piensa usted que uno puede hacer mas dinero?

☐   UNA MANZANA DE PASTURA   17.3%
☐   UNA MANZANA DE BOSQUE   50.6
☐   [LOS DOS IGUAL]   24.0
☐   [NINGUNA]   1.2
☐   NO SÉ   7.0

32. ¿Cual es mejor para el ambiente?

☐	UNA MANZANA DE CAFÉ O	70.5%
☐	UNA MANZANA DE PASTURA	6.0
☐	*[LOS DOS IGUAL]*	20.0
☐	*[NINGUNA]*	1.2
☐	NO SÉ	2.3

33. ¿Cual es mejor para el ambiente?

☐	UNA MANZANA DE CAFÉ O	10.6%
☐	UNA MANZANA DE BOSQUE	53.6
☐	*[LOS DOS IGUAL]*	35.3
☐	*[NINGUNA]*	—
☐	*NO SÉ*	0.5

34. ¿Cual es mejor para el ambiente?

☐	UNA MANZANA DE BOSQUE	76.2%
☐	UNA MANZANA DE PASTURA	4.3
☐	*[LOS DOS IGUAL]*	18.6
☐	*[NINGUNA]*	—
☐	*NO SÉ*	0.8

35. ¿Pensando en los árboles que hay en su propio terreno o finca, usted piensa que hay . . .?

☐	DEMASIADOS ÁRBOLES O	9.2%
☐	EXACTAMENTE LOS NECESARIOS O	34.4
☐	NO HAY SUFICIENTES ÁRBOLES	49.8
☐	*NO SÉ*	6.3

Ahora quisiera que usted me dijera de quién aprendió lo que usted sabe de los árboles y de los bosques.

APRENDIO SOBRE LOS BOSQUES	SI (%)	NO (%)	NO SÉ (%)
36. ¿De sus padres?	57.5	42.2	0.3
37. ¿De sus vecinos?	51.4	48.1	0.5
38. ¿De trabajar la tierra?	82.8	16.5	0.7
39. ¿En la iglesia?	62.2	37.5	0.3
40. ¿De los turistas?	46.1	52.9	1.0
41. ¿Escuchando la radio?	90.7	9.3	—
42. ¿Viendo televisión?	42.4	57.5	0.2
43. ¿De los guarda parques?	67.1	32.7	0.2
44. ¿De los extensionistas trabajando con alguna organización?	68.3	31.2	0.5
45. ¿Charlas que usted ha asistido?	60.1	39.7	0.2
46. ¿Del patronato o líderes locales?	53.9	45.8	0.3

47. ¿De todas estas fuentes de información acerca del bosque [lea las respuestas afirmativas], cual de éstas es la más importante para usted?

Padres (22.5%) LA MÁS IMPORTANTE (# de la tabla anterior)

48. ¿Después de cuántos años el guamil se convierte en bosque?

12.6 AÑOS [promedio]

☐   NO SÉ

49. ¿Cuántos años se tarda el guamil en crecer antes de que usted lo pueda volver a cortar o quemar para plantar un cultivo nuevo?

3.0 AÑOS [promedio]

☐   NO SÉ

Ahora voy a leerle algunas afirmaciones. Por favor dígame si está usted de acuerdo, en desacuerdo, o indiferente con cada una de ellas.

LA GENTE ASEGURA QUE	De acuerdo (%)	En desacuerdo (%)	Ni de acuerdo, ni en desacuerdo (me es indiferente) (%)	No sé (%)
50. Está bien quemar guamil si se va a cultivar ahí.	38.6	55.7	5.2	0.5
51. Cuando el guamil crece muy grande se convierte en bosque.	94.0	3.8	0.8	1.3
52. Está permitido descombrar bosque.	11.0	86.5	1.5	1.0
53. Las plantas de café son un tipo de árbol.	84.3	13.5	0.5	1.7
54. Es más fácil para los terratenientes conseguir permisos para cortar árboles, que para la gente común o pobre.	90.7	5.5	1.7	2.2
55. Si el guamil se convierte en bosque, el gobierno no te deja cultivar más esa tierra.	79.2	13.1	3.3	4.3
56. Está permitdo descombrar guamil.	47.3	46.8	3.5	2.5
57. Los árboles frutales son tan árboles como lo son los pinos.	84.5	12.6	1.8	1.0
58. Debería ser más fácil para el campesino común en esta comunidad conseguir el permiso para cortar un árbol para uso de la casa.	92.7	5.5	0.7	1.2
59. Los árboles pertenecen al gobierno.	63.8	30.2	1.3	4.7
60. Está permitido descombrar montaña.	7.0	91.3	0.5	1.2

61. Pequeños propietarios pueden conseguir permisos para cortar árboles tan fácilmente como los demás.	36.3	57.7	2.3	3.7
62. Si no tuviéramos leyes que protejen a los bosques, tendríamos muchos menos árboles.	96.5	3.2	0.2	0.2
63. Si a la gente se le permitiera cortar todos los árboles que quieran, no sabrían cuando parar.	95.0	4.3	0.3	0.3
64. La gente no hace quemas en sus tierra de cultivo porque tienen miedo del gobierno.	80.5	15.7	2.5	1.3
65. Debería ser más fácil para los dueños de tierra en esta comunidad conseguir un permiso para cortar árboles para su venta comercial.	53.4	42.4	2.2	2.0
66. Es la responsabilidad del gobierno de cuidar los árboles.	72.9	25.6	1.2	0.3
67. El gobierno no puede por si solo cuidar a los árboles y a los bosques, la gente de la comunidad debe ayudar también.	97.0	3.0	—	—
68. La mayoría de la gente que vive por aquí no le importa si se cortan los árboles.	41.6	53.7	3.2	1.5
69. La gente en esta comunidad puede, sin la ayuda del gobierno, cuidar los árboles.	65.7	31.8	1.3	1.2

Ahora quiero hacerle unas preguntas acerca de sus tierras.

TIENE USTED ALGUNA TIERRA EN ESTAS CONDICIONES	SI (%)	NO (%)	COMO CUÁNTAS MANZANAS TIENE USTED EN (promedio)
70. ¿Con bosque o montaña?	33.7	65.9	2.2
71. ¿Con guamil?	42.1	57.9	1.6
72. ¿Con café?	51.8	48.2	1.0
73. ¿Con pastura?	17.9	82.1	0.6
74. ¿Con hortalizas?	8.2	91.8	0.0
75. ¿Con cultivos como milpa o frijol?	58.4	41.6	1.2
76. ¿En otras condiciones? Especifique.	16.7	83.3	0.2
77. TOTAL. (Entonces, considerando todas sus tierras, usted tiene como (#) _____ manzanas, cierto? [Si no, revise las preguntas y reconfirme las manzanas en cada categoría.]			7.3

Ahora le voy a preguntar sobre la plantación de árboles o reforestación:

HA PLANTADO USTED	NO (%)	SÍ, EN MI PROPIA TIERRA (%)	SÍ, EN TIERRAS DE OTROS (%)
78. ¿Pinos?	61.1	11.7	27.2
79. ¿Otros árboles maderables?	46.7	34.3	19.1
80. ¿Árboles de frutas?	17.8	72.0	10.1
81. ¿Otros?	83.2	13.6	3.2

[Si ha plantado árboles:]

HA PLANTADO USTED ÁRBOLES	SI (%)	NO (%)	NO SÉ (%)
82. ¿A lo largo de quebradas y ríos?	42.0	58.0	—
83. ¿A lo largo de las orillas de las milpas?	36.1	63.9	—
84. ¿En pasturas?	17.5	81.5	—
85. ¿En el cafetal?	52.5	47.5	—
86. ¿Alrededor de la casa?	70.8	29.2	—
87. ¿A lo largo del camino?	25.3	74.7	—

88. ¿Ha conservado usted bosques en su propia tierra?

☐   SI   38.6% ==> 89. [¿Como cuántas manzanas ha conservado
            usted? 2.2 MANZANAS [promedio]
☐   NO   58.1
☐   NO SÉ   1.2

90. ¿Ha cortado alguna vez árboles o descombrado bosques en su propiedad?

☐   SI   58.3%
☐   NO   41.4
☐   NO LO SÉ   0.6

91. [Si cortó árboles] ¿Cortó usted estos árboles para . . .?   Si

☐   DESCOMBRAR BOSQUE PARA CULTIVAR LA TIERRA 52.7%
☐   PARA TENER MADERA PARA CONSTRUIR SU CASA 60.7
☐   PARA VENDER   4.6
☐   PARA LEÑA   69.9
☐   PARA RECLAMAR LA TIERRA   6.0
☐   OTRO, ESPECIFIQUE _____ 6.0

Voy a leerle mas comentarios que la gente hace sobre los bosques. Por favor dígame
si usted está de acuerdo, en desacuerdo, o si el comentario le es indiferente.

LA GENTE PIENSA QUE	De acuerdo (%)	En desacuerdo (%)	Ni de acuerdo, ni en desacuerdo (me es indiferente) (%)	No sé (%)
92. Debemos pensar en las generaciones futuras cuando tomamos decisiónes respecto al uso de nuestros bosques.	98.0	0.8	0.2	1.0
93. En estos días la gente de esta comunidad tiene más cuidado con los bosques que antes.	96.0	3.3	0.5	0.2
94. Cuando alguien corta un árbol, aunque lo corte en su propia tierra, nos perjudica a todos.	88.7	7.8	1.7	1.8
95. Cazar o matar animales silvestres está bien, si usted lo hace para alimentarse.	61.6	33.8	4.2	0.5
96. Las compañías madereras destruyen más bosque que la gente que vive en esta comunidad.	97.2	1.8	0.2	0.8
97. Los bosques por aquí benefician más a gente de afuera, como por ejemplo, científicos y turistas, que a la gente que vive aquí en esta comunidad.	48.8	39.0	9.2	3.0
98. Necesitamos primero alimentos y dinero antes de poder empezar a preocuparnos de cuidar los bosques.	70.4	22.8	6.5	0.3
99. Los seres humanos tienen que cortar árboles para poder vivir.	49.9	45.3	2.8	2.0

100. Es mejor usar la tierra para producir alimentos que dejarla así como bosque.	58.7	22.6	17.5	1.2
101. Por aquí estaríamos mejor económicamente si tuviéramos menos árboles.	14.0	78.4	3.8	3.8
102. Es muy importante que nuestros niños tengan la oportunidad de poder disfrutar de los bosques y los animales silvestres.	99.0	0.3	0.2	0.5
103. Se le debería permitir a la gente vender los árboles que están en su propia tierra sin ninguna restricción del gobierno.	26.8	69.3	2.0	1.8
104. Cazar o matar animales silvestres está bien, si usted necesita dinero.	18.8	80.0	1.0	0.2
105. Honduras está ayudando al resto del mundo preservando sus bosques.	93.3	2.2	0.8	3.7
106. Se le debería permitir a la gente descombrar bosque para cultivar o sembrar café sin ninguna restricción de parte del gobierno.	26.3	69.1	3.3	1.3
107. Si hay mucho bosque por aquí los animales que viven en el bosque pueden dañar mis cultivos o mis animales.	62.2	35.1	1.2	1.5
108. El gobierno debería prohibir a la gente el corte de árboles para vender la madera.	80.3	16.5	2.3	0.8

109. Se le debería permitir a la gente que corte árboles para construir su casa sin ninguna restricción del gobierno.	72.4	26.1	1.0	0.5
110. Se le debería permitir a la gente hacer lo que quieran con los árboles que se encuentran en su tierra.	17.2	81.8	1.0	0.2
111. Si nosotros fuéramos a conservar bosques por aquí, tenemos menos oportunidad de ganar dinero.	40.9	50.2	3.2	5.7
112. Nuestra comunidad estaría mejor a largo plazo si conservamos nuestros bosques en vez de cortarlos.	91.5	4.5	1.3	2.7
113. Hay muchas maneras de aprovechar nuestros bosques y hacer dinero, sin tener que cortarlos.	83.2	12.1	1.0	3.7
114. El gobierno debería prevenir que la gente corte bosque para cultivar café.	61.3	30.7	5.0	3.0

115. ¿Ha sido castigado o multado por acciones en contra de los reglamentos?

☐   SI   3.5%
☐   NO   96.0
☐   *NO SÉ*   0.8
☐   *REHUSÓ*   —

Ahora quiero hacerle algunas preguntas acerca del Parque Nacional Cerro Azul Meambar.

116. ¿Es bueno vivir cerca o dentro de un parque nacional?

☐   SI   80.4%
☐   ·NO   10.7
☐   *INDECISO*   5.9
☐   *NO LO SÉ*   3.5

¿Cuál de los siguientes grupos de gente se benefician del parque [*cheque todos los que se mencionen*]?

SE BENEFICIAN DEL PARQUE	SI (%)	NO (%)	NO SÉ (%)
117. ¿Usted mismo?	85.0	13.8	1.2
118. ¿Gente en la comunidad?	93.5	4.2	2.3
119. ¿Los guardas del parque?	94.3	2.2	3.3
120. ¿Turistas?	88.5	5.3	6.0
121. ¿Gente de todo el país?	90.7	3.7	5.7
122. ¿Gente en otras comunidades?	92.5	4.5	3.0
123. ¿Todo el mundo?	—	—	—

124. ¿Quién de ellos [*lea las respuestas afirmativas*] se beneficia más?

> Gente de la communidad (43.1%) BENEFICIA MÁS *(# de la tabla anterior).*

Dígame si usted piensa que el Parque es *muy importante, importante,* o *no es importante* para lo siguiente:

EL PARQUE	MUY IMPOR-TANTE (%)	IMPORTANTE (%)	NO ES IMPORTANTE (%)	NO SABE (%)
125. ¿Proteger los bosques y los árboles?	62.9	36.1	0.2	0.8
126. ¿Proteger fuentes de agua—calidad y cantidad de agua?	76.5	23.1	0.2	0.2
127. ¿Proteger biodiversidad— recursos genéticos?	64.1	33.6	0.2	2.2
128. ¿Proteger vida silvestre?	63.8	35.0	0.5	0.7

129. ¿Proteger los suelos—evitar la erosión?	61.6	36.6	0.2	1.7
130. ¿Fomentar el desarollo nacional?	56.7	39.3	0.7	3.3
131. ¿Fomentar turismo?	56.4	40.8	0.7	2.2
132. ¿Fomentar el desarrollo comunitario?	66.1	32.1	0.8	1.0
133. ¿Ciencia e investigaciones?	49.6	41.2	1.2	8.0
134. ¿Bajar impactos al ambiente?	61.3	33.5	1.2	4.0

Por último le voy a hacer algunas preguntas sobre usted:

135. [*Escriba género por observación*]

☐   HOMBRE   61.3%
☐   MUJER   38.4

136. ¿En que año nació usted? 19 <u>59</u> AÑO [*promedio*]

☐   NO SE
☐   *REHUSÓ*

137. ¿Usted nació aquí en _____ [*mencione el nombre de la comunidad donde está llevando a cabo la entrevista*]?

☐   SI   43.8%
☐   NO 56.3 ==> 138. En que año llegó usted a ésta comunidad por primera vez? 19 <u>74</u> AÑO [*promedio*]
☐   *NO SE*
☐   *REHUSÓ*

139. ¿Cuántos años asistió usted a la escuela?

3.2 AÑOS DE PRIMARIA *[promedio]*
0.8 AÑOS DE SECUNDARIA *[promedio]*
0.0 OTRO _____ (ESPECIFIQUE) *[promedio]*
□   *NO SÉ*
□   *REHUSÓ*

140. ¿Qué religión práctica usted?

□	CATÓLICA	47.5%
□	EVANGÉLICO	37.8
□	OTRA _____ (ESPECIFIQUE)	5.9
□	*NO SÉ*	2.8
□	*REHUSÓ*	1.2
□	NINGUNA	5.3

141. ¿Cuál es su nombre completo?

NOMBRE: _____

□	*REHUSÓ*	0.5%

142. ¿Mas o menos, cuál fue su ingreso total de la casa durante el año pasado?

L13.794 *[promedio]*

□	MENOS DE L30.000	45.7%
□	L30.000 a 59.000	4.0
□	L60.000 a 89.000	0.9
□	L90.000 a 120.000	0.2
□	MÁS DE 120.000	0.3
□	*NO SÉ*	46.1
□	*REHUSÓ*	7.5

143. Por favor dígame si usted o alguien en su famila recibe dinero. Por ejemplo de [*marque todos los que mencione*]:

□	AGRICULTURA	70.2%
□	NEGOCIOS COMO TIENDA O PULPERÍA	12.5
□	SALARIO DE OBRERO, JORNALERO	48.1
□	RECOGIENDO CAFÉ	36.3

☐	ALGÚN FAMILIAR QUE VIVE AQUÍ EN EL PAÍS PERO NO EN LA CASA	18.1
☐	ALGÚN FAMILIAR QUE VIVE FUERA DE HONDURAS	14.0
☐	OTRO _____	5.0
☐	*NO SÉ*	1.0
☐	*REHUSÓ*	0.2

144. ¿De todas estas fuentes de dinero [*lea las respuestas afirmativas*], cuál de éstas es la más importante para su casa?

<u>Agricultura (51.1%)</u> LA MÁS IMPORTANTE

145. ¿Cuantos hijos tiene usted (o el padre de la familia)?

<u>5 HIJOS</u> *[promedio]*

146. ¿Cuantos personas viven en esta casa?

<u>6 PERSONAS</u> *[promedio]*

147. ¿Fué usted entrevistado por una estudiante de nombre Mariela Fourli en 1995? Mariela era una estudiante de Cornell pero nacida en Grecia.

☐	SI	16.6%
☐	NO	60.0
☐	*NO SABE*	23.5

148. *Hora de finalización:* _____

Estas son todas mis preguntas. Muchas gracias por su ayuda.

Tendría usted otro comentario que agregar.

[Anote el comentario]

Le agredecemos infinitamente. Que pasa buen día.

Appendix E

Sociodemographic Data for Qualitative Interviewees Quoted

Costa Rica

	Years Here	Age	Gender	Religion[b]	Years School
CR1	10	33	M	E	5
CR2	23	23	M	C	8
CR3	5	70	M	C	—
CR4	26	26	F	C	—
CR5	25	54	F	C	2
CR6	14	42	M	C	—
CR7	23	56	M	C	4
CR8	24	78	M	C	1
CR9	18	48	F	E	4
CR10	25	69	M	C	1
CR11[a]	39	25	M	C	6
CR12	32	37	M	C	0
CR13	30	39	M	None	6
CR14	30	67	M	E	2
CR15	25	43	M	E	6
CR16	17	42	M	C	7
CR17	21	47	F	C	2
CR18	22	33	M	C	6
CR19	25	?	F	?	?
CR20	15	29	F	C	7
CR21	10	45	M	E	6
CR22	25	57	M	C	3
CR23	8	46	M	C	3
CR24	23	50	M	C (NA)	1
CR25	29	29	M	E (NA)	1
CR26[c]	12	50	M	C	?
CR27[c]	18	79	M	None	?

[a] Park guard
[b] Religion: C = Catholic; E = Evangelical, Pentecostal, or Adventist; (NA) = Not active
[c] Not recorded

Honduras

	Years Here	Age	Gender	Religion[b]	Years School
H1	18	18	M	C	6
H2	48	57	M	E	1
H3	50	50	M	C (NA)	6
H4	43	43	M	E	3
H5	22	39	F	E	6
H6	23	53	M	E	4
H7	21	27	M	C	6
H8[a]	29	29	M	E	3
H9	34	34	M	C (NA)	6
H10	36	69	M	Both	1
H11[a]	26	28	M	C (NA)	6
H12	20	50	F	E	0
H13	30	37	M	C	6
H14	31	39	F	C	6
H15[a]	10	45	M	C (NA)	3
H16	52	60	M	C	1
H17	26	26	F	C	8
H18	15	55	M	E	0
H19	38	38	M	General	1
H20	45	45	M	None	6
H21	3	31	M	E	9
H22	35	54	F	E	0
H23	15	41	M	None	2
H24	23	50	F	C (NA)	0
H25	2	28	M	C	12
H26[c]	24	69	F	Catholic	2

[a] Park guard
[b] Religion: C = Catholic; E = Evangelical, Pentecostal, or Adventist; (NA) = Not active
[c] Not recorded

Acronyms and Organizations

Aldea Global	Global Village, a nongovernmental organization
APRENABRUS	*Asociación Preservacionista de Coto Brus* (Preservation Association of Coto Brus)
CAMNP	Cerro Azul Meambar National Park
CIIFAD	Cornell International Institute for Food, Agriculture, and Development
COHDEFOR	*Corporación Hondureña de Desarollo Forestal* (Honduran Forestry Development Corporation)
ESNACIFOR	*Escuela Nacional de Ciencias Forestales*
GPS	Global positioning system
IDA	*Instituto de Desarollo Agrario* (Agrarian Development Institute)
IRS	Indian Remote Sensing Satellite
ITCO	*Instituto de Tierras y Colonización* (Land and Colonization Institute)
LAIP	La Amistad International Park
LCBS	Las Cruces Biological Station
LISS-3	Linear Imaging Self-Scanning Sensor
MINAE	*Ministerio de Ambiente y Energía* (Environment and Energy Ministry)
NGO	Nongovernmental organization
NSF	National Science Foundation
OTS	Organization for Tropical Studies
PANACAM	*Parque Nacional Cerro Azul Meambar* (CAMNP)
Patronato	Local community organization for governance
PILA	*Parque Internacional La Amistad* (LAIP)

Index

About the Authors

JOHN SCHELHAS is a research forester with the Southern Research Station of the U.S. Forest Service, located at Tuskegee University in Alabama. His research focuses on the relationships between people and forests, with interests in material determinants of land use choice, environmental values, social networks, race and ethnicity, and natural resource management. He has conducted research in Costa Rica since 1988. He has a Ph.D. in renewable natural resources, with a minor in anthropology, from the University of Arizona. He has worked as a researcher at Cornell University and the Smithsonian Migratory Bird Center. He also has worked for the U.S. National Park Service and served as a Peace Corps volunteer in Guatemala. He coedited the books *Forest Patches in Tropical Landscapes* (with Russell Greenberg) and *Biological Diversity: Balancing Interests through Adaptive Collaborative Management* (with Louise Buck, Charles Geisler, and Lini Wollenberg).

MAX J. PFEFFER is International Professor of Development Sociology and chair of the Department of Development Sociology at Cornell University. His teaching concentrates on environmental sociology and sociological theory. His research spans several areas, including land use and environmental planning, rural labor markets, and rural-to-urban and international migration. The empirical work covers a variety of rural and urban communities, including rural/urban fringe areas in New York, Mexico, and Central America. He has received competitive grant awards from the National Institutes of Health, the National Science Foundation, the U.S. Environmental Protection Agency, the U.S. Department of Agriculture's National Research Initiative, and the Fund for Rural America. Pfeffer has published a wide range of scholarly articles and has coedited three books and coauthored three National Research Council Reports. Pfeffer completed his Ph.D. in 1986 in sociology at the University of Wisconsin, Madison. He has also served as associate director of the Cornell University Agricultural Experiment Station and associate director and interim director of the Cornell Center for the Environment.

CPSIA information can be obtained at www.ICGtesting.com
Printed in the USA
235733LV00009B/91/P